Contents

Introduction   I

1. Am I Good For My Age?   5

2. What Do I Do About My Friends?   58

3. Am I Turning Into My Mother?   102

4. Is It Me, Or Is Everyone Showing Off?   134

5. Should They Have Written To Thank Me?   162

6. Can I Be Single And Happy?   196

7. How To Meet (The Right) Man After Forty   258

8. Now You Are A Stepmother   321

   Epilogue   355

   Acknowledgements   357

PENGUIN BOOKS

How To Meet A Man After Forty
And Other Midlife Dilemmas Solved

ıne Watson is a columnist for the *Sunday Times Style* magazine and is
ontributing editor to *Easy Living* and *Grazia* magazines. She is also
: author of two novels, *The One to Watch* and *Other People's Marriages*.

How To Meet A Man After Forty

After Forty

And Other Midlife Dilemmas Solved

SHANE WATSON

PENGUIN BOOKS

PENGUIN BOOKS

Published by the Penguin Group
Penguin Books Ltd, 80 Strand, London WC2R ORL, England
Penguin Group (USA) Inc., 375 Hudson Street, New York, New York 10014, USA
Penguin Group (Canada), 90 Eglinton Avenue East, Suite 700, Toronto, Ontario, Canada M4P 2Y3
(a division of Pearson Penguin Canada Inc.)
Penguin Ireland, 25 St Stephen's Green, Dublin 2, Ireland (a division of Penguin Books Ltd)
Penguin Group (Australia), 250 Camberwell Road,
Camberwell, Victoria 3124, Australia (a division of Pearson Australia Group Pty Ltd)
Penguin Books India Pvt Ltd, 11 Community Centre,
Panchsheel Park, New Delhi – 110 017, India
Penguin Group (NZ), 67 Apollo Drive, Rosedale, North Shore 0632, New Zealand
(a division of Pearson New Zealand Ltd)
Penguin Books (South Africa) (Pty) Ltd, 24 Sturdee Avenue, Rosebank, Johannesburg 2196, South Africa
Penguin Books Ltd, Registered Offices: 80 Strand, London WC2R ORL, England

www.penguin.com

First published 2009
1

Typeset in Garamond MT 11.5/16.5pt by Palimpsest Book Production Limited,
Grangemouth, Stirlingshire
Printed in England by Clays Ltd, St Ives plc

ISBN: 978-0-141-03674-8

www.greenpenguin.co.uk

Penguin Books is committed to a sustainable future
for our business, our readers and our planet.
The book in your hands is made from paper
certified by the Forest Stewardship Council.

For Tris

Introduction

Not long ago, I was mobbed on a visit to my local beauty parlour. 'Oh, it's you!' cried the receptionists, when I gave my name. 'Tell us. How did you manage it? You are our heroine!' The women sitting in the waiting room lifted their eyes from their glossy magazines, cocked their soon-to-be-threaded eyebrows and craned forward, eager to hear more. Passing girls in white gowns and flip flops, cotton wool woven between their toes, paused between appointments. Therapists (or is it technicians? I never know) poked their heads out of softly lit, scented rooms to see where all the clients had got to. Meanwhile, I turned to face my audience and began the story at the very beginning. (I should have been struck dumb by this frenzy of attention, but something similar had happened just the previous week at a party, and I was beginning to get used to my new role.)

In case you are not aware of the reason for my iconic status among certain members of the female population it is this: I got married, for the first time, in my mid forties. Tah dah! Not only that but I *met* the man I married in my mid forties. This, as you will know, is a rather different deal to, say, tying the knot in your forties having cohabited since college; or getting married for the second time – neither of which is any comfort to the terminally single. I am, in other words, the statistic-defying exception to the rule, a beacon of hope for the single woman who hadn't planned to be single indefinitely.

What's more, I have spent a significant part of a long career in journalism writing about being single. Not just the occasional gap between boyfriends, but long-term single for great tracts of my thirties and all of my early forties. I am not just a surprise late finisher; I was the spokesperson for the fulfilled single life for roughly fifteen years. The advocate of no compromise. The one who wrote an article entitled 'Why I'm Glad I'm Not Married', and more than I can count on the subject of the normal, and even desirable, state of living on your own. I had the mostly white apartment with the Polaroided shoeboxes, the glamorous jobs on fashion magazines and newspapers, and the 'full and active' life including yoga classes, spa breaks and plenty of journey-of-discovery holidays. Women I barely knew would call me up when their relationships ended to ask for tips on being single – I'm not even kidding. That's how contentedly, professionally manless I was when I met The One. So, it follows that people (mainly unattached women) are curious to know: How did it happen?

Not just how did it happen, but how did it happen to me? I'm not an heiress or a beauty. I haven't had my teeth done, or any part of me tweaked (apart from my hair, which is dyed to death and going a bit the way of Donald Trump's). I'm a very average cook, borderline slovenly, terrible in the mornings. (I could go on, but this probably isn't the place.) And we all know that, while it is *possible* for a woman in her forties to meet a man, she is now competing with Russian models, and superfit yummy divorcees (who look thirty, even if their passports say they're forty-four), and kids, and women who have been reconditioned from their roots to their toes by genius plastic surgeons. In other words, if someone like me can do it, then anyone can.

All of which explains how I came to be sharing the significant factors that led to me finding The One, with a roomful of strangers in white towelling robes.

And that was when it hit me that the problem of how to meet a man is just one of a whole host of new dilemmas facing women in their thirties and forties. Yes, women have been this age before, but not like *this* – not in a climate where aging is taboo and we are expected to be bikini fit into our sixties, and have fabulous style, and smart careers and hot sex lives and emotionally fulfilling relationships with everyone we know. Those women in the beauty parlour wanted to hear my story not because they were all looking for a man, but because they were conscious that this stage of our lives has changed beyond recognition and we're all (attached or not) trying to make sense of what it is to be a grown-up female in the twenty-first century when no one knows what the rules are any more.

Everyone is looking for direction and answers to the big questions – Who are we meant to be, actually? What do we want, really? – as well as all those thorny, medium-sized ones, like: How should I look at fortysomething? Do men now expect a Brazilian? Is it possible to humanely cull your friends? Are people getting ruder or is it just me? We'd ask our mothers for the answers but they can't help because when they were this age no one would have dreamt of removing all the hair from their bodies, never mind sharing changing rooms with teenagers, or living alone in flats strewn with glittery butterflies and fairy lights. We are living in uncharted territory, in uncertain times, and we have only ourselves to turn to.

And then I thought, if anyone is going to address the modern woman's many midlife crises, it might as well be someone who has first-hand experience of most of them – and plenty of time to think about what it takes to make us happy – so here goes ...

1.

Am I Good For My Age?

This question goes right to the heart of the modern midlifer's identity crisis – because the answer has to be, erm: that depends on where you are standing (and who's next to you). If you are at a ladies keep-fit class in Skegness, that's one thing. If you are waiting at the gates of an exclusive prep school in Chelsea, then that is another. There used to be a universal Good For Your Age Standard, back when Good For Your Age meant well preserved, considering how many years you'd been walking the planet. Now, how you rate on the GFYA scale depends on which micro planet you inhabit, and what the women in your world consider to be appropriate anti-aging maintenance. Is it regular exercise and plenty of fresh fruit and vegetables, or more like regular Botox, plus the occasional bit of lipo? You might be one of the lucky few who looks naturally GFYA, but, lined up next to your smart friends with the dermatologists and personal trainers, it could be a different story.

So, take a good look around. (If you are on a bus, it doesn't count: you should be in your natural environment, among your peers – the people who dictate whether you are GFYA, or more like Every Inch Your Age.)

Let me tell you where I am to get you started. I am sitting in Tom's cafe, in Notting Hill Gate, where I used to live and still work. The Notting Hill, as depicted in the Richard Curtis film, was a kind of spangly village inhabited by quirky characters. Now, it's more like a first-class lounge at Geneva airport – the temporary resting place of the international financial elite, and their expensively bought wives. Here, GFYA begins and ends at thirty-six. Before thirty-six, that's what you are. After thirty-six, that's what you stay. In this environment, if you look forty-six in the conventional sense – a few grey roots, a tiny bit of a tummy, fine lines around your eyes, one or two age spots – it means you are either visiting the area to drop something off, or working for one of the thirty-six-year-olds. This is not just a high-maintenance postcode, it is one of those postcodes that makes you look like a bag lady if you don't play by their rules.

Every night I head south on the bus to Battersea, which is in an entirely different GFYA postcode. In my local cafe on Battersea Park Road, the definition of GFYA is having your own teeth and two separate eyebrows. You can roll out of bed and slop along there in your pyjamas and still get the once over from the chef just because you don't have a moustache and nicotine-stained blonde hair.

So, back to Tom's and the table of women sitting to my left. This is the conversation I overhear:

'You need a project manager. You have to have a project manager.'

'I know. Bloody architects. We saw you and your gorgeous trainer in the park, by the way.'

'Isn't he fab. And he's got me on this incredible detox diet.'

'You are looking good.'

'Well, I found that two types of exercise just wasn't enough after the baby.'

'I know what you mean. I might get Xavier to come to the house a couple of times a week.'

'Or go to the club and do Power Plate. And they do great treatments there.'

'Mmm. But don't, whatever you do, try Doctor Zebedee [name changed to avoid law suit].'

'No, I wouldn't dream of going to anyone but my dermatologist. Although Jane's man is fantastic. He recommended the [indicates breast area]. Five pomegranate salads, please. And two fresh mint teas.'

These lunching ladies are pretty representative of affluent Notting Hill society, and they have their equivalent in every thriving city on the planet. They might look a bit undone by comparison with their New York sisters, and in Chelsea they'd have more jewellery between them but, still, these are the women who are raising the GFYA bar for each and every one of us. There are five of them, and they range from a gym bunny in Masai Barefoot Technology trainers and velour tracksuit, to a heavily made-up woman in a shearling coat and stiletto-heeled boots. The gym bunny could actually be thirty-six, possibly a lot younger; the rest of them are anywhere from mid thirties to late fifties. I would try to be more precise, but experience has taught me that it's too tough to call.

I am not one of the above types. I have not had a teeny breast boost or a bit of Botox (I once had Botox in my armpits, but that's another story). I am a member of a gym, though I hardly ever get there. I once paid for the moulds to whiten my teeth, only I couldn't get to sleep with them in, so that went out the window. I tried laser hair removal but then it turned out you can't have it if you get eczema (plus you need a six-figure salary if you want to see it through to the bitter end). I do get my hair dyed and my eyelashes tinted, I still buy clothes in Topshop and I am sometimes seduced by beauty products that promise to lift, tone and rejuvenate. I am as age conscious as the next person, in short, and I would like to stay looking as youthful as possible for as long as possible. I just don't want to undergo surgery or get my face syringed every couple of months in an effort to achieve that.

The women in Tom's would consider my attitude to be somewhere between social suicide and sluttishness. Meanwhile, there are plenty of women in my world who are even less anti-aging conscious than me – albeit not as many as there used to be. We are the Naturals (that's how we like to think of ourselves, anyway). They are the Plastics.

Aging used to be an accepted part of life – something women faced together, with a shrug and a Rich Tea biscuit. Now it is an ongoing bushtucker trial in which these two tribes are pitted against each other in a struggle to determine which will be the ultimate winner. Naturals have common sense on their side (potential health risks, the futility of trying to hold back the years). Plastics have an arsenal of lizard spleen and caviar extract and the whole nip/tuck repertoire, plus the time and the money to see us and raise us. It is war.

Are you one of them or one of us?

This is how weird things have got. Not long ago you would bump into a girlfriend who you hadn't seen for a while and you would talk about mutual friends, men, the credit crunch, giving up coffee, whatever. Now you get the preliminaries out of the way, fast, and then you are straight into the Where Do You Stand On The Big Issue conversation. It goes like this:

'You look great!'

'I look old!'

'You so don't!'

'I do! It's all starting to happen.'

'Tell me about it. Don't be tempted, though.'

'Have you?'

'Botox. Once. Didn't like it.'

'Really?'

'Just didn't feel right. And where do you stop once you've started?'

'I know.'

'Everyone around us is having stuff done. And they all have that *look*.'

'I know. Shiny. The light just bounces off them.'

'They look weird, actually.'

'I'm just not going there.'

'No, me neither. My sister had her tits done recently.'

'You're joking! But she's . . .'

'Normal. *I know.* But she's got this young boyfriend. And she has had three children, so . . .'

'The one thing I might be tempted to have, eventually, is an eyelid tuck.'

'But that's a proper operation!'

'I won't, *obviously.* I'm far too squeamish, apart from anything. But they say hooded eyes are the most aging thing of all . . .'

It is amazing how often you can have this conversation, and, as a matter of fact, you are guaranteed to have it with every significant female in your life at some point. You might not think of yourself as shallow and appearance obsessed – you may never have had a discussion about lip gloss or looking after your cashmere – but this is entirely different. The Will You Or Won't You conversation is really about revealing your colours and pledging your allegiance to one or other camp, because instinct tells us that this decision (to syringe or not to syringe) represents a fundamental parting of the ways. It is the beginning of a schism in the ranks of women – and we have to know who is on which side of the divide.

And here's the reason you need to have the conversation with everyone, and it gets repeated all over town, day after day: you just can't tell who is going to turn out to be a Plastic and who is a guaranteed Natural. There is no automatic rule that smart girls, or the women you respect, or feminists, will be Naturals. It isn't possible to say so-and-so would never go there – she's too fun/sexy/earthy/political/vegetarian. You might be able to say she would never fiddle her tax, or date a married man, or wear fur, but you can never say never when it comes to those stop-the-clock procedures.

This, in a nutshell, is why women are so mixed up about aging: the new rules have made us insecure but, far worse than that, they have alienated us from our own sex. In almost any area you care to mention you can say exactly where your girlfriends stand – on drugs, politics, thongs, waxing, the importance of sex, power showers versus baths – but aging has made us doubt each other's characters. It has fundamentally messed with our sense of sisterhood. We trust no one.

And everybody lies. The celebs who say, 'I certainly wouldn't rule it out,' (read, 'I've had some and I'm having more.'). The others who admit to a bit of Botox, (read full facelift and eyelid tuck). The women you know reasonably well who nod earnestly, their brows reflecting like wet marble, as you rant about the insidious pressure on us all to be totally crease-free. Even your close girlfriends have started lying to you, in case you happen to let slip in front of their husbands that they are having fillers. There is no precedent for this wholesale deception. We used to share everything – the state of our sex lives, the name of our hairdresser, the tiny tucked-away hotel that will be ruined for sure if everyone gets to hear about it – but the possibility of sneaking ahead in the race to stay young has made us (some of us) sly and secretive. (Did I mention that men are oblivious to the curse of cosmetic procedures?

However often you jab them in the ribs and alert them to another set of handlebar cheekbones, however often you roar, 'Oh, for God's sake, will you look at that! Look at the light bouncing off her! Look at those . . . ! Don't they make you feel physically ill?' you will never get quite the gagging response you were hoping for. They just don't find the treachery of our sex quite as terrible as we do.)

This is why getting old feels like it's a bigger deal for us than it has been in the past. It's one of the reasons anyway. Here are some of the others:

• Somewhere along the line, celebrities, models and women with senselessly rich husbands (women who get traded in if they don't stay looking the same as the day they married) got confused with regular people. Now we are all judged by the standards set by Cate Blanchett and Nicole Kidman (though she's starting to look weird, no?). Obviously not everyone is expected to achieve Hollywood perfection, outside LA, but we've learnt from the pros that age is very bad for business. You go to an ordinary civilian party in Shepherd's Bush and people are checking each other out like model bookers at a casting: 'Oh! She looks old. Doesn't she look old? Oh dear, oh dear.' What they mean is, 'She should look thirty-six. Why doesn't she look thirty-six? She may be fifty-two, but really . . . what can she be thinking of?' Looking old has become sort of grubby and negligent – like failing to brush your teeth or wash your hair. Don't you take care of yourself? Don't you change your underwear? Haven't you got any pride?

- We are more scared of getting old because old people have been outlawed. They aren't welcome. Anywhere. Not in fashion stores. Not in bars or restaurants. You go to a fabulous place of any description – a gorgeous hotel, a spa, a boutique, a party – where are the regular, grey-haired old people? Nowhere to be seen. When did you last notice one of them at the next-door table, or rifling through the sale rail? (Sometimes a grey-haired, Genuinely Old But Amazingly Well-preserved Person will be given a glamour outing – like that ancient model in the Gap ad. But that's a headline-making event.)

- Those who don't cheat can't avoid comparison with those who do. If you are a Natural, you are pretty confident, most of the time, that you don't want to look like a waxwork. But what you forget is that compared with the reflecting foreheads you look like the world's worst insomniac. They might look weird and inhuman but next to them you look crumpled and saggy and ill. And should you get yourself into a situation where you are outnumbered (like any situation in LA, for example) suddenly *you* are the odd one out – the knackered old crone who let herself go.

- Plastic surgery or youth worship, or both, has actually altered the way we look at people's faces. Get *Jules et Jim* out on DVD and you'll see what I mean. Jeanne Moreau, famous French beauty, thirty-four when she made the film, looks . . . quite old. She does. Gwyneth Paltrow could have played her teenage daughter.

- Finally, you no longer get that second chance to turn heads. The thing about being good for your age, in the old, unassisted sense, is that it was something everyone could achieve, regardless of how good-looking they were. You might be a fairly ordinary twentysomething and then, in your forties, come up on the inside (What glossy hair! What fabulous skin! What a neat little figure!) and pip the hot girls at the post. I was looking forward to lining up at the starting gate with the lookers and seeing if I couldn't edge up the ranks a bit myself. Why not? And no woman has ever begrudged one of her kind for being naturally well preserved: on the contrary, youthful beauty attracts envy, but those who age well win their right to be admired, fair and square. Or they did. The Botox culture – apart from creating a whole new set of criteria for looking good, based largely on ice-rink-smooth complexions – has usurped the naturally well preserved and denied them their moment.

One thing's for sure, aging isn't what it used to be.

❀ The Plastics

Who are they?

There are degrees of Plastics ranging from the serious pros (Cher) to your friend who has had Botox, but honestly only in her forehead, and she's never going to do anything else. Some Plastics you readily forgive, and even enjoy – like Lulu

– others make you want to scream, like Faye Dunaway (surely the naturally preserved sixtysomething Faye had to have been better than this?). It's given the Academy Awards a new lease of life, though. You used to sit there in front of the TV checking out the dresses and the on-loan Bulgari – now you're spotting the latest casualties: 'Oh ... she's gone. She's gone. Is that ... God, it is ... she's gone.' That's if you're a Natural, of course. If you're a Plastic, you're taking notes.

The Procedure Princess

Depending on when she started, the PP is either a dead ringer for Pete Best – half boiled egg, half cat – or she's like Demi Moore, an airbrushed, rejigged, streamlined and reconditioned version of her former self. You can't deny that the new army of procedure princesses coming off the conveyor belt look good, but you can't help straining to see the joins.

The Pincushion

So far, she is steering clear of actual surgery in favour of anything and everything that doesn't require an overnight stay. The pincushion looks decidedly spongey and puffy on certain days of the month, shiny and taut the rest, but, like all Plastics, she appears to be unaware of these drawbacks.

The Plastic Natural

Often she's married to someone older, who gets off on her barefoot and braless aesthetic, and the deal is that she is the breath of fresh air in their otherwise high-maintenance existence. Naturally, the PN cannot rely on nature alone to give her that youthful, fresh-faced edge, so she has a secret maintenance regime that involves plenty of Botox, teeth whitening and, lately, some smart lipo. She's as high maintenance as the rest, she just deliberately messes up her hair after her £60 blow-dry.

Philosophy

Anything is preferable to facing the fear. The Plastic wants to be employable in a glamorous job. She wants to prevent her husband leaving her for a woman who looks like she looked the day they met. (It's like that in Plastic world. And he's having a hair weave, possibly a moob job.) Your lesser Plastic has some underlying reservations, which are all health related. Your committed Plastic would eat the still-beating heart of a kangaroo if it was guaranteed to give her a smooth, wrinkle-free throat. But all Plastics think of their procedures as harmless little tricks, no different to a great bra or a magic under-eye concealer.

Years ago, I interviewed several of Harley Street's finest plastic practitioners, back when Botox was something that we still thought was for freaks and women with clinically low self-esteem. Apart from the fact that they almost winced (one did actually wince) when I said I wasn't personally interested, it was revealing because it taught me Plastics see the world differently. One of the surgeons, eager to demonstrate how much better a woman could look for a faceful of Botox and fillers, asked his favourite Pincushion to step by for my approval (she was somewhere in the building having something done – no surprise there). This woman looked younger than her forty-seven years, but she also looked distinctly uncomfortable in her skin. Like it was someone else's. I wanted to say, 'Yes, no lines. But she has a prosthetic head,' only what would have been the point? She was blissfully happy, proud to be paraded by her maker. He was incredibly smug and genuinely impressed with his handiwork. In Plastic Land beauty looks different.

Downsides

Looking very weird. Or totally unrecognizable. Apparently Plastics do not mind this, but their children and pets are suffering the effects. There is now a book, written by an American plastic surgeon (*My Beautiful Mommy*) to help children deal with the trauma of waking up to find their mother has traded bodies with someone else. For the dog who thinks a stranger is in the house, nothing as yet.

How do they do it?

How much time have you got? There are so many anti-aging procedures you could give up the day job and still have trouble fitting them all in. But even a half-hearted Plastic has weekly commitments that will include Boxtox injections, Restylane or hyaluronic acid injections, face peels, carboxytherapy (for stretch marks and bums), laser hair removal, maybe some smart lipo for saddlebags. And you know what they say: the more you top up one area, the more the others look like they're in need of work.

❀ The Naturals

Who are they?

Naturals are realists, purists, sceptics, refuseniks, women who don't think about their looks much and women (*moi* included) who think there has to be more to life than obsessing about your marionette lines (and who, more to the point, recognize that if we have to add line-plumping to the list of things we need to do in order to compete, we might well combust). Naturals are also quite confused. Sometimes we assume the moral high ground, other times we feel like those women who are still using sanitary towels seventy years after the invention of tampons.

Anti-maintenance Woman

Hard line AMs shave rather than wax, don't bother with pedicures or manicures and their only anti-aging strategy is a hair dye once in a while. A lot of people assume that fresh-faced types with unbrushed hair are AMs, but that's like assuming that because Kate Moss scruffs around in Minnetonkas she's low maintenance. It's hard work looking naturally undone past the age of thirty, and Anti-maintenance Woman tends to look more frazzled than fetching (though ten years ago she'd have looked absolutely normal). AM Woman gets away with it if she is a) skinny, b) glamorous, in terms of her job or connections, or c) attractive. As a matter of fact, she can end up getting more attention than her Plastic peers – but not often.

Old-fashioned Girl

She looks after herself, eats well, loves a beauty treatment, can't resist an anti-aging product, lives to get her hair done, but she's not going to fall for the serum that restricts body-hair growth or the eyelash-elongating formula. Also she's a firm believer in dressing to disguise the parts of your figure that you don't want to advertise, rather than paying someone to vacuum them away. You wouldn't have any trouble guessing her age, but you might think she was doing okay.

Everything-but-the-syringe Girl

That's me! Well, not quite everything (hate facials, hate eyebrow threading and I have definitely grown out of charlatans with inflatable pressure boots and magnetized water), but that leaves plenty of options to play with. I've been hosed down and wrapped in seaweed and buried in clay and colonically irrigated and Hollywood waxed and walked on by Thai ladies and presented with a special washcloth by Eve Lom. For the money I've spent over the years I could have bought a small château in the Loire, but that's fine by me. Part of being a Natural is accepting that this stuff can make your day; it just doesn't stop you getting older.

Philosophy

Sometimes being a Natural seems like common sense (who knows what the long-term effects of Botox will be?). Sometimes it feels like a point of principle (what does it say if we're too scared to let anyone see what we actually look like?). Other times it just seems that the alternative is selling out, and starting to think like the sort of woman who would sleep with anything to get her hands on a Mercedes SLR. But, mainly, to be a Natural you just have to feel in your gut that you would rather look old than scary, and believe that you have every chance of looking better than your Plastic contemporaries down the line. (Something we forget about the Plastic look is that in a way it is aging, because having it at all suggests you have crossed a threshold. It's like joining an exclusive club that, nonetheless, is a club for people who can no longer cut it.)

Still, no one's saying the lot of a Natural is easy. Your faith is tested roughly once a day. It is rocked every time you see Sharon Osbourne on the TV (Britain's most successful midlife makeover . . . what a top-quality facelift that is!). Sometimes Naturals can feel smug, of course – especially in the presence of someone whose Restylane lips have gone pufferfish on them – but other times we're not so sure. In a showdown with a woman who is considering defecting to the Plastics, sooner or later she will say: 'Tell me. What exactly is the difference between injecting your smile lines and dyeing your hair, or whitening your teeth?' And sooner or later you will think, I give in. What is the difference? Why am I even taking this stand?

It's not unlike what happens to Donald Sutherland and company in the *Invasion of the Bodysnatchers*. The real people start out determined not to fall asleep and get turned into zombies, but then they get so worn down and bored of fighting they simply haven't got the energy to resist any more.

Downsides

You are aging at a normal rate in a culture where that is becoming as eccentric as living without electricity. The Plastics used to be the big joke, but now mocking them is like laughing at people using BlackBerries: they are just too commonplace, and the work has got too good. Also, it's all very well taking a position against cosmetic procedures if you look like Isabella Rossellini. But if you look like you, can you really afford to take a stand?

How do they do it?

The sensible Natural, who has no agenda and an average amount of vanity, says no to the white coats, scalpels and syringes, and really pulls out the stops in every other department. But the secret of being a successful Natural is knowing what *not* to do.

❊ Looking GFYA: Know Your Style

We eat better, exercise harder and are more health conscious than any previous generation, with the result that there are now plenty of thirty- and fortysomething women who can dress like Kate Moss if they want to. Not only that, but we all aspire to a youthful aesthetic. It is cool for a grown woman to wear the clothes, second time round, that she was wearing when she was eighteen (and most of us would give that woman more brownie points than the one in the 'age-appropriate' skirt suit and sensible heels). This is all good news: it means more fun for us, more freedom, more choice. But if you want to look GFYA you must first recognize that, just because you Can doesn't mean you Should. This is the most important rule of dressing your age – don't confuse a good body with a young one.

Here are some others:

• Everyone has to adapt her style some day. Stevie Nicks is the only exception and no one else could get away with what she does.

• If you fancy yourself wearing something, then that automatically takes seven years off your age. If you happen to actually look good in it, make that ten.

• What you wear is just a part of how you come across. You could be working the groovy minidress and the five-inch heels, and look like Alexa Chung from the neck down, and then ... whoops. That grim I-have-a-lot-on-my-plate expression will kill it dead as surely as if you'd hit the town in a tweed suit and orthopaedic lace-ups.

Now you need to beware of the following style traps, which can be more aging than knee socks on Sarah Jessica Parker. (We've all been victims of at least one of them.)

Too Body Conscious

If you happen to have a good figure, it is tempting to go down the 'check out my bmi' path. We're talking low-cut Lycra tops, push-up bras, super-tight jeans or short jean skirts, stretch jersey dresses and high-heeled boots with everything. No one is left in any doubt as to this woman's impressively toned assets, but this look is aging because it only appeals to fortysomethings with expensive gym memberships. (And, obviously, too much flesh on display is never a good idea. Wear a strapless top, by all means, but not with a miniskirt.)

Avoid: Tight on top and bottom. Too much cleavage (a little goes a long way).*

Instead: Show off one aspect of your fabulous bod. It's okay, we can still see you're a size ten.

* A while back I went to a wedding wearing a super-tight dress I had just bought (I fancied it flattered my figure more than the one that actually fitted). All was fine until, walking down the aisle to my seat, I suddenly felt horribly exposed. Naked and not that hot. And a bit of a slut. And slightly sick. Being in the sober atmosphere of a church, with several pairs of eyes following my progress, taught me a lesson in six seconds that might not have sunk in for another decade – that tight is cute on girls, and sexy on vamps with personal trainers, but it can look desperate on a regular woman wearing ordinary underwear. I bolted back to the shop as soon as the service had ended and exchanged the dress for the bigger size (the assistant was very sporting about swapping them: she knew a TBC purchase a mile off) and ever since then I have been careful not to mistake tighter for better.

Too Youth

It's true that the whole concept of clothes for different generations has been blown away – kids wear pearls and women wear Ugg boots – but it's mostly one-way traffic, and you have got to feel for the younger generation. Every day they share changing rooms on the high street with women old enough to be their mothers (I have actually tussled over a jacket in Topshop with a fellow shopper who turned out to be a child in school uniform). But here's something to remember: not all of these clothes are meant for us. Great if you look good in the loons and the wedges and the military jacket but it is not – as some of us like to think – okay to duplicate everything your niece is wearing, right down to the shell ankle bracelet and the Stranglers' T-shirt. Apart from anything, it makes you look like you are having an identity crisis.

Avoid: The rule used to be don't go there if you were wearing it first time round. Now it's more like don't go there if you know your eighteen-year-old god-daughter would kill for it – especially the season's throwaway must-have (like a skull scarf) and anything that you might wear to a festival or prom. Also steer clear of logos (what are you even doing in Abercrombie & Fitch?).

Instead: Check if the clothes you fancy could conceivably be prefixed with the word chic, so: jackets, sunglasses, boots, bags, a sheath dress, a military coat. But not: the smock dress, harem pants, playsuit, strapless sundress, flying suit, leggings, etc.

I think I can still do Scruffy Rock Chick

I am standing in Rough Trade, a record shop on Portobello Road, and there is a girl wearing a man's cardigan over a T-shirt, a denim miniskirt and biker boots. She is not wearing make-up, or a bra, she has long, ropey hair and bare legs and she looks exactly like a young Jane Birkin – which is, as far as I am concerned, about as good as it gets. This look is also deceptively easy: the skirt is not too short, there's not a lot of flesh on show. Then I notice two things. One, her legs, which are demerara golden and Barbie-doll smooth. Two, another woman, maybe ten years older, who is also doing a Birkin – unbrushed hair, boyfriend's shirt – and managing to look like she just got out of bed, possibly after a bout of flu. This look is actually harder to pull off than a pvc catsuit, because it relies on youthful skin and a certain kind of dreamy, unselfconscious attitude. A good figure and a tan are not enough to get you into the club. For this look you actually do have to be young.

Avoid: Bare legs and miniskirts, unless you have one in a million legs. Boyfriend's cast offs (now strictly for the bedroom).

Instead: Get some opaque tights. Better still, don't go there.

I'm doing Old-school Glamour

Well, you'd better be careful. The trouble with Glamour with a capital G – unreconstructed cocktail dresses, jewel colours, expensive jewellery and fur wraps, not to mention the ready-for-my-close-up panstick make-up – is you automatically look like a woman who predates the sixties fashion revolution. Think Nancy Dell'Olio. No one knows how old she is – fiftysomething? – but she's looked it for as long as anyone can remember.

Avoid: All those clothes marked 'evening wear' that hang in the no-go areas of department stores. High-impact block colours, like turquoise and scarlet and candyfloss pink. Ginger with a sparkle make-up. Fur, and done, teased hair (see hair).

Instead: Wear a vamp dress without the jewels.

Note: Quantities of precious rings, trophy watches, more rings, charm bracelets, are as much of an age giveaway as a crêpey cleavage. Everyone knows that women who feel their sexual power slipping away are unwisely attracted to plunging necklines and serious jewellery, especially hand booty. You don't want to be one of them. Red nail varnish is another giveaway.

I'm a Chic Lady

As in neat and formal in a navy-blue shift dress and a princess coat with a snappy little bag to match. This look wasn't aging when Jackie O was laying down the formula, but please, the woman was unique and it was more than forty years ago. Can we get over it? Carla Bruni – who has a head start over most mortals – has started to look every inch her age since she married her pocket-sized president and ditched the jeans and ponchos for cable-knit cashmere, loafers, chinos and grey dress-and-coat ensembles. (Yes, yes, we're meant to think she's the epitome of European elegance, but who cares if she's added on a decade?) A pristine coordinated outfit is more aging than a blue rinse.

Avoid: Covering up (you need *some* flesh on show, whether it's your arms or your neckline). Uninterrupted grey and navy and beige. Pashminas (you can still wear them, just not proudly, in a slip knot, out to dinner). Jackets with gold buttons. Flat pumps with below-the-knee hemlines. Sunglasses on the head: it's the wooshy, to-the-manor-born thing it does to your hair; suddenly you are Princess Anne at the Burghley Horse Trials.

Instead: Break up the tailoring, go for quirky shoes and Françoise Hardy hair (Bruni's pre-Sarkozy fashion muse).

Floaty and Feminine

You think it's a sexy, bias-cut, floral tea dress that will look just like it did a decade ago. But floaty and feminine flips over into mumsy and blowsy, quite suddenly, at about the same time your lower legs start to look stiltony at the start of summer. And beware slinging a cardigan on top unless it is tiny and in a fashion colour such as watermelon.

Avoid: If you are going to wear a pretty dress, then everything else has to be the opposite of pretty. Steer clear of cashmere wraps, straw baskets, subtle gold jewellery, nude stockings and kitten-heeled sandals.

Instead: A denim biker jacket, clashing wedges and a flash of brilliant orange bra strap is more like it.

Kitten Girl

Who knows what you're thinking? I suit bows? I am adorable? The cut off for good girl cutesiness is twenty-five.

Avoid: Bows. Broderie anglaise. Cloying pastels. Gingham. Puffed sleeves. Note: Even if the sleeves look perfectly okay when you are standing in front of the changing-room mirror, you will be out in these puffed sleeves, reach for your martini glass and – *whoosh!* Suddenly you will feel like a maid of honour at Ivana Trump's wedding. Or worse (and I know this feeling), Grayson Perry.

Instead: Just get over it. And put away that flowergirl handbag with the appliquéd roses.

Some more things that are surprisingly aging (and they're not what you think they are)

• Make-up. As with hair (which we are coming to), what is aging is overdoing it. Bizarrely, the only people who suit lashings of make-up are the very young and fresh faced. When you start to really need the cover is when you have to step back from the dark eyeshadows and strong lipsticks and resist that bronzer. Orangey foundation automatically adds years. It's like wearing your Spanx on your face.

• Chiffon. The little chiffon dress will take you everywhere until one day, not that long after your fortieth birthday, you will put it on, look in the mirror and looking back will be the sort of woman who wears half slips and carries a pack of Wet Ones in her handbag. It is amazing how this dress can go from being your Holly Golightly facilitator to a total whistleblower.

• Teeth. Everyone assumes that whiter teeth are the key, and it's true yellow teeth do no one any favours. But please. That wall of glaring white porcelain just screams, 'I was born before 1966.'

• Black. You can still wear black, of course. It's just that it has to be the deep, quality, light-reflecting sort – Oscar Night black, not a black T-shirt you have had in your drawer for a couple of years, or, God forbid, a cotton polo neck.

• Leather. You can still wear leather – just not the hardcore Girl On A Motorcycle sort. Or the shiny, tailored Alaia sort. Or trousers (unless you're Honor Blackman). It has to be soft, and it can't be bulky or feature any hardware. I have a faded black men's Gap leather jacket and so far, so good. But that could change any day. Leather is borderline.

• Cheap when it needs to be Real – as in the vinyl, high street version of the leather jacket. Poor quality will age you before it makes you look hip.

• Hats. I have a fortysomething friend who looks dazzling in a woolly beanie, à la Ali MacGraw in *Love Story*. Even so, on the whole, the hats you used to wear – fedoras, trilbys, wide-brimmed felt hats, berets – make you look considerably older than you would bare headed. It is a sad fact that once you reach the stage of life when you can afford the giant coyote trapper's hat, that is the moment when you start to resemble the Russian oligarch's dowdy first wife (the one who's been banished to the dacha in the Crimea).

• Back fat. I mean that spare bulge above the horizontal strap of your bra just before it snakes round under your armpit. This can be solved by buying a nice new bra.

• Underwear. If your bra strap is liable to show, and it's last year's white, or this year's flesh, then that's telling everyone that your underparts are being protected in a functional, joyless manner, and that feeling sexy doesn't rank high on your list of priorities. It's so easy to get a bra in shocking sherbet pink or canary yellow, and then whey hey!

• Practicality. Never give in to the temptations of practicality: the easy fleece, the sloppy cardi, the really useful blazer (and then you complain that you're becoming invisible?).

• The one-piece swimsuit. If you've always worn them, fine. If you're a natural bikini girl, then a one piece will make you feel like you've been branded 'It's All Over'. Stick with it. Joan Collins does.

• The knee-to-shoe zone. Strange though it may sound, the knee to toe area is the number one danger zone. Your hem to heel ratio is crucial. A below-the-knee hem with flatish heels adds years (and pounds). Midcalf-length is miserable and, however chic the outfit, automatically makes you look dowdy. Maxi is a devil to pull off, but, if you're going for it, make sure you are wearing dangerously high wedges. And, if you happen to have the legs for short, resist wearing ultra high heels – that's a young girls' game.

All stockings are aging if the weather is good enough to go

bare, but sheer and coloured or, God forbid, patterned are worst of all.

Shoes must have flair and on no account should be practical or safe. (That said, there is nothing more aging than the Theresa May 'Do You Think I'm Racey?' leopard-print shoe stuck on the bottom of a boring old suit. Jazzy shoes are the equivalent of jolly spotted wellies, and you don't want to go there.)

• Veiny feet. Unfortunately there comes a time when heels make the veins in your feet bulge. The solution is to wear them for less time, or to drop an inch. But watch this one: the engorged foot is as aging as dentures.

Things you should ditch before you turn forty

- Glitter make-up
- High street jewellery
- Plaits
- Dungarees
- Tiered skirts
- Hairbands and bandanas
- Ankle bracelets
- Rock-band T-shirts
- Tattoos
- Leggings

Things you must get into by the time you turn forty

- Grooming (now it's not so much grooming as survival: one single stray hair on your lower leg will look like decay).
- Waxing your moustache. Unless it really is a downy bit of blonde, for God's sake do it. Bleaching only advertises the lady 'tache.
- Pedicures. Even if you are hairy as a bear under your clothes, a nice pedicure suggests that all is shipshape and tidy.
- Proper specs. The Boots £3 jobs make everyone look like Uncle Bulgaria.
- Big sunglasses. These should be worn whenever possible. Not only do they do wonders for disguising the appearance of fine lines, but underneath a pair of Oliver Peoples, you too can be an A-list star hunted by paparazzi.
- Colour. You can't get away with the plain white T-shirt any more.
- Feminine. Even the poster girls for utility dressing soften up in their mid thirties and add a bit of detail – you could start with some earrings.
- Make-up. Go easy, but your days of getting an eyelash tint and leaving it at that are numbered.

- Ironing. You need to be totally crease free yourself to get away with crumpled clothes.
- Exercise. You really should. I fully intend to.

❀ Know How to Shop

Remember, the sales assistant is not your friend

She doesn't know you, or the people you hang out with, or the places you go. She is not equipped to say, 'Hang on, but where exactly are you planning to wear this full-length kaftan, madam? I assume you've been asked to the Missonis' holiday villa, because, otherwise, what could you possibly be thinking?' The assistant is not aware that you already have three pairs of white jeans in your wardrobe, two of them unworn, because every time you try them on you feel like the third wife of a hedge-fund manager. She can't tell that you are allergic to wool (how could she guess – you keep trying on wool?). She doesn't know that silk makes you break out in a muck sweat, or that, flattering though the four-inch heels may look when you're standing in front of the changing-room mirror, you can't walk in anything over three. And all of this is no problem whatsoever, so long as you don't expect the sales assistant to tell you what you should be wearing.

The problem is, you lean on sales assistants more now than you ever did. There was a time when you might ask the girl serving you if she thought you could do with the smaller size. Now you say things like, 'You don't think it's a bit too pale for me?' or, 'This doesn't remind you of Miss Piggy, does it?' There are some wonderful sales assistants out there, but, on the whole, this makes no more sense than asking your boyfriend if you look okay in what you're wearing when you're already two hours late for the party. Not only that, but you are inviting the sales girl to bamboozle you with her stylist's know how: '. . . not if you dress it up with heels and maybe a sparkly shrug . . . not if you belt it and add a rabbit's foot on the lapel . . . not if you wear it with a special low-backed bra and a slip'. The assistant doesn't know that you can't belt anything, and that you are more likely to leave the dress hanging at the back of the wardrobe than get round to buying the novelty bra (why is it so depressing to shop for those things?). She assumes that you know what suits you and what doesn't, what works with your life and what doesn't, what is within your budget and what isn't, what is already in your wardrobe and what you actually need. She is pushing you a) because she is on commission and b) because it has never occurred to her that a grown woman might abdicate all responsibility for her appearance to a stranger. I repeat, she doesn't know you.

My favourite person to take shopping is Mentor Friend (of whom you will be hearing more). She once said, 'I know what you think you look like – Jane Fonda in *Klute* – and you don't. Trust me.' You just can't argue with that.

What you look good in is not the same as what you want to look good in

Here is the basic problem. When you start out on your shopping career, what might actually suit you doesn't even feature on your list of priorities. Stuff is either cool or not cool, fashion or not fashion, the same as your best friend's or not the same as your best friend's. Considerations like whether it brings out the colour of your eyes are for losers. The clothes are what count and you, the one wearing them, just have to carry them off as best you can (drainpipe jeans – fat legs – oh well). It is these formative shopping experiences that make it possible for you to stand in a changing room, several years after your thirtieth birthday, and ask yourself if the dress in the mirror is hot, not if *you look hot* in the dress. It's what makes you turn your nose up at the cute tailored jacket and the pretty skirt that also comes in pale pink (pale pink – As If) and it's the reason you have so much black in your wardrobe. You have muddled through this far, but as of now you need to adjust your taste radar and focus on the big four:

Your ideal shape.

Your ideal hem length.

Your best colours.

Your best feature.

Yes, it sounds like the end of shopping fun as we know it, but it must be done.

Note: Your shopping friend is invaluable when it comes to sorting out what looks good on you from what looks good on the hanger. She knows your weaknesses and your strong points and whether or not you can risk having your knees on show. I have got to the point with MF when we can do the whole thing over the phone, in roughly fifteen seconds:

MF: Where are you?

Me: Oasis. In the changing room.

MF: Not the print maxi halterneck? You're not trying that on, are you?

Me: Um. Well. It's actually quite . . .

MF: Put it back.

Me: What about the shorter one?

MF: I'm ringing off now. You need a coat.

Honestly. The woman has saved me a fortune.

What she looks good in is not the same as what you look good in

You may develop a fashion crush on someone you know, or it may be triggered by a split-second sighting on the tube. The female brain has a surprisingly un-Darwinian ability to bypass the details that matter (for example the age of your fashion crush, size, height, skin tone, etc.) and go directly to 'I want what she's got'. Whatever this girl is wearing, you have to have it: wide-leg sailor pants and boob tube, why the devil not? So what if the outfit is more appropriate for a six-foot teenager with a bmi of sixteen – you are not defeated. It's your crush you can see in the changing-room mirror.

Beware those candy-trap shops

These shops will make you buy things when you are feeling the opposite of twinkly and feminine and scrumptious. You go into them hating yourself for being so shallow and sissy, and then you find yourself sucked into all the gossamer butterfly prettiness and end up buying a dress designed for a butterfly in which you look like a caterpillar's mother.

There is a time for the ridiculously expensive and impractical purchase

Like, for example, the Chloé wooden-soled, pale beige sandals with the slingbacks that were obviously going to lose their sling grip after half an hour's wear, making them harder to manoeuvre than bricks attached with Sellotape. But that didn't matter because the shoes did their work and shunted a very ordinary dress into the 'I Know The Score, Thank You' category. Very expensive, in terms of value per wear, granted. On the other hand, simple, effective, fast track to an updated look with none of the stress involved in finding an entire new outfit. Perfect.

Shoes and bags can make it or kill it

Lately, shoes have become the most radical, extrovert element in fashion. It wouldn't be too much to say it's all about the shoes. This is excellent news for women like us who want to look like we still get it, but are probably not in the market for a playsuit. What it means is that you can wear something fairly unremarkable – a little black dress or a sweater and jeans – and then whack a pair of these heartstarters on the bottom, and – *boosh!* No one could possibly question your lust for life, your confidence or your commitment to all things modern. Suddenly you look like you know it all. And, of course, it works the other way round too: wear the safe, low-heeled pumps and it doesn't matter how much effort you have put into your outfit you will – until further notice – look like an undercover policewoman.

(Similarly, a bag will not actually make you look younger, but it allows you to do sharp-end fashion without changing your clothes, and it's easier to carry off than a gladiator sandal.)

Never shop with a man

At the start of every relationship you think you will be safe shopping with *this* man. He really gets you! He loves the way you dress! And, besides, he'd never let you buy something that didn't make you look terrific. As a matter of fact, he has a vested interest in you looking hot, so what better person to go shopping with? Oh dear God. This is more dangerous than believing the sales assistant is your friend.

First of all, a man who is mad about you will think you look great in anything, including a cocoon minidress. Worse than that, he will make *you* think you look good in anything. As it is, you are already in a 'How sexy am I?' fever, which will compromise your normally reliable instincts. You are no longer focused on the merits of the dress (brilliant Balenciaga rip off, in a useful colour), only whether it makes him look hungry – and male hunger takes no account of fashionability, or good proportions, or what the people who count (i.e. stylish women) will think. Men get hot for stuff that reminds them of their first English teacher or nurses or Joanne Whalley-Kilmer, floaty handkerchief-hemmed skirts, fifties-style shirt-waisters, cheesecloth shirts. They take against perfectly flattering articles like black velvet jackets. They do not have your best interests at heart.

On top of this you will get, despite yourself, a bit Julia Roberts in *Pretty Woman* and he will be somewhat channelling Richard Gere:

You: 'But it's red and satin and short, with puffed sleeves, and a cape. I could never wear something like this.'

Him: [*settling into the chequebook chair*] 'Try it on. I want to see you in it. What the hell. We'll throw a party for it.'

This kind of shopping is good for your sex life but bad for your image.

Then, after the honeymoon period, the man you shop with will lose his unlimited appetite for watching you twirl in front of shop mirrors and, henceforth, will be mainly concerned with hurrying you up, and the next thing you know you will have a wardrobe of things you literally cannot wear. Note: Only a man says, 'Why not get both?' and they only say this because they think that will mean one less shopping trip down the line.

Never shop with someone much richer or thinner than you

You will think you are too big (in the personality sense) for this stuff to count. And it won't count, until you can't find anything to wear for the party, but every single thing she tries on makes her look like Sienna Miller, and you know she could afford the lot, including the £3,700 Alexander McQueen.

10 things to own if you want to stay in the loop (that you don't have to be Kate Moss to carry off)

- The sunglasses of the season
- Black boots with a chunky heel
- A pair of conversation piece shoes
- A tight black tuxedo jacket
- A shawl/scarf that's more dazzling than a pashmina but as versatile
- Several pairs of Wolford opaques
- A pair of £200 jeans
- A white bag and a tan or red bag (black if you must) with style enough to attract glances
- A chunky watch
- A simple LBD equivalent in a brilliant colour or print
- Something gold or silver: jacket, shoes . . . turban if you're Zadie Smith

You can't anticipate when what used to look sexily dishevelled, in a French, Gitanes-over-breakfast-in-your-boyfriend's-shirt kind of way, will tip over into scary dog breeder – but no one gets away with bed hair forever. That said, the one thing guaranteed to age you faster than no-maintenance hair is a blow-dried, smoothed out, hairsprayed, collarbone-length bob. It's the tidiness that does it, and the manageable, safe, neither short nor long length. On no account go there, even if it does make you look cleaner and tidier. Yes, so? You'd look cleaner and tidier in a skirt suit and pussybow blouse, but you'd also look *a lot older.*

And that's not all. The extraordinary thing about tidy, shorter, ultra-groomed hair is it automatically casts a dowdy pall over every other aspect of your appearance. You could be working a Gwyneth Paltrow minidress with six-inch heels and all anyone would see is the hair of a lady mayoress or senior politician, possibly a retired tennis champion. Why do women fall for it? Because we think we need more grooming as time goes on. And we do – the more the better – but not the full on, country club sort. You want to find the hairdresser who knows you have to keep that length, who has the good sense not to swoosh it back off your face in creamy, deluxe waves, who understands that backcombing and starchiness and thick, tonged curls and turned up ends might look okay on Mischa Barton but will make you look like Mischa Barton's mother. It's all in the detail.

The dye issue

Besides cutting it too short, and coiffing it too thoroughly, there is the whole monster issue of getting the colour wrong.

They have yet to invent the dark hair dye (capable of covering grey) that doesn't make the average woman look like Ozzy Osbourne, with the result that every fortysomething greying woman now has highlights, somewhere on the spectrum from creamy light brown to surf-bum white. Blonde – or certain types of blonde – is the new grey, so you want to be very careful that you pick a shade that still has the right sun and Scandinavia connotations. For example, a full head of closely packed, bright platinum highlights, à la Camilla Parker Bowles, tells the world you have three children, one dog, a husband called Toby, a weekly Bums, Tums and Thighs keep fit class and an interest in gardening. If you go a bit more radical with the bleach (you may be aiming for the Debbie Harry studiedly unnatural look) you run the risk of looking like a rock 'n' roll survivor. The only way forward is as natural as possible. You want uplights and downlights and plenty of your natural colour showing through. And you want to pay good money for it. Straw hair is the most aging blonde of all. Texture, at this stage, is everything.

The grey debate

Lately there have been some vociferous converts to the virtues of going grey. Their argument is – more or less – that it is both undignified and impractical to keep covering up the inevitable. Going grey is liberating, they say, particularly since it's hardly the end of the world. I say it's very simple. If you are striking and dark and you have thick hair, cut in a clean, definite style, like Betty Jackson or Emmylou Harris, and your natural grey colour is a little bit gunmetal rather than snowy pensioner white, then you might want to go grey. But if you have thin, wispy, not much of anything hair, and a pale complexion, then going grey will undoubtedly make you look like a washed-out flannel, and it's not worth even considering. Grey hair is aging, period. If you are great-looking and uncommonly young to be grey, it can add a frisson of glamour, but only for as long as your face remains out of step with your hair. If you are Anna Ford, you've got so much going for you it doesn't make much difference either way. But if you're Ann Widdecombe, you might as well reach for the bottle and be damned.

Note: Women who have gone grey will often feel an urge to convert those around them to the path of true hair colour. They are genuinely perplexed by the time and money you are prepared to waste in order to cover up something so inoffensive. But don't be swayed. You can still be a good Natural and shell out £1,000 a year on hair dye without feeling a twinge of guilt. Hair is important. It's very important. And men are scared stiff of grey hair, unless it's on the over seventies.

Finding the hairdresser who will change your life
About seven years ago, John Frieda introduced me to his discovery, a hairdresser called Sally Hershberger. (Note the

way I casually drop these names! This is one of the major perks of working on glossy magazines – you get access to the people who have the means to change the way you look forever. You can have your hair snipped by Sam McKnight in between breaks on photo shoots! You get your make-up done by Ruby of Ruby and Millie! It never actually changes the way you look, but you get to glimpse how things could be, if only you made the effort.) Anyway, we were on a press trip and my hair was crying out for a serious overhaul, so Sally was volunteered for the job.

Sally was everything the hairdresser who will change your life should be: bristling with attitude, best friend to the stars (she was looking after Liz Hurley's dog at the time), impossibly booked up, fabulously expensive (I can't even tell you what she charged; you would choke). She arrived at half her appointments by helicopter, always wore a cowboy hat and rarely spoke when she was working. Sally cut my hair in roughly twenty minutes, and I was smitten. It was like being picked out of a line-up as mousey Norma Jean and reborn in the chair as platinum Marilyn. Did I mention she was based in New York, so any further cuts would have cost $**** plus the airfare, and the hotel, but was that going to stop me from making her my hairdresser for life? As if. And then a few months passed, I went on a photo shoot and fell in love with Michael the stylist . . . or was it Derek?

The search for the ultimate hairdresser is an ongoing project, with no finish date. It begins when we start to work out our position on the looks chart, relative to other girls, and realize that hair is the big part you can change. Then we get our first proper, radical, unsupervised haircut, and it is a disaster. We go in looking like an angel and come out looking like the killer in *No Country for Old Men*, only less symmetrical and glossy. And that, basically, seals it. If a haircut can make you look that bad, then it must have the opposite potential, or that is how we choose to see it. Plus, at some point during those forty-five agonizing minutes in the chair – watching some snake-hipped, gum-chewing poseur abuse our trust and destroy our chances of getting a boyfriend – our inner romantic has been roused. It is only female to dream that one day you will find the hairdresser who will press his cheek close to yours, meet your eyes in the mirror, separate your fringe with his expert fingers and say, 'My God, but you'd be lovely if we just got rid of some of the weight and layered it through the front.'

Then you find him, or her. And it's all coming together (you're growing out the layers, working on breaking up the colour) when you meet a girl at a party who has a fabulous sort of early Rod Stewart cut, and she gives you the number of her stylist, and the cycle starts all over again. It doesn't matter that your hair could not be more different from her hair, or that her head is a totally different shape from your head, or that she's a twenty-one-year-old backing singer and you're not. You want a change. You want a haircut like Rod Stewart girl. Mainly you want to be younger, prettier, thinner and groovier with more interesting friends and better clothes. This is the stuff we invest in haircuts. It is complex and irrational and it is the reason why you can be Condoleezza Rice and still searching for the hairdresser who will change your life. (There are some well-adjusted women who know what suits them and who *really are* just looking for a couple of inches off – but most of us are sick freaks who are still wondering if a *Rosemary's Baby* crop wouldn't unleash our inner Mia.)

Note: Your loyalty to your hairdresser is a fairly accurate gauge of your grasp on reality in general. I have a friend, S, who I introduced to my hairdresser fifteen years ago (that's seven hairdressers ago), and she's still with him. How grounded is that? And it's no coincidence that this friend has never bought a seriously expensive coat with a Mongolian lamb collar that she wore only once. She has never fallen in love with a boy solely because of his prowess at skiing. And when summoned to help decide if I should buy my flat she was the one who checked the boiler and the electrics and the neighbours while I drifted around wondering if I could live with the paint colour in the kitchen. But then she is exceptional.

❀ The Big One: Are You Too Fat To Be Good For Your Age?

All you need to know about the way we view fat now is that 'fit' is the word boys and girls use to describe someone who is attractive. Not fit and pretty or fit and sexy, just fit, because fit says it all. Fit is what really counts. Lately, the most average-looking girls are getting serious attention in the media for no other reason than that they have the slim, slight, willowy figure necessary to carry off a blowsy minishift and gladiator sandals. Which means, of course, that they are very young.

To be attractive, according to this modern definition, you need to have a figure that – at least covered up – could be a twenty-five-year-old's. You must be up to wearing tight jeans, and a bikini, and shorts on the beach. If you have a lovely face, so much the better. But the test is the figure. This is why we are all obsessed with size: not because we think it's gross to be voluptuous, or because we believe that the female body looks better smaller, but because we want to look good in clothes. And the reason we want to look good in clothes is because we want to look like contenders. We want to be considered for the jobs that younger women are considered for. We want to be attractive to the men that younger women are attractive to. We don't, in other words, want to be thought of as getting any older. And so, by extension, we have reached the point where we now actually believe that narrow hips and a pert bum and a flat stomach and arms with definition are the first defence against aging. (And they are the first. Even the Plastics worry about their figures before they worry about their faces. If you asked them to choose between getting fat and having Botox, or taking a year off Botox and staying skinny, they would take the lines and the pert body every time.)

This is what it boils down to: if you're thin enough, you can wear the skin-tight trousers and skinnier jacket and stride up to the door of the new club in the Meatpacking District in New York and, providing your eyeliner is dark enough and your air of entitlement just right, you will be granted entry – regardless of your age. People will take it on trust that you have a right to be there, because you look the part. If, however, you are something of a beauty, but more of a curve-packing, big-busted, forty-seven-year-old – well, you'll be lucky. Don't get me wrong. Beth Ditto can go to this club. Big and medium-sized women are welcome, providing they are hip and young. But if you're past the first flush of youth thin is your ticket to credibility.

Naturally, this means thin has come in for a bit of a recategorization in recent years. If you were to do a fat/thin perception chart, beginning in 1973 and ending up now, you would discover two quite remarkable things. One, that the sex sirens back then (I give you Agnetha in Abba with her fabulous turquoise upholstered bottom and curved tummy) would be classed as fat in the noughties. Two, that women past their prime childbearing years, grown-up women – women for whom aspiring to have the hip measurements of an adolescent boy is not just peculiar but medically unwise – are shrinking before our eyes. If you're forty and affluent in the twenty-first century you are quite likely to be thinner than you were a decade ago and, if you're not, then the chances are you would like to be.

Wanting to look good in clothes applies to all females, but

something particular happens to women when they reach their late thirties and get the scent of a generation coming up behind them. One minute they're competing using their personalities, their brains, their sex appeal *and* their bodies, and then, click clack, they shift tracks and the focus becomes *all about* size. How big they are in relation to each other, or rather how small. You can go for decades not minding that much about your weight, but cross the forty threshold and size becomes a pressing issue, whether you like it or not. You want to come on holiday? We'll all be wearing bikinis! You want to come to the party? We'll all be wearing sleeveless tops and cheeky little denim skirts! The competition at this stage is not just to look fit but to look more fabulously fit for your age than anyone, ever, with the possible exception of Madonna. It's the modern antidote to the old fear of becoming invisible – get older, but get back to the size you were fifteen years ago. Or considerably smaller. Show the world that you can exist on a diet of San Pellegrino and celery.

What is too thin and what is too fat?

That depends, once again, on where you're standing. If you're a Plastic, too thin is Amy Winehouse (but even then it's more about her scuzziness than the lack of flesh on those bones). Too fat is being any bigger than the hottest girl in your circle (who used to be a model and is just back from the LA fit camp, so, you can imagine). In Plastic Land, no one is ever really thin enough and no one acknowledges the obvious fact that the skinnier you are in later life the more haggard you will look. Because, as we've established, this isn't about Actually Looking Young. This is about staying in the competition, and winning.

Too fat, from a Natural's point of view, is a size or two bigger than their normal weight. It's when we start looming in photographs and ripping cap-sleeve dresses under the armpits and getting dent marks from the seams of our jeans. Too thin is the point at which women lose their sense of humour.

An awful lot has been written about our peculiar attitude to weight, but people rarely discuss the terrible effect that controlled eating has on the female personality. Never mind the so-called drinkorexics who fall over after two cocktails because they haven't swallowed any solids since yesterday, what about all the women you know who are tired and snappy and permanently run down and still insist on refuelling with a handful of grapes? Who's to say these silent dieters aren't blighting the nation's future as much as boozy youths and selfish bankers? Lots of people are naturally thin. *Too* thin is when there's an almighty internal struggle going on to keep off those extra pounds – and it just so happens that this is more likely to be the case with a thirty-nine-year-old size six than a twenty-one-year-old size six.

The best measure of what is and isn't too thin is the story of Twiggy. Twiggy was twig thin as a teenager and now, pushing sixty, is fit and slim enough to be modelling, but nothing like as skinny as Teri Hatcher or Candace Bushnell or a thousand grown-up women you could mention. She looks comfortable and radiant. They look gaunt. She's always looked the size she was meant to be. They look the size they think they need to be in order to keep on fitting in where they want to be.

Are you too fat or too thin?

Who knows? Yesterday I felt really fat. Today I feel sort of normal. It has also come to my attention that I am several pounds thinner than I was when I met The One (a certain pair of jeans that were tight on me then are almost baggy) and yet I haven't really noticed it. This tells you just enough, I think, because it's the same story for all of us. You are only as fat or as thin as you feel, and if you feel good, you actually forget about your size. (Something else that says it all: when I met The One, everyone kept telling me how thin I looked. What they meant was I looked radiant/happy/glowing/whatever and – because all the comments came from women – they naturally equated that with weight loss.)

How to look just thin enough

There is something called your perceived fat level, which goes right down provided you show off a bit of a waist and dress to complement your curves rather than disguising them. For example, Charlotte Church is large by modern standards but is generally regarded as nicely voluptuous because she favours an hourglass frock with lots of cleavage. However, were she to dabble in tight designer jeans and skinny-girl gear, the fat police would be on to her like a shot. Other ways of reducing your PFL include:

- Not wearing long jackets or voluminous tops and cardigans that cover your bum. The reality is always preferable.

- Show forearms, calves and ankles and a bit of cleavage. Too much coverage creates the illusion of bulk.

- Avoid scoop necks. Sharp Vs or round necks are better.

- Steer clear of tight trousers and focus on figure-hugging dresses (see the Nigella uniform: a gipsy-style hourglass dress that advertises all her best assets).

- Black always works (if it's quality black).

- Forget belted coats, full skirts, cap sleeves, leather, sheepskin, bulky woollen cardis and sweaters, frills and froth and tiers. And beware wearing knee boots with dresses, if there's no gap between the top of the boot and the hem.

- Avoid a bob.

- Stick to heels.

- Never fall for on-show fastenings, like laces or hooks and eyes.

- Avoid masculine clothes, big linen shirts, pleat-front pants, unless you are super tall.

- Watch those big prints. They can work, but only if they're more Missoni than flower power.

❀ And now for the important anti-aging stuff

I saw a magazine editor at a party recently whom I have known on and off over the years and remarked to a friend how lovely she was looking:

'She definitely hasn't had anything done,' I said.

'Hmm.'

'Maybe she's grown into her looks.'

'Hmm.'

'I wonder if she's given up drinking . . . She's definitely given up smoking. That could be it.'

'Maybe she's just happy.'

'What?'

'Maybe she's happy, and that's why she looks good.'

'Oh.'

In our efforts to do everything right and eat enough tomatoes and drink enough water and restrict our caffeine intake and get enough sleep, it's easy to forget that nothing makes you look quite so youthful as feeling good about life.

There was a follow-up to this conversation:

Me: 'X is looking fantastic and we all think it's because she's happy.' (Notice I am now taking the credit.)

D: 'It's success, definitely. She is on a roll.'

M: 'She took that long break over Christmas. Recharged her batteries.'

C: 'You lot! What are you like? She's going out with Daniel whatsit. She's totally loved up. That's why she looks so good.'

And there you have it. How you get your youthful glow entirely depends on what makes *you* tick. Also, you will notice, not one of us suggested the magazine editor might have been seeing an electro-magnetic therapist, or eating only celery and almonds, or borrowing Gwyneth's personal trainer. When it comes down to it, everyone knows that it takes more than diet, treatments and exercise to look good for your age.

So are you good for your age?
Yes if you can say:

- I can touch my toes.

- I draw the line at leggings.

- I have my own teeth.

- I have stopped home dyeing my hair.

- I only have friends who make me laugh.

- I still buy albums.

- I crave fashion (sometimes).

- I own nothing beige.

- I never compromise on shoes.

- I have danced in the kitchen in the last six months.

No if you would say:

- I still want to look like Sarah Jessica Parker.

- I never eat carbs after six.

- I sometimes wear overknee socks and heels.

- I lie to everyone about my age.

- I never touch my face with my hands because it's bad for the complexion. (This is something Glenn Close once told me in an interview. I have literally never got over it.)

- I won't allow animals in my house.

- I am always in bed by midnight.

- I need my own room.

- I cannot see the point of ear-splittingly loud music.

Anti-aging tips that have nothing to do with your appearance

- Don't move to the country. You'll be cold and damp all the time. You'll forget about exfoliating. You'll get toenails like Howard Hughes, and then one day a hair will grow on your chin and you won't even notice it.

- Do not go to the serious side. There is a dangerous assumption that growing up means rejecting silliness. Not long ago I went to a dinner at which there were brains and beauty on every side. All the conversations were clever and important and worthy of noting down and delivering as mini lectures, but no one was having any actual *fun*. I don't think I heard anyone laugh all night. At that dinner, for the first time ever, I felt really old.

- Force yourself to be spontaneous. Of course you can get ready in half an hour. Of course you can go to Spain for a long weekend. What's stopping you from having a party? Nothing.

- Never stand in front of mirrors with brutal overhead lighting (okay, this one is appearance related). The ex-model who co-owns the Soneva chain of hotels once told me that she insists all the mirrors in their properties are lit to flatter women (i.e. badly) because feeling good in your bikini/skimpy dress is what makes the difference between a happy holiday and a week of self-flagellation. You risk injuring yourself in those bathrooms, but what the heck: you go out to the restaurant wearing practically nothing, and you feel Great.

- Don't worry so much about the pointless stuff. That's what's giving you that clumpy nobble between your eyebrows.

You know all this. And, remember, you could be
dead tomorrow! So stop beating yourself
up. Who cares!

2.

What Do I Do About
My Friends?

There is one big problem with friendship at this stage of life: circumstances have conspired to give you way too many of them. Even if you're not that much fun to be around, life has expanded, and the friendship years – as in the pre-settling-down years – have roughly doubled for most of us. I went to a wedding recently at which the groom had not one but two best men. No one batted an eyelid: two seemed just enough, given that he was almost forty and had already lived several lives, on at least two continents. This abundance of friends is definitely something to celebrate, in theory. It is also the reason why you wake in the night with a racing heart thinking: 'Shit. Yesterday was Sarah's fortieth birthday/ the day her decree nisi came through/my god-daughter's christening.' (I particularly worry about being a bad godmother to my thirteen god-children. Not only do I have trouble remembering how old they all are, I have actually written the wrong name on a god-child's Christmas present and had to be reprimanded by her mother. That, in a roundabout way, I put down to friendship overload.)

Here's something else that puts a strain on modern friend-ships: we are all at completely different life stages. I mean, look around you and spot the friend whose life is totally in sync with yours. I have friends with one-year-old children, and friends with teenagers, and single, childless friends and friends who are pregnant. At 7 p.m. on an average night, one is dealing with headlice and homework, one is on a conference call at the office and one is guzzling mojitos on a date. It is a mystery how we could have been born at roughly the same time when we have so little in common. You try and meet up at the weekend, but your different priorities – park and zoo, gym and rest, heavy drinking followed by dancing – make settling on a plan a lot harder than it used to be. Not only that, but these friends are spread out all over the country and every one of them is determined to stay put and get the others to come to them. (Otherwise what, exactly, was the point of paying all that money to put in a kitchen extension?) Oh, and it goes without saying that all of us are *incredibly* busy. You send each other those emails, 'Can do August, first two weekends, or Thursday week, or Friday, can you do any of those?' But they can't. Or you can't. Or they can, and then the dog's ill.

To complicate matters further (if that's possible), we're conditioned to aspire to unmanageable amounts of friends. In the twenty-first century your worth is measured by the number of people you know. Power is important, status is crucial, but if you can summon two hundred people to your wedding – all of whom appreciate that it would be pointless giving you a fondue set – that is the modern definition of success. (Facebook is the ultimate expression of this need to feel connected to hundreds, preferably thousands of people. I happen to be allergic to Facebook – unless it's being used by students, the demographic it was invented for – because it encourages people to collect pals like trophies, and it's all about looking good in photographs). Still, this highmindedness doesn't mean I don't want seas of Christmas cards covering every surface of my house come December – even if they're from my dentist and the guy who mends my computer. And it definitely doesn't mean I don't want to be asked to the party by the person I barely know and get greeted on arrival at the party by endless near strangers. Like I said, we've all got friendship problems.

Your mother never had these problems because she did not accumulate friends in the compulsive, competitive way that you do, and she did not marry your father after twenty-odd years of relying on her friendship network for life support. Also, let's face it, she needed less attention, and her friends did too. Whatever, you have a situation. You suffer from guilt that you are not a good enough friend, and sometimes you suspect that your friends are not performing as well as they might. It's time to take stock. First of all, you need to know who your friends are.

❀ Know Your Friends

Have you noticed how people have started using the prefix 'my friend'? This only used to happen in junior school, but the habit has spread, post Facebook, since we've all become conscious that the 'friend' word has been abused to the point where it is almost meaningless. Now, when you say, 'Have you met my friend Sue?' what you mean is, 'This person is someone I have a genuine history with, as opposed to someone I just happen to know, and I wish that distinction to be noted because I'm aware that this friendship lark is way out of control.'

When you're young, you don't need to think about who your Real Friends are, as distinct from your Regular Friends, but, as you get older, your friend radar becomes corrupted: expediency and vanity and all kinds of stuff, like the fact that they have a nice house in the south of France, gets in the way of your pure gut instincts and you may find yourself confusing Regular Friends with Real Friends. This is normal. We've all done it from time to time. But it's important to get the distinction straight, because not differentiating between the two is what leads to these feelings of overload, and guilt, and generally messing up your friendship priorities.

The definition of a Regular Friend

- You dress up for them.

- You worry about who they are sitting next to at supper.

- You are always 'up' on the phone to them.

- You have never had a conversation that begins 'that fucking bitch'.

- You compliment them on their weight.

- You buy them quite expensive presents.

- You ask them to the theatre.

- You are conscious of paying them back for every invitation.

- You can't shop with them; it's embarrassing.

- They take you seriously.

- They think you have good taste.

- They can look at your clothes without looking at you.

As for Real Friends

- You can tell them when you have threadworms, or similar. In fact, you probably call them up especially to tell them.

- They never comment on your appearance, unless you have done something radical with your hair.

- They always call you back even though you have established that the urgent conversation you need to have is about what you should wear on Saturday.

- You can cry on the phone to them just because you feel like crying.

- You talk to them about your parents.

- They think nothing of being rude about your New Friends.

- They don't confuse you with your job.

- They will perform for you in public if necessary.

- They will occasionally say hurtful things to you and follow them up with, 'Sorry, but you know what I mean.' You do. (One of the definitions of a Real Friend is someone who can say things to you that you might, just, take from your mother. For example: 'You've got really bad breath.')

- They never take offence if you cancel.

- They tease you, about the right stuff.

- They listen when you say you are busy, but if there is a thinly disguised cry for help in there – as in 'I am drowning and maybe I'd be better for a pep talk' – they will hear it.

- They have been known to cry when you are happy and when you are sad.

- When you say, 'But *why* doesn't he love me?' they do not say, 'Well, maybe because . . .' and proceed to list the ways in which you might be unlovable (there is someone in your life who is prepared to do this, see The Friends You Don't Need).

They say that a Real Friend is someone you could trust with your life, but then that rules out all your impractical friends, and the cowards. I think a Real Friend is someone who could speak for you if you were in a *The Diving Bell and the Butterfly* situation (i.e. stroke bound and only able to move one eyelid). They would say, 'Hold on, I think she wants the TV on. Yes. Not that! She hates that! Leave it on *Strictly Come Dancing*. Or *Scrubs*. Don't try to give her the salmon. Oh, that was close. She hates salmon. Especially blended. And she's allergic to ketchup. Are you washing the sheets in non-biological, by the way? She's allergic to biological. And soap. And lilies. Better take those sunflowers away, now that I think about it, they remind her of that arse Richard. Yes. Thought so. And she *always* has a cappuccino after lunch, no chocolate dusting. Could that be delivered intravenously?' A Regular Friend, you see, would have no idea.

There is nothing wrong with cultivating lots and lots of friends, but here is the potential pitfall: you may find you are spending considerably *more* time on your Regular Friends because your Real Friends simply don't require the same degree of maintenance. When did you last take flowers when you were asked to a Real Friend's house for dinner? Or spend a lunchtime choosing a lovely birthday card to go with the bottle of Jo Malone? Exactly. They get a text if they're lucky. Possibly a day late. To be fair, Real Friends don't expect this kind of VIP treatment, but this isn't really the point. We've already established that you have way too many people in your address book – so, if you're going to neglect some of them, it probably shouldn't be one of those you may need to ask for a kidney.

❋ The Friends You Need

Old Friends

You met through the bars of your playpen, or in the college bar – it doesn't matter exactly when the friendship was formed – what matters is you go back far enough for this person to know the unedited version of your story. Unlike friends you meet later in life, they have been privy to the really embarrassing stuff, the round-the-family-table stuff, the stuff you can't remember on account of the Malibu, many of your major rites of passage (first break up, first seriously traumatic haircut, first sacking, second break up, second sacking, etc.) and vice versa. This stuff automatically creates a bond and allows you to communicate on a subliminal level.

Here is a typical telephone conversation with an Old Friend:

'Did you get the dress?' (Old Friends have no need to introduce themselves.)

'No.'

'Why not?'

'I looked like fat Wonder Woman.'

'I knew you reminded me of someone. So, what are you going to wear?'

'Don't really care.'

'Are you busy?'

'Yes.'

'Shall we have a drink, then?'

'When?'

'Now by the sounds of it.'

'Okay.'

Now the same conversation with a Regular Friend would have gone something like this:

'Hi, it's me, Anna. How *are* you?'

'Oh, hiiiii. Fine. How about *you*?'

'Great, thanks. Did you get that lovely dress I saw you trying on?'

'I didn't in the end. I thought it was a bit ... Wonder Woman.'

'No! You are funny! You looked great! So, what are you going to wear?'

'I'm not quite sure. I need to go through my wardrobe.'

'You sound a bit distracted.'

'Do I? Sorry. So how is everything? How's Jack ...'

Old Friends, as everyone knows, are irreplaceable and surveys have shown that spending time with them lowers stress levels, though not quite as much as stroking a donkey. You do not have to be on your best behaviour with Old Friends, or even your second best. They will rally round in times of crisis. They always help clear the plates and load the dishwasher. They will stay up and listen to you going on and on about the look He gave you, and what it might have meant, even if they have an important meeting in the morning. That said, let's be clear. Old Friends have their disadvantages, namely, their refusal to acknowledge the passage of time and the possibility of change.

So, for example, when you breeze in and say, 'Hey, guess what? I've been nominated for an Oscar!' they will say, 'Great!' and then, 'Right. Are we going to get a curry or what?' This is all part of the Old Friend's job description. They aren't interested in the slimmed-down, madeover you, or the you with the glamorous job involving first-class travel. (They're not *not* interested, they're just not impressed. Why would they be? They have known you since you were dyeing your own shoes and working in a sandwich shop.)

The thing is, your Old Friends love you in much the same way as your family – and they are, to an extent, in loco familiac – so it follows that they reserve the right to keep you in your place. If they shared a house with you at university, it's inevitable that they will honk with laughter when you say you 'can't cook' on electric (yes, you can). And if you were called Pudge at school, then they're hardly going to call you Priscilla now – what would be the point? It's not the job of an Old Friend to make you feel good. It's their job to keep the bullshit detector turned up to ten and then follow you around with it, prodding you in the small of your back. This is all brilliant and healthy. You wouldn't change them for the world. But a girl needs to get some rapt attention now and then. She needs to charm and be charmed, to be thought witty and interesting and special. And for this she needs New Friends.

New Friends

New Friends are like lovers at the start of a relationship. They want to know everything and anything about you; they think you look great, smell great, live in a fabulous place and they can't believe how lucky they are to have discovered you. ('Isn't she amazing!' they will say to your Old Friends and your Old Friends will nod enthusiastically while shooting you a glance that says, 'Where'd you find this one?')

Crucially, which is precisely why they are such a seductive prospect, New Friends are getting to know you *now*. They are arriving in your story at the good part, when you have finally worked out who you are and got together something approaching a personal style (you've given up accessorizing, in a nutshell). Unlike the people you have known most of your life, these friends have no inkling of how many mullets and waitressing jobs and nights covered in tears and snot it took to get to this point. They don't know that you once had a boyfriend who looked like Bill Gates, or that you used to dress like Princess Anne, and the beauty of it is *they never need to*. This is intoxicating, naturally, because it allows you to be the improved, up-to-date, sorted version of yourself, and to get some genuine feedback. The trouble with Old Friends is they are no gauge of how you are perceived, because they'd be along for the ride, regardless.

There's another big advantage with New Friends. You can hand-pick them to fit your current life – choosing them for their geographical proximity, house in the south of France, staggering array of single male friends, whatever. You've got your Old Friends for the nitty gritty stuff, so your New Friends can afford to be nominated for really superficial reasons. (It is perfectly possible to make a New Friend solely because she looks fabulous in her yeti-hair jacket and thigh boots, and is guaranteed to add glamour to your party in a way that a disco ball and some more candles just couldn't. You can't rely on Old Friends for that kind of input.)

New Friends can make the conversion to Old Friends, but generally only if you work side by side with them, solidly, for years on end. It's been tried. We've all tried it. You meet this couple on holiday and they're great, so you try to keep the momentum going when you get home, with impromptu Friday night parties and meeting in bars for cocktails. And then, after a few months (when real life resumes and there just isn't the time for all that flirting) the NF affair fizzles out. Or, alternatively, it limps on for a couple of years, with each of you in turn valiantly issuing invitations in the hope that you can get the relationship to the stage where it can chug along, more or less unmaintained. But that's just it. You can't do no maintenance with New Friends.

I made friends with a couple not long ago, and I could have sworn we'd cracked it: enough people in common, enough opportunities to bump into each other, enough reasons to bother. And then one day she uttered the fatal words, 'You must come over one night and just watch TV,' and that killed it stone dead. In that moment we all knew the game was up, because we could no more hang out and 'just watch TV' than join in each other's family Christmas celebrations. All of us wanted to stop doing the intense, dating part of the relationship and move on to the cosy, taking each other for granted part, but there wasn't – and never would be – the time to get that comfortable. (Now, whenever we meet, there's that same frisson of embarrassment you get with men you accidentally slept with and really shouldn't have.) Some New Friends will become Old Friends, given enough exposure, but it's better to accept that most have a short lifespan and will need to be replaced.

Note: As a rule, you don't want to mix Old Friends and New Friends. Old Friends are the equivalent of long-term partners who don't have a lot of sex, but have been through so much together that their bond is unshakeable. New Friends, of either sex, are the twenty-three-year-old Argentinian polo player who always comes down to breakfast without his shirt on. They are rivals, in short, with very different styles.

Work Friends

Work Friends may have as strong a bond as Old Friends – possibly stronger, if they have to lean on/cover for each other in times of crisis – but only for as long as they are working in the same job. Just one in twenty work friendships survives a job move. (I made that statistic up, but I think it's probably a generous estimate. How many colleagues' leaving cards have you signed with the words 'Keep in touch!' and you've never, ever, seen them again?) The demise of the work friendship is something you have to get used to in life – like the fact that people you love have loved other people, and slept with them – but it's always tough. You've been through the highs, the lows, the cutbacks and the power cut that wiped everything, the incredible drinking sessions, the motivational weekends (aka incredible drinking sessions) and you've spent more time with these people than you've ever spent with your family, let alone your friends. Why wouldn't you stay together forever? But a) you have a new set of work friendships in your new job, and lo ... they fill the gap. And b) because you've never shared the lying-around-eating-pizza-draped-in-a-bedspread for-days-on-end stage of the friendship, you haven't reached the point at which you can just let it coast and pick it up later (see New Friends).

That said, if you work together for long enough, and you tend to go out together after work instead of going home, and you are all slightly in love with each other, and this working relationship comes at a formative stage of your life, then your Work Friends will definitely become Real Friends. I have slept in a kingsize bed with the entire editorial team of a magazine I once worked on, and I am still in close touch with almost all of them.

Trophy Friends

Unlike a New Friend, a Trophy Friend doesn't necessarily have a lot of time for you – but that couldn't matter less. Trophy Friends, like trophy wives, don't need to do much to earn their keep, apart from make you look good. She, or he, is the adult version of a schoolgirl crush combined with a shot of social ambition. It may be that your Trophy Friend is a bit famous, very good-looking or unusually talented (though then they would have to be slightly famous too –

unless people can spot the Trophy in their midst, it doesn't work). Either way, you use this Trophy Friend to beef up a social occasion, as bait for other Trophy types, or just to give you that very special glow that comes with knowing someone other people would like to know. (These are shallow times. The two things guaranteed to put people in the party mood – besides the obvious stuff – are a man with a camera and a couple of people whose faces are recognizable from the TV or the pages of *Grazia*.)

Note: Trophy Friends are only too happy to play their role. They have a whole set of other superior friends, and far sexier places to be, but they like to pop in on the real world and see the jaws drop and the eyes widen. It's like recharging an electric car.

The friendship survival pack

There is no rule as to the number of friends a person needs. According to MSN surveys, six true friends is the average, but you might feel comfortable with more or less. What counts is having the complete survival pack, as listed below and, if you're like me, you will want two in each category.

Wise Married Friend (WMF)

This friend needs to be married, as well as wise, because her life must be a complete contrast to yours and her home a domesticated haven you can retreat to and lick your wounds. The WMF always has a full fridge and an open door, but above all she has the answer to every practical and emotional problem – including where to buy a rug for the bedroom (trickier than it sounds) and what to do if a man doesn't call when he says he will. Most likely to say: 'Why don't I make us osso bucco and you can talk to me while I'm cooking?'

Mentor Friend (MF)

If you have to shop for an important dress, buy a flat or decide on a job offer, you don't even think about doing it without first consulting MF. Her job is to provide the no-nonsense Simon Cowell perspective and an antidote to your occasional fecklessness. At the outset her input was mostly career-related, but lately she gets dragged into any decisions that require a bit of steel: whether you should buy the Miu Miu boots, whether you should go on a second date with the ghastly photographer, whether you should give up drinking during the week or just Sunday to Tuesday, etc. Most likely to say: 'You are ten years too old for a fringe. Get over it.'

Angry Single (AS)

The Angry Single is not actually angry, or even necessarily single, just ready to get angry if anyone makes assumptions concerning women's capabilities. She is a bonus friend for women who are in a relationship and absolutely essential if you are not, since she is never too tired or too busy to drop everything, and has not compromised her lifestyle since the day you met (although she does now have to wear a knee support in certain situations). Most likely to say: 'Oh, have a baby, so what. I'll look after it at weekends. Let's get on a plane tomorrow; it will be a laugh. Oh, fuck him – he was too short anyway. Can you put another shot in this? I can't taste the alcohol.'

(Optional, but desirable) Available Attractive Male Friend
Your AA Male Friend – aka Platonic Friend – is invaluable during those fallow periods when you can go for months without glimpsing a single man. He escorts you to parties. Helps shift heavy stuff in your flat. Helps shift you, if you happen to get tired and emotional. Vets any available talent, and provides that all important masculine perspective, for example: 'Someone would have to love you very much to put up with that swimsuit.'

Note: My own survival pack will be cropping up at regular intervals throughout this book, because that's the nature of these friends: they are never far out of the picture and they are involved in all the significant dealings in your life. (WMF likes me to go to the hairdresser with her and stand over the colourist, to avoid a repeat of the highlighting debacle of 2004, but personally I don't go as far as taking any of the pack to the hairdresser. Shopping, yes.)

I hate my Best Friend
Even in this friend-saturated climate, you will probably have a Best Friend, and what distinguishes her from your other friends is her ability to make you hate her. Usually these feelings will arise because:

- She has told you something you don't want to hear. For example, that the man you have been going on about for weeks, as if there is some possibility of something actually coming of it, is clearly a two night stand.

- She has been deceitful (i.e. not told you, the morning after the party, that she got off with the man at the party. Her excuse is that he was in bed next to her when you rang, but still).

- She has lost weight and started throwing her (lesser) weight around and adopted a really irritating hips-thrust-out pose.

- She has developed a girl crush on someone at work and is always having a drink with her whenever you phone. Also, when she picks up, she is giggly and offhand, as if she's been liberated from the suffocating monogamy of your friendship and is now having a really cool affair.

- She borrowed your silk dress and sweated in it and didn't bother dry-cleaning it.

- She has been monstrously disloyal (at a supper party at your house she ganged up on you and teased you about your Sienna wannabe waistcoat, when the unwritten rule is 'you never break ranks').

- She bought the same shoes that you bought and didn't tell you.

- You tried to make her have a bitch about a mutual acquaintance and she looked disapproving and wouldn't join in, thereby breaking the other unwritten rule: any enemy of mine is an enemy of yours.

• She met your ex at a party and talked to him for *an hour and a half* and yet she can only report back one minute of edited highlights.

• Neither of you cook (sort of by agreement) but now she is cooking and pretending it is *second nature*, and she's bought a mezzaluna.

• She completely denies that it was you who got her into yoga and claims it was some girl at work.

• She has cut back on drinking to the point of not drinking and pretends she hasn't, just like she does when she is on a diet.

• She fancies she has a special relationship with your on-off (okay, probably ex) boyfriend and says things like, 'Yes, but he'd hate that,' and, 'I can see him really hitting it off with Jane.'

The reason your Best Friend gives you so much cause to hate her is because she is treading a fine line between being your friend and your dedicated soulmate. As she whisks away from the registry office, in the taxi cab bedecked in white silk ribbon, you imagine that the thought bubble above her head will read: Oh, I love her. I love him too. But I'm so lucky to have her. I hope she'll be okay. I'm going to really miss her.

When in reality what the thought bubble actually says is, Shit! Did I remember to say goodbye to his mother? Am I creasing this? I am! That's better. Now, who did I give my bag to? Oh, that's right, Best Friend. Phew. Well, she'd better remember to bring it to the hotel, or there'll be trouble.

Your Best Friend thinks about you exactly the way you think about her, which isn't always good enough.

Also, your Best Friend knows too much. She doesn't just know all the Old Friend stuff, she knows *everything*. Only toxic women (see below) would dream of actually using privileged information against you, but your Best Friend reserves the right to gently prick your Achilles heels (you have eight, and she's on to every one of them) when she feels it's appropriate. It's like a perk for all those hours spent buoying up your fragile ego, advising you what to do and then, when you go ahead and do the opposite, starting all over again. You know the stuff she does that drives you stark raving mad? Sixty per cent of it is entirely deliberate.

❀ The Friends You Don't Need

There are only two reasons to cull a friend: a) if their presence in your life is having a negative effect, or b) if you have come to the realization that you are not actually friends, even in the loosest sense of the word, and so maintaining the pretence of friendship seems pointless. For example:

- You have an email address for her but no phone number.

- Her husband always mispronounces your name.

- You can't actually recall his name.

- You know no one in common, except for your ex.

- You find it genuinely awkward when you bump into her in the street, especially after you've said, 'So how's Rick?' and it turns out Rick went off with the au pair in 2005.

- Neither of you has ever been to the other's house.

- You definitely saw her dodging you in the street.

- Last time she sent you a text you couldn't work out who it was from, even though she signed off with an initial and the message contained the words 'Jack sends love'.

- You feel relieved when you call her and she doesn't pick up, which means you can just leave a message.

- She had a huge party and didn't invite you.

This category of friend doesn't actually require culling. Here the *missing believed dead* rules apply. You don't contact them; they don't contact you. A couple of years pass and you are officially acquaintances. Toxic Friends (i.e. the ones having a negative impact on your life) may require more decisive action.

The Drain

You know her. She's had a hard year. Her car got broken into. Her cat got ill. The flat she wanted to buy fell through. Then her pipes leaked and the kitchen ceiling had to come down. It's one thing after another (even if there are gaps of several months in between crises, it feels like one thing after another). She can be funny, but the deal with the Drain is you listen to her problems and marvel at her resilience even if you are on the brink of losing your job and covered in shingles. And the problems used to be funnier, and involve men.

How to cope: Look sympathetic then change the subject. Say, 'Oh well. Looking on the bright side, you could have bird flu.'

How to cull: Tell her that you've got a lot on. Then don't answer your phone.

The Mrs Ripley

A while back you made the decision not to wear your new purchases in front of Mrs R because, sure as eggs is eggs, she'll have one in the same colour before the day is out. And she wants your curtains. And your earrings. And the name of your upholsterer. And the recipe for the chilli. Imitation may be the sincerest form of flattery, but this is ridiculous. Mrs R will also ask the friends she met at your place to dinner, without telling you, and then book the house you booked last summer, for the same two weeks. This is bordering on identity theft. Maybe if she owned up to her Single White Female tendencies it would be different and you could laugh it off, but maybe not. It's got to the point where you are hiding cushions and coats and dimming the lights whenever she comes round for fear that your whole life could be cloned.

How to cope: Get vague. Withhold. When she asks where something came from say, 'Do you know, I really can't remember.'

How to cull: Be unavailable.

The Princess

There was a time when you were in thrall to the Princess's delicate charms and were often to be found dragging both your suitcases through the airport, elbowing your way to the bar to get two drinks (champagne for her), standing in puddles to hail cabs while she sheltered in a doorway clutching her fur collar to her throat (her hair and her shoes have somehow always been a higher priority than yours). In the past you didn't care because the Princess was always entertaining and had one of those Tardis address books containing the numbers of the best ever waxer and hairdresser. But now you don't have the time or the inclination to indulge her, and what was quite cute in your youth is starting to look manipulative. Meanwhile – and here's where the problem really starts – the men in your life simply don't see it. They love it when she gets them to hail her a cab. They assume that she needs an arm to steady her and another to carry her umbrella. And, if you protest that you never get the same attention, they just laugh and say 'but you're perfectly capable of looking after yourself', which is meant to be a compliment, but makes you feel like the ugly sister.

How to cope: Don't put up with it. Hail your own goddamn cab and leave her in the rain.

How to cull: Make her do the walking and the planning and the paying. She'll soon give up.

The Competitress

She hated it when you got your flat, your last boyfriend, your job. She moved when you moved and redecorated when you redecorated. She has decided that you are the barometer against which she measures her own success and she must be ten points ahead, at all times, or she cannot sleep at night. (The Competitress carries this on through life: she will need to have more children than you, more money, a bigger dog, whatever it takes.) So far so just about tolerable (you don't have to pay attention), but when you're in public together the Competitress can't resist trying to undermine you. She'll tell your new cool friends that you've always voted Tory. She'll tell your boss that you were bottom of the class at school. She'll remind the room of the time you were sent home from the fashion assistant's job to get your look together. She can't help herself: if things are going well for you, she feels threatened and, if necessary, will try to bring you down. When I met The One, an arch Competitress of my acquaintance found an early opportunity to draw him to one side and inform him, in confidential tones, that I had been single for ten years (true, but, you know, not *absolutely* single and, anyway, I was hoping to leave the timescale somewhat vague). Not only that, she strongly implied that before he came along I had been sad, lonely and . . . wait for it . . . quite a bit fatter. The One, being a man and therefore having only loyal friends, was curious to know what I had done to deserve such treachery. But you will know that my only crime was getting loved up late in the day, thereby messing with her ten-point lead, and sending her into a scrabbling fever of sabotage.

How to cope: Laugh.

How to cull: Cut off her oxygen. Steer well clear.

The Patronizer

It is a rule that, whatever you do or say, the Patronizer makes you feel like a sixteen-year-old at a grown-ups' party. She'll interrupt your rambling stories to ask you what you're trying to say. She'll remove your hand from the neck of the olive oil bottle and take over making the salad dressing. She'll remark on your quaint choice of music, or widen her eyes in faux interest when you're talking about some trivial episode in the life of a mutual friend. It's every little thing. If you smoke around her, she makes you feel like a gibbering neurotic; if you offer her olives to go with her drink, she makes you feel bourgeois and sad. Idle chat sounds like gossip; less idle chat sounds like trying, and failing, to be smart. New clothes are evidence of your shallowness and profligacy. Old clothes are evidence of your tired life and slipping standards. She'll get you, whatever way you play it. You put up with the Patronizer because you think it might be your problem, but then she comes up in conversation with someone else equally glamorous and sophisticated and they say, 'God, she is soooo patronizing.

Who can put up with it?' So now you know it's not just that you deserve it.

How to cope: Patronize her right back, if you dare.

How to cull: If you won't play her game she will probably go elsewhere.

The Bully

This one is tricky because the bullying looks, from a certain angle, a bit like constructive life coaching. The Bully even thinks that's what she's doing. But she's angry, and she's angry with you for some reason. You should be doing more to get your life together. You should be planning, organizing, getting together an exercise plan, sorting out your priorities, finding a goal and working towards it. These conversations – about how much improvement your life could do with – generally start because you tell her you are feeling low, or struggling at work, or slightly missing the presence of an attractive man in your life, and – *bam!* In she roars with all the ways in which you must conquer these mindsets. There's a part of you that quite likes a positive, plain-speaking approach, which is why you put up with the Bully in the first place. But the thing is she doesn't seem to really care about your situation, only that you should do as she says. If you're lucky, there will come a crunch point when you phone her, one night, looking for reassurance and she gives it to you right in the solar plexus: 'You're just going to have to pull yourself together.' No friend could use these words. You are now free to leave.

How to cope: Don't ask for advice.

How to cull: Walk.

Note: It is not possible to cull Old Friends unless there has been some major crisis (i.e. they have sneaked in at the eleventh hour and gazumped you on the house of your dreams, and even then you'll probably forgive them in a couple of years). The whole point of Old Friends is that not seeing them for months on end, or having a blazing row, is nothing out of the ordinary. So, even if you wanted to dump them, they just wouldn't get the hint.

Some things you would think are reasons for friend culling, but aren't necessarily

• They have married someone unspeakable. At the start you will think this is an insurmountable problem, and it does seriously compromise your opportunities for enjoying life. But, if you follow the rules (listed later on), you may survive.

• They have a dog that has attacked you. This is unacceptable in some cultures, but in Britain the attackee, toddlers included, always takes the blame for having strayed too close to the dog when the dog was having a bad day.

• They have made a pass at your boyfriend. Amazing what you can blame on alcohol, if you so choose.

• They have given up alcohol. This is tough, but it doesn't stop you drinking.

- They have made a load of new friends whom you cannot stick. These friends will probably fall by the wayside (see above). And if not you should be able to say to them, 'Look, don't ask me to spend seven days straight in an isolated cottage with Mandy and Marco because they bring me out in hives, and no good will come of it.'
- You are pretty sure they stole your sunglasses. This is weird, admittedly. But some people have that klepto streak and you have to ask yourself, is it worth sacrificing the friendship for a pair of Oliver Peoples? Better by far to keep buying fakes and leave them lying around.
- They keep asking you over with their third-division friends. (Choose to take this as a compliment. You don't need to be impressed.)
- They repeated something you told them about someone, who told someone, and it got back to the original someone, and now you have some explaining to do. Some friends just happen to be terribly leaky, and are not to be trusted with sensitive information.
- They insist on being sexy during down time. I'm referring to those weekends in Wales when you have an understanding that it is strictly grimy fleeces, cagoules and wellington boots but She brings the entire Toast catalogue, plus ultra tight jeans for the evenings, and a capsule collection of fresh, outdoorsy

make-up. Her backwoodsy, thermal-with-a-lace-trim underwear is on show the whole bloody time.

- They jealously guard useful information. You just wanted the number of a plumber/curtain maker/whatever, but will She give it up? Chalk it up to a childhood spent sharing toys.

❀ How To Keep The Friends You Want

Be easily abused

The last thing any of us needs is another person to disappoint or irritate, let alone nurture. Your close friends, and you in return, should be consistently available (on the phone, anyway), easy-going and above all undemanding. When you get your first boyfriend, your girlfriend is entitled to say, 'I never see you any more,' but this is not appropriate when you are both forty-one and you've got a stye and a deadline and you really can't face her annual Christmas lunch party. The most welcome phrase in a friend's vocabulary has got to be: 'No Problem.' At this stage none of us needs to hear, 'I will be very, very disappointed. I am relying on you. This is a very difficult time for me.' All that stuff just makes you want to run in the opposite direction, and phone a friend.

Don't waste each other

This is the Old Friend's worst fear: that they will arrive at the house by the sea, all set for a weekend of boozy reminiscing in the manner of *The Big Chill*, and be greeted by ... other people. Or worse, other local people. There is an extended period of our lives when this mix-them-up approach is very welcome, but there comes a point when strangers – unless they are celebrities – are just so much flotsam in the way of you enjoying your real chums. (As we've established, the last thing you need in your life is *more* people.) The reason Old Friends do this to each other (i.e. scupper your one chance in twelve months of having a meaningful exchange by turning the weekend into a hair-raising catering challenge) is habit. They think introducing new blood will make it more of an occasion. Or, alternatively, they want to show off. ('Look, we know the delightful Swintons! Well enough for them to be here, in our house, round our table!') It's also, frequently, because they owe the couple down the road, who always look after the dog when they are away, and are using your visit as an opportunity to pay them back. Whatever the reason, this sort of knee-jerk socializing gets in the way of the real thing and is to be avoided.

Beware the money gap

Guess what? Not only are you all at different life stages, you are all living off radically different incomes. Your oldest girlfriend has a real Chloé handbag and doesn't think it is a hilarious state of affairs that warrants a lot of snorting and nudging. She and her husband drink the wine you had on Christmas Day, *all year round*. There is a king-size bottle of the scent you wear in their downstairs bathroom (plus the candle and the roomspray). The entire basement of their house is floored in the slate you looked at – and decided you couldn't afford – for the splashbacks in the kitchen. And the fact that you are able to make these comparisons is where the problem lies. You are travelling to the same destinations, in roughly the same taste zones, only you are always one quality grade behind them: their life is business class to your economy. This keeps you nicely within envy range at all times.

Meanwhile, among your group of friends there will be a few who think *you* are loaded and who cannot believe you bought your kitchen chairs from a shop, when you could have gone to Spitalfields Market at 4 a.m. and bartered with a man under a dripping tarpaulin. The potential for friction is there, in other words, even among old mates. One woman's hard-earned bubbly is another woman's something for the school raffle. This girl's new shearling coat is that girl's cast off. All of you need to be vigilant and respect that there are rules when it comes to money and friendship, for example: never talk about money with a friend unless their financial situation is more or less identical to yours; never use emotive words like 'broke' – your broke may be very different to theirs, and then they will want to hit you; only holiday with people whose attitude to money is the same as yours, then keep a kitty; if friends bring wine to dinner, make sure you drink it (the affluent ones will be gagging for something decent, the not so affluent will worry, if it gets whisked away never to be seen again, that it was the vino equivalent of

Ferrero Rocher). And always consider the adults when buying for their children (don't get your godson the guitar, on a whim, that his parents have been saving up all year to buy him for Christmas).

Note: Friends can be too rich.

I have a friend whose eleven-year-old son was asked on a family holiday, with a gang of senselessly rich people and minor celebrities. At some point this boy was bet, by one of the adults, that he couldn't swim round a rock, which he duly did and was rewarded with a prize of £500. (On advice from a civilian who was present this sum was reduced to a more manageable £200.) When the boy got home, he went straight out and blew all his winnings on everything he had ever wanted, including all the gadgets and games that his mother had been planning to buy for his birthday, six weeks later. Meanwhile, his older sister, who had been saving up all year, and had £67.50 to show for it, retired to her bedroom, where she sobbed for days. They're going camping this year.

Living with the children

It's at about this stage that you wake up one day and realize it doesn't matter how much you like your friends any more – what counts is whether you can tolerate their children.

This is not something that would have occurred to your mother, because her friends' children would all have had more or less the same routines, and dietary requirements, and number of toys, and respect for authority, so there would have been no reason to notice how tolerable they were, one way or the other. The situation is not the same for you because your friends have radically different ideas as to how to bring up their families.

Some are totally hands off and happy for their children to dictate the terms of their upbringing from the moment they can walk. Some are full-time hands on and convinced that if their four-year-old doesn't eat at precisely twelve thirty (the organic medley that they have brought with them, not trusting anyone else to provide the right balance of nutrients) there will be emotional consequences later in life. And some are in the good place in between, but not as many as you would hope, with the result that roughly one third of your friends are unseeable. I don't just mean the prospect is no longer attractive – although that does come into it – I mean you can't actually see them, in any meaningful sense of the word, because their children entirely dominate the proceedings so that they, and you, are incapable of concentrating on anything else.

At first you think there must be ways around this. You try turning up for supper at ten in the hope that the coast is clear. (Jason and Milo, five and four, have decided to stay up and eat with the grown-ups.) You try summoning them to cocktails at your flat. (They bring them, all of them! And the baby gym.) You volunteer the phone numbers of willing babysitters. (But you are made to feel like you've suggested leaving them chained to the kitchen table leg.) You fix to meet them in ludicrously expensive restaurants. (They bring them.) You point out that the kids look like they've been clubbing for two nights on the trot, and that their parents don't look much better. Finally you admit defeat.

Note: No one is so good a friend that you can tell them their children are hell to be around. You can hint, but why volunteer for the grief? That stuff is best left to the grandparents. What you can do, if you are desperate, is approach the problem head on by roping in another child for cover (one you are related to, for example, and so entitled to boss around) and then giving them both a piece of your mind. Also, I have a friend who recommends pinching when no one is looking. Nothing nasty, mind you, just a little grip of the wrist and a focused gaze. Apparently it works wonders.

Rules of the married–single friendship

No one ever discusses how married women with children and single women manage to maintain their friendships, but it is pretty astonishing, when you think that your average fortysomething childless single probably has more in common with her teenage god-daughters than with their mothers. And I'm not even exaggerating. Hangovers; handbag obsession; hopeless, unsuitable boyfriends; ambitious 'lifetime experience' travel; TV addiction; hanging out in coffee bars; shoes; cosmetics; sunglasses; the best sort of strings of butterflies to drape around mirrors – these are the preoccupations of single women. Your married friends with three under five go to sleep worrying about food additives and MMR and the au pair's imminent week off, and you go to sleep vaguely wondering if you'll be able to get the candle wax off your Topshop Mongolian lamb waistcoat. Yes, you've known each other since you were twelve, but there is now a bloody great chasm separating your two worlds and there's no use pretending love alone will get you through. From now on this relationship requires careful handling.

For example: when your married girlfriend asks you on holiday she must volunteer, up front, the child saturation levels. The correct procedure is as follows: married girlfriend says, 'Come the first week when it's just us, and we've got help. You're welcome the second week but the Browns are turning up, with the quads, and the Parkers with their three. It will be a nightmare.' If she were speaking to another married friend she might easily say, 'Come whenever you want – either week is fine,' but this would not be enough information for a single friend. To the single woman, 'Come whenever you want,' sounds like a trap. And single girls live in fear of being trapped in situations where there is no one on their wavelength – say, a summer holiday when the swimming pool is invisible under a thick crust of pool toys and everyone retires early so that they can wake up all refreshed to do wholesome, family-centric things.

The key is respecting each other's priorities. It would, for example, be tactless of the single friend to go on holiday with a bunch of nursing mothers, stay up late with the music cranked up to full volume, then lie in a hammock all day, sleeping off her hangover, while they're expressing milk and changing nappies. But it's equally bad news if baby domination stretches into dinner, Thomas the Tank Engine is on the stereo, little Max is crawling all over the table, and all the adults have to eat off their knees just in case he gets burnt.

Acknowledging and celebrating your differences is really what the successful single/married relationship is all about. You can't help out on the school run and she can't throw the Bacchanalian singles party; you aren't much good for teething tips and she's no use for the lastminute.com to Ibiza. But what you can offer each other is *escape*. In fact, this is the big unspoken obligation of these relationships. The single friend's role is to provide responsibility-free fun – a self-indulgent break from the real adult world – and, in return, the married friend does nurture and advice and practical back up. It's like this: when your lives are rattling down very different paths the secret is to provide something that the other one is missing – which means, on occasion, a bit of role playing.

The best married friend knows that what she can provide is domestic sanctuary: a cosy kitchen buzzing with activity; a table groaning with proper food (including carbs); some picturesque, affectionate children and the presence of a sympathetic, neurosis-defusing husband. Her role is to provide warmth, comfort and lots of soothing surrogate parental attention (and, if she's a really good friend, she'll condone some serious ego-boosting flirting on the part of her husband).

Meanwhile, the good single friend acts as a conduit for her married friends' fantasies. You arrive in their lives like a cross between Withnail and Sienna Miller (well, Withnail anyway) bringing scandalous stories, hilarious escapades, real-life emotional drama and all the preoccupations that are but a distant dream to them. You're like the wayward teenage daughter they can afford to find amusing. Likewise, if a married friend and husband come to you, then you have a duty to make it a decadent experience and deliberately overplay all the stuff they can no longer get away with at home, namely, thumping music, smoke-filled rooms, plenty of sharp corners and non-dishwasher-friendly glasses.

Inevitably married friends' lives are not all floury hands and Radio 4, just as single friends' aren't all sex, cocktails and shopping, but so what. The extremes are what makes this relationship a treat rather than a trial. And one more thing: it relies on an unspoken agreement to envy, rather than merely tolerate, each other's lifestyle. This is very important to the smooth running of the friendship, because nothing will kill it faster than the whiff of smugness or exasperation or a teeny bit of a lecture on getting your act together/getting out more. The idea is to make each other feel special, not alien.

You don't always get it right. There have been times when I have sat in the back seat of a married couples' car and felt like the special needs child who refuses to leave home. (It makes perfect sense to put the single woman in the back, but letting us ride up front, now and then, helps). More than once I've sat round my own table and listened to married friends talking animatedly about schools and unreliable au pairs and wondered if I should shuffle off to bed or just set fire to myself. And, likewise, I've muscled in with plenty of unwanted observations about childcare, fresh from watching *Supernanny*. I've coaxed married friends' husbands into staying up into the small hours, thereby making them unfit for any domestic duties the following day. I've stayed way too late at the houses of knackered new parents, and smoked (back in the old days) in the presence of tiny, pink-lunged infants. And once my friend Caroline caught me using the baby bottle brush to get the mud out of the treads of my trainers (I thought it was just a really narrow brush). But if you make an effort to see the world through each other's eyes, most of the time it works.

How to be a good platonic friend

In all platonic friendships there will be a deciding moment when the door closes shut on any possibility of romance. Up until then, you are ninety-nine per cent positive nothing could ever happen, but there is always that teeny sliver of a chance, if only because he's a man and you're a woman (and you both like a cocktail). Generally the Decider will take the form of a near snog that one of you dodges. Or an actual snog that one of you backs out of as soon as it has got underway. Or a mutual friend will loudly observe that it's high time you got together, because boyfriends come and go but you appear to still be joined at the hip, and one of you will look panicked, and change the subject.

Alternatively it will take the form of a conversation that goes like this:

'Imagine if we slept together.'

'What?'

'It would be embarrassing if we did. Don't you think? Imagine.'

'It would be hilarious'

'That's what I thought'.

Or:

'Wouldn't it be simpler if *we* were going out. It would just be a lot easier.'

'Us?'

'We spend so much time together. I don't know.'

'But we don't fancy each other.'

'No. That's true.'

The Decider can go the other way, in which case you're talking a *When Harry Met Sally* ending. (But Note: Their friendship never had the hallmark of a genuine platonic friendship. She was just too girly and he was just too blokey. A proper platonic friendship requires a man with girly tendencies and a woman with boyish tastes, otherwise one is humouring the other, for reasons of mutual attraction, and that's not a friendship, that's an arrangement between two people who fancy each other but just haven't got it together.)

No platonic friendship is evenly matched at the outset. It will go through phases when each of you thinks (or maybe just you), Hang on. Why exactly haven't we? But all platonic friendships settle down and turn into friendships that, even if your mother isn't convinced, have nothing whatsoever to do with sex.

Even so, it's a good idea to establish some rules, namely:

• Anything goes in public: dancing, squeezing, hugging, but not once you are alone together in the privacy of your flat. (Dancing is sometimes okay, providing it is to bad music, and you are making total arses of yourselves.)

• Application of suncream must be swift and undertaken with clinical efficiency. It's just a weird area, suncream.

• No spontaneous neck/head massages.

• Bed sharing may be done but only if a) the bed is big enough for you to get plenty of distance and b) at least one of you is incapable of finding their own bed or c) you are in a foreign country and saving on room bills. Otherwise he goes on the sofa. (Note: When sharing a room in a foreign country you will want to stagger your bedtimes. That wandering around semi-dressed, brushing-teeth stage of proceedings is weirdly intimate.)

• Room sharing – that is – in two separate single beds, is absolutely fine, but it goes without saying that you should not drift about in a little something you have just spent £300 on in La Perla. This is just common sense – not because you are guaranteed to arouse his ardour – but because it would be just plain inappropriate. Platonic friendships rely on both of you behaving more like brother and sister than saucy, will-we-or-won't-we singles. That's just creepy.

How to stay friends with married men

The problem with close, straight male friends is they all hook up with a woman in the end. In roughly one out of three cases, this woman will embrace you like a sister, and vice versa. In the other two she will regard you with some suspicion or, alternatively, outright hostility. You were hanging out with her husband for fifteen-plus years, and in that time you never so much as touched pinkies, yet this woman is convinced that you are a ruthless home wrecker (in the movie you would be played by Sharon Stone) poised to strike at any moment.

If she tires of that particular fantasy – as she must when the strike never happens – then she'll find some other reason to make it impossible for you all to be friends: you are a bad influence (you smoked in front of the children); you are pleased with yourself (you came straight from work); you look down on their friends (you couldn't make dinner at the weekend); you are competitive (you asked them back for dinner); you are mean (you brought chocolates); you are ostentatious (you brought champagne); you are overdressed (trying to show her up) or underdressed (slob) . . . You get the picture. If your friend really wants to see you, he will have to sign a disclaimer and meet you in a neutral environment, wearing a wire. And, guess what – you are quite a laugh, but you're not worth that much effort.

However, if he teams up with just an averagely tricky one, and you have a long-standing friendship that is worth fighting for, then there are some things you can do to make the situation almost bearable (although there are no guarantees).

For a start you must, henceforth, treat your friend as if he is mildly deluded and a bit of a nuisance: the idea you want to convey is that you will tolerate seeing him but the person you are really interested in is her. (However unlikely this scenario, it's the only one she'll go for.) Refuse to respond if he mentions TBH (time before her). Ignore him if he is in any way affectionate towards you, particularly if he tries to flatter you. Gang up on him whenever possible, for example: if she moans about his attempts at clearing up, roll your eyes and say, 'You are amazing the way you cope. I don't know how you do it.' On no account comment on his appearance, or anything personal relating to him, especially not in a manner that is teasing. (Teasing enrages them. They think it is foreplay.) And as of now only ever make plans through her; if he happens to get to the phone first, slam it down immediately.

After all this, you may feel you don't have much in the way of a friendship. The only consolation is you can probably afford to ease up on the tough tactics and resume cordial relations in the next ten or so years.

Actually having a history with a man makes it almost easier to maintain a friendship. This is partly because the 'what if?' element has been removed (so you are less of a threat, paradoxically, to any woman on the scene) and because a man can be dismissive of an ex in a way that he can't be about a friend without seeming disloyal. Also, women are naturally intrigued by their partner's exes, and they long to share, even though they know they shouldn't. ('Did you find he was a bit weird about . . . ?' 'Oh God, the thing with the two towels and the smaller towel . . . is it OCD, do you think?')

Even so, you will want to avoid the following: any conversations about sex; any conversations that begin, 'Yes, you remember, it was that New Year's Eve when we went to the party dressed as horny little devils . . .'; finishing each other's sentences and/or dissolving into giggles for reasons that are not clear to anyone else. Equally you mustn't ignore each other because that can look like brooding, or being so comfortable in each other's presence that you don't need to try.

It is well worth cultivating friendships with ex-boyfriends because after a suitable cooling-off period ex-boyfriends (who don't hate you) are invaluable sounding boards for current relationships. This is an actual transcript of a conversation I had with an ex:

'So. He rang and I only saw him this morning. What do you think?'

'He's keen.'

'Do you think so? But why does he want to have *lunch*?'

'Because lunch is stress free.'

'I'm too nervous to have lunch. In broad daylight. I need lots of alcohol for this. And I've got cystitis.'

'Whatever you do, don't tell him you've got cystitis.'

'Okay.'

'And don't wear that jacket.'

'What's wrong with it?'

'He'll be wearing it. He's got the same one.'

'Oh.'

'You know he lives in Papua New Guinea, don't you?'

See. How useful was that? (Though he was wrong on the lunch call. Lunch means 'I'd better see you again, out of courtesy, and because we know people in common, but I don't want to give out the wrong signals.')

Maybe the feeling that you are not giving enough time to your friendships is just part of the human condition. I once worked on a magazine edited by a distinguished older man who every so often would take me out to lunch and give me the benefit of his sixtysomething years of experience. On one occasion I asked him what I should do about my friends. 'I never see half of them,' I said. 'There are only so many days in the week and I spend the whole time feeling guilty.' This was in the early eighties, by the way. I had no conception of the scale of the problem we were facing. 'Don't be foolish,' chuckled Distinguished Boss. 'You will always see the people you really want to see. And if you don't see them often, you make it count.' I find that if you repeat this, it helps you to feel calmer.

3.

Am I Turning Into My Mother?

Nooo. Your mother darned socks. She *made* the Christmas pudding. She ironed her husband's shirts and *did his packing*. Not only that, but when your father voiced an opinion about the financial crisis, she would never have dreamt of saying, 'Oh, for fuck's sake. That is bollocks.' But these are just details. What makes you profoundly unlike your mother is this: your mother did not expect to be the priority in her life story. First there would be a husband to consider, then children, then pets. So far you have none of the above. Your mother expected to become something like her mother. You do not.

Before we go any further I should explain that my mother is not like a lot of mothers. On numerous occasions I've been asked to write an article about the prickly, sometimes competitive, often complicated relationship between mothers and daughters. 'Come on,' the editor will say, 'what about all that jealousy when you start doing the things they never had the chance to do? What about the control? You can never please them.' And every time I have to say, 'Sorry, that's not my mother.' My mother is not my best friend, or my sternest critic, or someone whose approval I seek daily. She isn't an Edina to my Saffy, or a career role model. I have never been on a spa break with her (she wouldn't see the point, and what would we do with Dad?) and she has never sought to influence any aspect of my life, other than to forbid me from using cotton buds – so I'm aware my experience might not ring true for you. But all relationships between mothers and single daughters are alike in one important sense – our life experience is completely different.

All our mothers have had to adjust to the possibility that we will never, ever become like them, but naturally they still live in hope. In my mother's case, this hope has become focused on the small amount of jewellery given to me on the occasion of my Christening, which she has kept, tucked away in its velvet boxes, waiting for the day when I show some interest in wearing it. Every couple of years she tests the water, to see if that day has arrived. The conversation goes as follows:

My mother: 'Darling. You know I've still got all your jewellery.'

Me: [*Silence*]

MM: 'The brooch your uncle gave you would look lovely with that. Shall I bring it next time I come?'

Me: [*Sidelong menacing glance*]

MM: 'I'm just saying. You could be wearing it.'

Me: 'I *will* wear it. Just not now.'

MM: 'Well, when?'

Me: 'I *doon't knoow*. When I'm older.'

MM: 'But, darling. You ARE OLDER.'

*

Here's what we think. We think we look nothing like our mothers. And we're absolutely right. They had puffy pink arms and tidy hair, we have toned arms and floppy fringes. They wore stockings in summer, we have glossy waxed legs and wet-look pedicures. They used foundation, we favour dewy tinted moisturizer. Never mind cosmetic intervention, ours is a more youthful aesthetic. And we eat better. And we go to Pilates and Power Plate and glug down bottled water and sit with our legs tucked up under us on the sofa and wear tops that reveal a few inches of midriff when we reach for the coffee on the top shelf. Still. We may not look like our mothers did at our age (when did you ever see your mother's midriff on show, other than at the beach?), but that doesn't mean we aren't getting any older. Most of us are so carried away with the project of not looking like our mothers that we have forgotten this is not the same as *being* young. Your mother hasn't.

She is quite clear in her mind that you are officially middle-aged: the same age she was when she was starching shirts and stuffing turkeys and making curtains and sewing on name tapes and driving here and there, to swimming lessons and ballet lessons, and hosting cocktail parties and generally running a family of five. At your age she had a fifteen-year-old son. And yet you think *wearing a brooch* is too grown up for a frisky young kid like you.

It must be strange for your mother, if you think about it. She is at the stage when she could reasonably have expected to be sitting in your kitchen dandling a grandchild on her knee, swapping stories about awkward husbands (like a scene out of *Mad Men,* only with less smoking), whereas the reality is rather different. The reality is that she meets you at your flat after work, you arrive staggering under a heap of Topshop bags wearing four-inch heels and a man's leather jacket, there isn't any milk in the house and your mother (if you're lucky) gets busy tidying up your bedroom.

Things your mother does that you would never consider

- Makes sandwiches and a flask of coffee for a car journey, rather than stop at a service station and pay through the nose for the supermarket equivalent
- Recycles Christmas paper
- Posts things that people have left behind, such as a single glove
- Keeps vegetables outside the fridge
- Keeps shoes in a shoe bag and shoe trees in shoes
- Saves jars
- Takes cuttings
- Sews
- Uses a proper handkerchief
- Plays the Lottery

Things you do that your mother would never have considered

- Pay to have your toenails painted (or paint your toenails in the first place)
- Paint the house six carefully selected different shades of white, including the floors
- Wear four-inch-high-heeled, red-soled shoes
- Own more than one handbag
- Own a thong
- Drink on an empty stomach
- Chuck out a chicken carcass (with quite a lot of meat on it)
- Describe someone as 'anally retentive' or 'controlling'
- Read *Grazia* from cover to cover
- Take a taxi back from the supermarket
- Suck down ten vitamin pills a day
- Wear a funny metal button that is supposed to ward off radioactive rays
- Wear a man's leather jacket

You are definitely not turning into your mother, for all these reasons, and because . . .

You are bohemian

This definition of bohemian has nothing to do with gipsy skirts and free love and everything to do with relaxed standards on everything from childcare to the state of your car. In your mother's day, a woman who never brushed her hair was a woman who had lost the plot – whereas now unruly hair is perfectly normal if you have made a certain lifestyle choice, like eating soya if you're a vegetarian.

Dinner served at 9.30: in your mother's day a colossal screw up (now bohemian). Long hair and floaty clothes on a grown woman: in your mother's day self-delusion (now bohemian). Un-housetrained dog: IYMD just that (now bohemian). Children asleep under the dinner table at midnight: IYMD negligent parenting (now bohemian). Car with broken exhaust, seats covered in dog hairs and sandwich wrappers in the foot-well: IYMD slovenly (now bohemian). Likewise not bothering much with domestic hygiene, staying in bed until 12.00 at the weekends, failing to observe dress codes, recreational drug use – all of this and more are features commonly associated with the underclass, and the new bohemians.

Most of us are too squeamish and fond of comfort to really embrace the full boho lifestyle; we just cherry pick from the available options. And this is the big advantage of being some-what bohemian – it allows you to fall way short of your mother's standards, as and when you choose. According to these flexible rules, being houseproud is uptight, but having nice possessions is important. Order is over-rated, but luxury is very welcome. Punctuality is for control freaks and observing traditional etiquette is for snobs, though we still like to be asked to a smart party. We don't take care of our clothes or our property (so there are wet rings on the table. It's only a table), which we think makes us less precious and more open minded. Your mother reckons it's all just an excuse never to iron anything, or tidy up properly, or clean your shoes, but what does she know.

You are worth it

The really staggering difference between you and your mother, however, boils down to your relative levels of self indulgence. (My mother feels guilty when she spends money on an essential purchase, such as a hat to wear to a family wedding, whereas I only really feel guilty if I pay for a pedicure and then muck it up because I was too impatient to wait the extra five minutes and then do the thing with the cling film.) Similarly:

• You have been buying cashmere sweaters like they were Gap T-shirts for the past five years. Your mother still thinks it's a treat (mine has one cashmere sweater, which I gave her for her birthday, and she treats it like the Turin Shroud).

• You might easily spend on a Moroccan rug covered in coins (and therefore impossible to vacuum) what your parents would spend on a week's holiday in Spain.

• When you are feeling run down, you have been known to take the morning off work to give yourself time to recover. Your mother would have to be running a temperature to change her plans.

• Somewhere along the line you persuaded yourself that £28

scented candles were household essentials. Your mother would be pleased with one Diptyque candle for Christmas.

• When you go out to dinner you might order a glass of champagne to kick off – why not! Your mother could be persuaded, if it were a special occasion, but mine would be wondering if the money couldn't have been better spent replacing the iron.

Bottom line, your mother has never, even for an instant, confused her existence with that of a rock star, whereas you make no distinction between Them and Us. You may not be rock star – or even backing-singer – rich, but that doesn't mean you can't drink the same antioxidant health-food supplement as Jennifer Aniston, and wear the same brand of jeans as Kate Moss, and do the same yoga as Gwyneth Paltrow, and go to the same cocktail bars as Mick Jagger and L'Wren Scott.

Over the past decade, I have tried all of the following: yoga, Pilates, reflexology, gym training (I think that's what it's called), swimming, meditation, every single type of massage known to woman (and the cellulite-busting ones, repeatedly), Eve Lom facials, regular facials, t'ai chi and kick boxing. For three years I had regular appointments with a woman who rebalanced my system with the aid of inflatable reflexology boots and I used to see Bhati Vyas (one of Cherie Blair's gurus) who is also a fan of boots, though hers are different. I've had iridology, colonic irrigation, countless food intolerance tests, several courses of Chinese medicines and spa treatments a-go-go. While a lot of this has been conducted in the name of research for articles, even so, the money and time invested in fine-tuning my body is getting on for second-wife-of-major-Hollywood-executive levels. Meanwhile, my mother has never had so much as a massage.

Conscious of this imbalance, I have sometimes tried to pass on whatever wisdom my current charlatan is peddling. Once I sent my mother rare vitamin pills, guaranteed to extend her life expectancy (she didn't like the look of them and refused to take them, even though they cost me roughly £5 a pop). I gave her a duplicate of the diet sheet specially formulated for me by the medical staff at Chiva-Som spa, which she claimed was too complicated to follow ('they've never heard of soya yogurt in the shops round us'). I tried to introduce her to green tea, during my green-tea phase, and to interest her in hula hooping (after I bought a giant, weighted hula hoop on eBay, and then couldn't fit it through my front door) but she was having none of any of it.

The fact is my mother is just not interested in holistic wellness. She is bored by the news (which I devour and act on instantly) that almonds/broccoli/blueberries guarantee longevity. She can't understand why I flip from evangelically practising yoga to Power Plate, then back to Pilates, when a bit of weeding the garden and scrubbing the bath has stood her in perfectly good stead all these years. And it is mysterious to her that someone with a university degree is willing to hand over good money (thank God she has no idea of the actual figures) to be told that wearing purple while working at a computer will repel bad energy.

Come to that, what really amazes your mother is the stuff you are prepared to pay other people to do. A windowcleaner maybe, but a woman to paint your toenails? A man to deliver organic vegetables? Someone to sort out your wardrobe? (You haven't actually gone this far, but the point is you could.) Your mother cannot comprehend why you employ so many 'experts' to give advice that she'd be happy to give herself.

And she's got a point. Who did your mother turn to when she had a baby? Her mother! Now, were you to have a baby, your mother would be involved, naturally, but mainly you would rely on the latest literature and Mumsnet and the opinions of mothers your age who work – because your own mother couldn't possibly be expected to know what's involved in bringing up a baby in the twenty-first century. She has no idea about the risks involved in eating sushi, never mind the latest thoughts on baby massage and cranial osteopathy or the Maclaren Turbo buggy versus the Bugaboo. If you were going to have a baby, you would need advice from professionals, preferably several.

Who did your mother call up when she had to cook supper for twenty? Her mother! But now you crave the latest thinking from Nigel or Nigella or Gordon. Even if you're cooking a stew – something your mother has made for years – you want it to be the very latest rebranded, modern stew, illustrated in bright scrumptious pictures. And when it comes to sorting out the garden, do you rely on your mother's forty-something years of rose-pruning experience? Nooo. You think, Better call in a landscape gardener to get the up-to-the-minute take. Better call up ten people who have put in gardens in the last two years. Better look in magazines and read the gardening columns, because there are bound to be some hot new must-have pot plants or radical theories on growing your own herbs.

Your mother has a lot of life experience, it's true, and she's only too willing to pass it on. But there is so much new information out there, so much beautifully packaged advice for every situation, so many people waiting to focus on your every little need.

You are too clever to trust common sense

Our mothers were happy to trust the wisdom of the past whereas our generation thinks all knowledge must be in a constant state of revision. We keep tearing up the rules, rewriting them, then revising them in the light of new findings and ending up in exactly the same place. In the last two years I have: made my mother stop drinking tap water and then forbidden her to drink bottled water; insisted she take supplements and then advised her not to bother; encouraged her to cut down on alcohol, then urged her to start drinking red wine, in moderation. Got her on aspirin, off aspirin and on again. The latest crusade is anti waste. My mother has been recycling for decades (carefully folding and keeping the Christmas wrapping paper, saving saucers of carrots, turning leftovers into soup, etc.) and now I – who never so much as remembers to turn off the hot water when I go on holiday – am lecturing her on the virtues of sorting out her cans from her bottles.

It's the same with everything. Tomatoes are good for you. Wash your hands if you've been touching raw chicken. Air beds to kill bedbugs. Get a dog to boost your immune system. A brisk walk in the fresh air is the best way to lift mild depression. This is all news-breaking stuff to us, stuff which mothers have known since infancy.

Your mother doesn't care that you flip from one fad to another, depending on what the latest, research-endorsed revelation happens to be, but she could do without you trying to convert her. This is how it goes:

You: 'Hi, Mum.'

Your mum: 'Hello, darling.'

Y: 'Listen, Mum. You need to start taking selenium.'

YM: 'Oh? What is it?'

Y: 'Well. It was in the soil, and now it isn't, so you have to take it. Especially if you don't automatically buy organic, which, as we know, you don't. Despite my advice. And you have to stop eating red meat more than once a week. And sausages. And bacon. Stop Dad eating bacon and sausages, immediately.'

YM: 'Oh. That's a pity; he loves sausages.'

Y: 'Well, it's very serious. And you have Got To Get a Water Filter.'

YM: 'But we have lovely water, darling. It's icy cold right out of the tap.'

Y: 'Well, it is full of contraceptive pills, and that's not all. Is Dad depressed, do you think?'

YM: 'No, darling, he's watching *Neighbours*.'

Y: 'No. *Depressed*. A lot of men are undiagnosed. It's called late . . . early something. Also, Mum, you have to keep taking the aspirin, but it has to be *at night*, before you go to bed. One aspirin, and evening primrose oil . . .'

Your mother has got used to this ongoing attempt to make her look at life differently, but her least favourite aspect of the New World According to Us is our generation's preoccupation with the psychological dimension. We are particularly fierce when it comes to analysing other people's motives (your mother calls it maddening; we call it passive aggressive. She calls it chippy; we call it insecure. She calls it fastidious; we call it anally retentive) and she thinks this new way of looking at the world makes normal human behaviour seem alien and a bit scary. But the key difference in our approach to the human condition (besides the terminology and the amount of time we spend dishing out labels) is that we believe no one can be happy until they confront their demons, whereas your mother thinks it's probably better not to go there and get lots of fresh air instead. As for self-medicating, in her day it was called 'needing a drink' and no one was ashamed to admit that a lot of everyday stresses and strains, not to mention relationships, were made much more bearable by a stiff gin and tonic.

Talking of which, as far as your mother is concerned, all of this – including the selenium obsession, the yoga and the dissection of other people's motives – is one big fat distraction to compensate for the absence in your life of A Husband.

You are not your mother ... mainly because you are single

Let's be absolutely clear here. Your mother is totally supportive of everything you do and has taken your eternally single state entirely in her stride. She has never once cracked and started screaming, 'For Pity's Sake Consider A Haircut At Least!' But the fact is at your age she had a husband and children, as did all her friends, and you can't blame her for wondering every once in a while if you might be doing something wrong when it comes to men.

Many mothers, mine included, start from the perspective that men are men, just as they always have been, and there is no point kidding ourselves that they have changed. You, on the other hand, operate on the principle that the world has changed beyond recognition and that men are strapping baby papooses to their chests, and rustling up Jamie Oliver recipes for their loved ones, because they really want to. Everybody's lives are richer for it. They are happier; we are happier. Your mother thinks this is mere wishful thinking. She also thinks this false representation of men is making them resentful and secretive and will keep you single more surely than a full beard and a pointy finger. Here are some things your mother knows about the opposite sex:

• That men find mundane domestic tasks much harder than women. So it is unkind, not to mention counterproductive to ask them to put on a double duvet cover, alone and un-supervised. (They are capable of tasks such as hoovering, providing you don't mind them missing the corners.)

• That men need to feel looked up to, so – unless they have actually left a pan on a lit gas ring, overnight – you should resist pointing out their shortcomings. Likewise you should not be actually better than a man at a sport if you want him to find you attractive.

• That men need to be protected from trivia, especially at the weekend, when they are relaxing. (She thinks that it is mean, for example, to make a man discuss the paint colour in the bathroom, even if you really need a decision.) According to your mother the little stuff impacts harder on men. A woman's head can be clogged with shopping lists and work commitments and mortgage worries, but a man's head starts to spin if you fill it with domestic trivia. (Note: Your mother has a whole category of cruelty to men that you do not recognize and she regards men of your generation as she would an unfairly disinherited son – with a mixture of pity and protectiveness.)

None of this actually applies to you, because you are not in a serious relationship, but there are plenty of things you do which, your mother suspects, may be standing in the way of you ever having one.

Things that it probably is cruel to subject a man to, although we might think otherwise

Girls' nights out. For some reason women have got the idea that when two or more girlfriends are gathered together it is a good idea to include a boyfriend in the mix. He will love it! Three hours of eavesdropping on the workings of the female mind and marvelling at how naughty and funny and rude we are. No, he won't. He is bored of the Botox conversation. He couldn't care less that so and so's marriage is going through a bad patch or that X has lost two stone and everyone thinks it's because she's taking speed. He doesn't particularly want to eat mini portions out of steam baskets and drink peach and elderflower martinis. Better by far to leave him at home.

Stopping for a coffee. Stopping for a coffee may be the underlying reason we go shopping in the first place. Men do not have the same cappuccino cravings and they rarely want to draw out the shopping trip for any longer than is necessary.

Socializing with your ex. He doesn't want to. Why would he want to? Why do you want to?

Pointless shopping. Men don't do purposeless shopping. They never, for example, wander into somewhere just to absorb the fairylight-draped, tuber-rose-scented atmosphere. They wouldn't dream of taking a detour through the soft-furnishing section of Habitat, simply to see what's there. And, so, when they go shopping with you, they may become overwhelmed by a sense of wasted time and opportunities, and you could tip them into a midlife crisis just by saying, 'No, but do you *really* like these?'

Sharing in your gynaecological issues. Your modern man is one hundred per cent geared up on periods and the timing therof, PMT, MT, post-MT (as far as he's concerned there's not much in it), bloating, cramps, the different absorbency ratings of Lil-lets, but do not ask him to share in specifics relating to your gynaecological issues. Modern girl can get lured into thinking that because 360-degree openness is the Holy Grail of relationships, and she is accustomed to doing her toilet in front of her man (often literally), he will be as interested as her girlfriends are in the pros and cons of a Mirena coil, etc. No, no and no again. And he really doesn't want to know how many women wielding electrically charged wands it takes to rid your bikini line of hair, or the details of your sister's labour (aka 'the most horrific and drawn-out birth the midwife had ever witnessed during her thirty-year career'). It is a common twenty-first-century misconception – fuelled by men laughing at the Bridget Jones movies and liking Beth Ditto and knowing about Kate Moss at Topshop and the incredible price of handbags – that they are comfortable talking about anything and everything. Your mother knows better.

Wardrobe advice. It's one of the great injustices of life that if you ask a trusted girlfriend what you should wear to a party and she gives you a preference you will go with it, but if you ask a man to choose, whatever he says will be wrong. This is because we want male approval, but we do not trust men to take all the relevant factors into consideration. For example: that there will be ultra fashion-conscious girls at the party, so sexy/pretty/flattering will simply not cut the mustard. That you've recently lost half a stone, so that needs to be advertised, whatever else happens. That even though this top might exaggerate the worst part of your arms, it could be worth it, because it is Brand Spanking New Balenciaga. That the heels must show, or else it's not worth putting up with the pain caused by the heels.

Your trusted girlfriend's judgement will have taken all these points into consideration, plus the walk from the car, the above the table rating (that's how you will look when sitting down at dinner) and the potential for VPL. No one can compete with her attention to detail, least of all a man who is acutely conscious of the no-win situation he's in.

Other related subjects to save for your girlfriends

- Your digestion
- Your nail fungal infection
- Your receding gums
- Your facial hair
- So and so's IVF hell, including details of injections
- Your ex's career progress

✿ *Reasons Why Your Mother Thinks You Might Still Be Single (although she'd never say it)*

It mildly pains your mother that most of the time, from a distance, you could be a long-haired adolescent boy. And then, when you make the effort to dress up, you're so tall! You even frighten your father in those stonking great heels and jagged pointy rings. Added to this is your refusal to edit your conversation in the company of men. Your mother doesn't mind the story about the time you ate the contents of an ashtray for a bet, or the plate of chillies, and she loves the one about you getting arrested for being caught peeing on MOD property, but she questions the wisdom of telling those stories in front of available men. You can protest all you like that these are your friends and they don't need special treatment, but the way she sees it there is no harm in erring on the side of caution, just in case.

Here's where your mother is pretty sure you're going wrong. In her opinion, platonic friendships are not as common as you would like to believe, and all your male friends – including those with girlfriends – are merely going along with the friendship routine in the expectation that, some day soon, you will wake up and give them a sign. If one or two of them genuinely aren't interested, well then that's only because you have worked so tirelessly at getting them to think of you as one of the boys. In a nutshell, your mother doesn't believe that you can tell the difference between a friend and a potential suitor.

The definition of a male friend, according to your mother, is a man who will drive you back from the party and wait to see you safely through the front door. The ones who accompany you clothes shopping, and on holiday, who meet you in bars after parties and will happily dash off to buy you tampons in emergencies – those are could-be suitors. She doesn't know the half of it but, from what she can see, these so-called friendships are mini marriages, without the sex, and the only reason they exist at all is because your generation are mistakenly hung up on the 'extra factor' required to make a life with someone. You have plenty of 'friends' who would make perfectly good husbands: attractive, available, considerate, employed. What's not to marry? Then again, why would you marry one of your friends since you don't seem to be interested in choosing a man who might, conceivably, be marriageable.

Of all the rules that our generation has thrown out, your mother finds the abandonment of any sense of appropriate dating the most perplexing. The way she sees it, we all go out with men, one after the other, sometimes for three or four years at a stretch (as if you wouldn't know whether you were with the right man after a matter of months) who appear to need nothing much to recommend them besides reasonably good looks and a head for alcohol. Any of the qualities you might expect in a life partner don't come into it. They don't have to be particularly responsible, or committed, or solvent, or have a plan of any sort. Our mothers assumed that we would have the same survival gene they had and that, in due course, we would wave goodbye to the struggling artists and the wannabe pop stars and the boys who look good on motorbikes. But no. We just carry on dating people we fancy and then we're surprised when the time comes to organize our fortieth birthday celebrations and ... lo! We are no further along the path to finding The One than we were at eighteen. When, your mother would like to know, did 'suitable' become an optional extra?

You have explained to your mother that it all boils down to chemistry – the chemistry isn't there with your friends, whereas it is with the boyfriends – but she just looks at you as if you are unwell. You have told her you simply haven't met The One (she gets this, she just doesn't necessarily believe that you have any concept of who The One might be). And you have reminded her that you can't conjure love up out of nowhere; you can only live in hope. Your mother has a healthy respect for love. However, she is mildly anxious that there is a world of difference between feeling nothing for a man and waiting for a big orange lightning bolt to singe your socks off. In short your mother is worried, and increasingly so, that you have unrealistic expectations.

Eventually there comes a point when all mothers of terminally single girls decide that it is their fault for not having adequately prepared their daughters – i.e. told them in no uncertain terms to get out there and pick a man before it's too late. This is the moment when you will have the 'There is no such thing as the perfect man' conversation. In my case it went like this:

Mum: 'Darling.'

Me: 'Hmm.'

Mum: 'You do know that all marriages are hard work, don't you?'

Me: 'Hmm.'

Mum: 'There is no such thing as the perfect man. None of them are perfect. Your father isn't easy to be married to all the time. Your father is not perfect.'

Me: 'Hmm.'

Mum: 'You can't expect too much, is what I'm saying. In the end all you want is someone who is kind. (Pause.) And who has a sense of humour.'

Me: 'So that's why you married Dad? Because he was kind and had a sense of humour?'

Mum: 'Yes, and because we fitted together when we danced.'

Ha! He must be kind and have a sense of humour and there must be *chemistry* I think you'll find she said. For a minute there I thought she was trying to tell me to compromise.

The question is, though, does your mother have a point? She's wrong about the friends. The friends are just a red herring. But what if she's right, in general?

❀ Some Things Your Mother Told You That Are True (even if you don't want to admit it)

Your hair is your crowning glory

And how annoying was *that* at the time? All that nagging you to brush it and wincing whenever you doused it in peroxide. Would she never get the message that you wanted to look evil – that was the whole point? But now you could weep when you think of how you squandered all that natural shine and bounce with all the endless feathering and perming and bleaching and tugging strands through rubber caps with a crochet hook. Who knew you'd get to be forty and the height of fashion would be smooth, sleek, hot-rollered hair like a ¬eventies beauty queen's? Too late! The Cossacks have done their worst. Only scorched stubble here.

Don't shave your legs; you don't need to

They were tiny blonde hairs! You couldn't see them with the naked eye! Why don't they have public information broadcasts warning against the folly of shaving at an age when a) you have no hairs – and if you think those are hairs, then just you wait; b) no one is going to see them apart from your best friend Jill? Just Say No or that first innocent dalliance with a Bic razor will lead to more Bic razors, and then Epiladys, and those sandpaper mitt things, and wax strips, and hot wax, and a lifetime spent worrying about when to book your next appointment – the day before the party, so they're just growing back on holiday, or just before the holiday, in which case they'll need covering up for the party . . . because, one thing's for sure, *you can't have nice legs for both.*

Beware of very good-looking men

And how true was that. What you want is an extremely attractive man, as opposed to a drop-dead dazzler. This is partly because the latter are catnip for other women, and you will spend your whole time saying, 'Excuse me, no – that is his crotch, not your handbag.' But the real reason to avoid senselessly good-looking men, is that they are all Adoreds.

The world divides up into Adorers (whose primary function is to lavish attention on their partner) and Adoreds (who need plenty of it). You get two Adoreds in a relationship and you have two needy, unhappy people who both feel neglected. Princess Diana, for example, was an Adored who married another Adored, HRH Prince Charles. Camilla Parker Bowles, on the other hand, is a classic Adorer, who is only too happy to undertake the gargantuan levels of ego massaging and cajoling required (allegedly) to keep her husband on an even keel. Hence the happy ending.

Every successful relationship requires an Adorer and an Adored: David Cameron (Adorer); Samantha (Adored). Nigella (Adored); Charles Saatchi (Adorer). Jamie Oliver (Adorer); Jules Oliver (Adored). It's just so obvious once you get the hang of it. The trouble is some of us don't discover the opposite A rule until pretty late in life. And there is a further complication, which is that women can mistake low self-esteem and a blossoming maternal instinct, for a natural Adorer's personality. It's the reason smart, funny, independent girls fall for narcissistic, selfish boys, or tortured married men (and Adoreds are adept at spotting females who are looking for someone to love, and prepared to blame themselves for everything that goes wrong).

Your mother will tell you that most women, in order to be truly happy, need to be adored.* Even if they start out determined to give, give, give, there will come a point when they get tired of all the stroking and soothing and nurturing and ego boosting and want a bit of attention themselves. It's just human nature. (Whenever you read a news story about

* There are exceptions to this rule. All women who are married to writers, actors and artists are Adorers, but they tell themselves that they are subordinating their own needs for the sake of a higher purpose. Which probably helps.

a fiftysomething housewife who has gone awol with a nineteen-year-old beach bum and is planning to uproot her life, sell her house and give him all her savings, you assume that's lust. But, more often, it's the desperate act of a woman who has never been adored and thinks she may have one last chance to experience the feeling.) The impulse to be adored is even stronger than sex.

Never chase a man

This one really sank in. I must have been about eleven. We were watching a black-and-white bodice ripper on the TV and my mother was less than impressed with the scene unfolding before our eyes. On the screen a sobbing woman, skirts trailing in the mud, was clutching at the leg of a man on a horse wearing a top hat and a cold sneer. The wind howled, the rain lashed, the horse reared. I think there might have been lightning. My mother looked up from her crossword, caught my eye and said, 'Never run after a man like that. They're not worth it.' (She meant never run after a man in that manner, not never run after a cold-blooded toff.) Eventually the man on the horse shouted, 'Stand aside,' steadied his mount and galloped off into the night leaving the woman slumped in a pool of skirts on the wet heath/cobbles/driveway. I did think at the time my mother was probably right – better not to beg and avoid the humiliation. And she was.

Obviously there are plenty of ways of running after men that don't involve actually locking on to their lower leg. You can phone them, even when you promised yourself you wouldn't. You can meet them for a coffee to check if you have really broken up. You can try to go to the same parties as them, and get everyone you know involved in finding out where they are, and how you can contrive to bump into them. But there are several problems with these modern forms of man chasing. First of all, men are allergic to it. To paraphrase Woody Allen, they think that any woman who's prepared to blatantly stalk them is not worth having. Secondly, it will make you behave in a way guaranteed to repel men – that is wild eyed and on edge rather than languid and flirty. And, thirdly, it's a waste of time because your persistence will never change the man on the horse into the right man for you. If anything, it will make him behave more like the man on the horse. You are looking for a man to adore you. Chasing is strictly for adorers.

Don't make it too easy for men

She meant don't sleep with them. She meant they are only interested in One Thing and if you give them that One Thing they won't respect you (she meant marry you). This is a very old-fashioned theory, but the underlying principle is spot on. You must sleep with men whenever the mood takes you, but if you want to see them again, you must not make it too easy. I'm not suggesting you hide somewhere in the house Sellotaped into your clothes, more that it pays not to be too eager and available. For example: don't offer to bicycle over to his house in the rain. Don't do all the washing up at his flat, clean the bath and then pop out to stock up on food. Don't arrange to meet him after the party he hasn't asked you to, or otherwise act as though, whatever his plans are, you will be delighted to fit in around them. Even the most chivalrous of men will take advantage of this and then go looking for the girl who drives a harder bargain.

Men like a woman who looks good on their arm

Unfortunately there is an element of truth in this. It couldn't matter less if you look like hell most of the time, but they notice if you stop bothering to scrub up when required. It's not big bums or bingo wings that depress men, it's absence of self-love: discoloured toenails, hair the texture of coconut fibre, straggly eyebrows, last year's washed-out cardi. They fear dowdy. (Exactly how old are you?) They don't like rough. (Exactly how much do you smoke at work?) And they have a subliminal fear of a colleague spotting the two of you and thinking, 'Aww, what a nice bloke taking his auntie out for a jaunt.' Also (oh dear) men like girls in dresses or skirts, once in a while. They like to be able to stroke the back of your knee if you happen to be passing.

All you want is a man who is kind, has a sense of humour and who fits with you when you dance

This is pretty close. Though you might want him to have a job as well. And nice hands.

By the way, whatever my mother says, for the first twenty-odd years of their marriage, she worshipped my father – mainly because of the ease with which he topped up the oil in their car. Dad was always grateful for, though slightly perplexed by, the herogramming which accompanied this relatively simple task. And then, one day, he came home from some trip to find my mother in the garage, bent over the open bonnet of the car, gripping an icing bag and painstakingly dripping oil into the tiny dipstick hole. (I have to tell you that my father, instead of stepping in and demonstrating where she was going wrong, crept away from the scene, and continued to play the role of heroic oil-replenisher for several years to come.)

❀ Things Your Mother Told You That Are No Longer True (probably)

Put these aside somewhere safe; you will need them later in life
You won't. It all goes into those cupboards you never dare look in – the photo frames, the cutlery trays, the thermos flasks, the hand-whisk thing, the place mats, the money belts, the waterproof cushions – and it never comes out again.

No one is looking at your feet
Actually, they are. No one these days can avoid noticing shoes – they are right there, centre stage, and frequently the most eye-catching, not to mention expensive, part of your look. Meanwhile feet are now neck and neck with breasts – if that isn't too confusing – in the sexual availability messaging stakes.

'Yeah, I'm six foot two in these, so can you handle it, big boy?/ Ooh, look, I'm wearing darling little ballet pumps; you could just scoop me up and carry me upstairs.' Yes, they *are so* looking at your feet and you don't want to waste the opportunity to send a clear signal.

Men don't notice what you are wearing

Oh yes, they do. The world is saturated with fashion and they've been indoctrinated just like the rest of us. It's not like they know one label from another, but they've moved on from 'that's a pretty frock' to 'whatever you do on no account buy one of those pod coats'. A lot of men, for example, are very anti high-waisted jeans. And clogs. And double-strap Birkenstocks. And harem pants. And shoe boots. And city shorts. They really don't like city shorts. Also most men have a strong aversion to clothes that vaguely remind them of their mothers, such as velvet jackets and satin shirts with pussy bow ties. You can't say exactly what will do it for a man, but there is no question that what you wear can make the difference between 'blank blank blank' and, 'Hello. I wouldn't mind seeing what's under there.' My mother doesn't get this at all, on account of having managed very well in a WRNS uniform, followed by a wedding dress bought with coupons in the fifties and shared between a group of her friends. Even the shoes were one size fits all.

There are two types of girls

There *are*, but not the ones your mother meant: the two types are Us and Focus Woman. You know her. She's the one who has always had a plan. She knew, for example, that she wanted four children by the time she was forty and, guess what, that's exactly what she's got. And she knew where she wanted to live, to the nearest street, and where she wanted to spend her summer holidays, and how she intended to celebrate her tenth wedding anniversary (this was all decided when she was twenty-three, or thereabouts). While you've been drooping around wondering if you might fancy the new boy in the post room, Focus Woman has been out making a grown-up life, and good for her. (It is a bit easier for Focus Woman because she was looking for a backer rather than a soulmate, but, whatever. You've got to give her points for sheer . . . focus.) Your mother still thinks girls who sleep with everyone come to grief in the end but Focus Woman can be pretty slutty if that's what's required, and it hasn't done her any harm.

Still, on balance, your mother is more right than wrong – and you are becoming increasingly aware of this with every passing year. In other words, notwithstanding all the differences between you, yes – you probably are turning into your mother.

Here are some of the early warning signs:

• You are permanently alert to the possibility of things being spilt.

• You have started asking total strangers their opinions, especially shop assistants.

• You challenge people to keep quiet in cinemas and engage people in conversation in bus queues – as in 'Unbelievable! Did I have my hand out or not?' This is behaviour that would have made you cringe a couple of years ago.

• You have a new-found attraction to pretty colours.

• You have started offloading clothes/objects you no longer have any use for on to your friends.

• You mind where things go in the fridge.

• You would quite like to be good at gardening.

• You have developed a conscience about the neighbours and keep wondering if you should ask them for a drink.

• You are collecting Christmas tree ornaments.

• You want to go on a cruise (just kidding . . . you are not quite there yet).

• And the big one. You have started to quote your mother. She likes to 'quote' you when she wants to say something contro-versial, but you have taken to using her in conversation as an example of incorruptible common sense and feminine intuition. You never thought you would, but now you just can't resist. It's the beginning.

4.

Is It Me, Or Is Everyone Showing Off?

Are you kidding? It's horrendous. Everywhere you look women are juggling careers and children and renovating their houses and running marathons, all while looking like their hair has been glazed with honey and their bodies toned by Madonna's personal trainer. Typically they might start the day with a jog in the park (wearing MBTs or pushing a Bugaboo) and end it – after the supper party featuring something light and delicious they threw together earlier – checking their emails on their BlackBerries. In between there will be work, shopping, a blow-dry, endless phone calls to the builders. And this is not Stella McCartney we're talking about here, it's women we know. Women who make those of us who can only do three things a day – and one of those is ordering lunch – feel increasingly inadequate.

The normal level of female competition that sustained our mothers through the long, boring winters (who had the flashiest hotplate, who had the best roses) has turned into something altogether more serious, not to mention in your face. There isn't an hour of the day that this Show-off woman isn't milking for maximum return. If she's walking, she's simultaneously toning her core muscles. If she's at home looking after her baby, she's also setting up a little online business from her sofa. (When she lies stock still, for three hours at a stretch, watching DVDs of *Green Wing*, God only knows.) There are just two rules if you want to be a contender in the noughties and you also happen to be a woman. Everything you do – even the stuff that has always gone with the territory, such as running a house or raising a family must be a statement. If you have children, you have to have four, because three is just too easy and what does it prove? If you buy a house you have to gut it and then completely make it over in a style entirely your own. Then, at all times, you must be looking around, keeping an eye on the progress of your contemporaries, and the minute you see someone else cramming more into their day you must step up to the plate and do more too.

If you are, by any chance, thinking, What is she on about? then welcome, younger reader, but don't, whatever you do, skip this chapter because you think this is some freakish syndrome that bears no relation to your life experience. Trust me, you will not escape the urge to Show Off altogether, not unless you have a sex change. Even if you don't have an inkling of it now, you will hit thirty-eight, or forty-two, and suddenly you will find yourself sneaking to bed with property magazines and going shopping for household props in the run-up to having people for supper, possibly even rearranging the books on your shelves so that the smart, fashionable writers are in pole position and the endless shlock is hidden from view. Besides, there are degrees of Show Offs and you might turn out to be just averagely afflicted, like me. (By current standards I am definitely an amateur Show Off, although, at my peak, I did go as far as buying some very uncomfortable vintage cowboy boots because I figured that, even if I didn't get around to wearing them much, they would look good lying around the place. See? Quite sick.) Still, the point is we are not all pounding the parks in our MBTs and exercising our pelvic floor muscles while working on small business plans. Some of us are struggling Show Offs whose hearts aren't really in it, though none of us is immune.

❧ How did we get here?

Blame Helen Mirren for looking so hot in a bikini in her sixties. Blame Gwyneth Paltrow for being a hands-on mother and a legs-out, red-carpet celebrity. Blame Cherie Blair for juggling a career, a prime minister, children and a memoir. Women like these have certainly played their part in raising the bar and making the rest of us wonder why we are so knackered all the time. But this new brand of showing off is really about the fact that we no longer have everything in common with the women we know.

Take Betty Draper in *Mad Men*. Lovely Betty shares a similar lifestyle to all her friends, so their competitive reference points are identical. First there's your husband (must be good-looking and a good provider with a high-status job); then your home (must have a nursery and a Wendy house in the garden and newly fitted air-con); then your appearance; and, last but not least, your housekeeping and mothering skills. The difference between Betty's experience and that of her friends boils down to where they take their holidays, so any competition between them is neatly contained. It's all about a pot roast, a lipstick, a husband's promotion, a new frock. They all know exactly where they stand. For us girls it's rather different. Our reference points extend way beyond the street where we live and the people whose lives are more or less like ours. I have friends who work in finance and friends who work in fashion. I know women who are film producers and housewives and gardeners and teachers. Some go to work in Manolos, some go to work in flip flops and some, like Betty, don't go to work at all.

What this means is that we are rattled by all the different lives being lived around us and each of us feels a pressure to showcase our particular choices in the best possible light. When our friends drop in to check out our world, it's got to stand up to the scrutiny of an outsider with completely different priorities. So, for example, if you live in the country, in bucolic middle-of-nowhere isolation, it needs to be the picturesque magazine spread ideal as conceived by Annie Leibovitz, with a teepee in the garden and a terrace over-looking rolling hills and black sheep. You must grow your own organic vegetables and have several decorative children who are running slightly wild (in contrast to their more timid urban cousins) and there must be lots of dogs, possibly a donkey, and some chickens.

Once they've created their particular idyll, some women

stop there, but not a lot. And this is where the real showing off starts. These days you don't think, Okay. That's her life, because she is who she is, and she's married to a hedge-fund manager. You simply keep adding to the list of things you must do in order to compete. Jill has a lot of pastel cashmere and a figure like a model's. Must have that. Jade Jagger has pearlized rubber flooring throughout her house in Ibiza. Should consider that. Anna is starting up her own small business selling imported jewellery. Right. Need to have an extra string to bow such as jewellery business. Caroline has her own cutting garden. Don't have much in the way of a garden, but could there be room, in that strip of earth down by the fence? (Notice how I slipped Jade Jagger in there. *Why not?* Now there is no one too remote – in terms of age, job or income – for us to measure our lives against.) This means the showing off has reached staggering, mind-boggling proportions. It is totally crazy. And yet it's accepted as quite normal.

There was an issue of *Vogue,* a while back, which featured an interview with Sheherazade Goldsmith, thirty-four-year-old wife of Zac Goldsmith, ecologist and extremely wealthy young man. It was one of those articles that have always formed the backbone of glossy magazines – the Duchess of Devonshire talks about her chickens; Nicole Kidman opens up about juggling motherhood and movie commitments – and Sheherazade was duly photographed drifting around various properties, talking about managing her family, and the horses, and the organic vegetable gardens, and the organic meat farm, and the books she is writing, and the houses she is doing up. So far, so normal. But there has been a subtle change in how these articles are written over the last few years. Before, you got the broad brushstroke view and we were invited to gaze in awe from a discreet distance. Now, the brief is to get the hard detail: where the star of the piece gets her crockery. How she stores her clothes. What she eats for breakfast. Exercise routines, favourite beauty products, heel heights, rug suppliers. The difference is that we, the humble reader, are expected to try to emulate this lifestyle in whatever ways we can manage without actually ending up in prison. The magazine's editor knows that we are long past pressing our faces against the bars of the wrought-iron gates and gazing up dreamily at the life we can never have. We want to get the look – for less, on a shoestring, whatever – just like we want WAGs bags and Kate Moss's clothes and the skinny on Catherine Zeta Jones's new diet. We are buying the bloody cushions, at least!

❈ The Show-off Chart

Still at Number One: Bodies and aging

We've dealt with this in the chapter Am I Good For My Age? Having the body of someone half your age is currently the Show Offs number-one priority.

In at Number Two: Decorexia (or, My house is better than yours)

See if this scenario rings any bells. A while back I was asked to dinner by a glamorous New Friend who lives in a street that I often walk down – craning my neck to get a glimpse of how the other half lives through the ground-floor windows. You have to have taste to live in this street and, if you don't, you pay someone else to deliver it. The interiors of the houses are guaranteed to die for. Had this friend said, 'Robert Downey Jnr will be there, and Leonardo DiCaprio,' I could not have been more eager to get through that front door.

As I crossed the threshold I had that same heart-racing, panicky feeling you get when falling in love with a ludicrously attractive and unattainable man. Those pale grey walls (just the right shade). That bold rug in a Bloomsbury-esque print that somehow didn't clash with the pale-raspberry-striped chairs. The bookcases made out of old floorboards (oh, such genius!). Ten years ago I'd have been mesmerized by the man with the floppy fringe lounging next to the fire (carved mantelpiece, possibly painted in John Oliver Historic White), but now I only had eyes for the eau de Nil velvet sofa on which he sat.

And then, the moment I had been waiting for – the Tour! (*Of course* there was a tour. There's always a tour. You think this woman went to all this trouble for the love of it? A house like this is created to impress *other women*. That is the whole point of having a beautiful house and beautiful possessions: to Show Them Off.) What I wouldn't have given for a camera, a notebook and a measuring tape. But that would be too much. The deal is, you look and marvel and memorize and, just occasionally, enquire as to the origin of something (not too often, or you risk looking like a house stalker) and then you go home and dream about recreating your own version on an Ikea budget.

I will have you know that I bought my last flat – of which we will be hearing more later – entirely on the basis of the exquisite taste of its previous owner. And when I went round to see it for the second and third times, it wasn't (as I told the estate agent) to look at the water tanks, or to double-check the hefty cracks in the ceiling, but to note down the exact shape and shade of her sofa, and the scale of the table under the window, and the shape of the mirror over the mantelpiece and the colours she used in the bedroom, and (pity me) the arrangement of her lilies. This, ladies, is Decorexia. And if you haven't experienced something like it then you've got it all to look forward to.

As you know, there are something like five phases of drunken behaviour. And, as sure as eggs is eggs, you will pass from one (shrill observations) to five (uninhibited solo dancing) just so long as you keep drinking. Well, there is an equivalent sequence of passionate attachments that all females experience during the course of a lifetime. It starts for everyone with ponies and/or dogs, then moves on to rock stars, girls in the sixth form and clothes, before drifting into boys and more clothes. Stage four kicks in around your early to mid twenties, when there should be a shift from boys to men (though some get stuck at boys) and clothes are still level pegging.

At this point your lifestyle envy is confined to women who

can flip through an Oxfam rail and come out looking like Lindsay Lohan. You would happily chase a girl down the street to find out where she got her boots. You obsess about other women's haircuts and how they are wearing their skirts with their shoes with their belts with what earrings. And then – *bam!* One day – somewhere in your mid thirties – you turn a corner and a whole new section of your brain has been activated (who knew you even cared about mattress ticking?), and now the stuff that makes each other's living spaces stylish is what matters. Never mind, 'Who's that girl at the window? I love what she's wearing.' You've moved on to, 'Who's that girl? I love her curtains. And the shutters. And the light fitting.'

You cannot believe this will ever happen to you until it does. When you are in your twenties you marvel at the insensitivity of your father giving your mother a set of lamps for her birthday. What next? A full tank of petrol? A roll of boiler insulation? But now it starts to make sense. Decorating combines all our favourite things – shopping, rearranging and showing off our resourcefulness – all without having to strip off in a changing room. And there is nothing quite so tantalizing as the prospect – however remote – of becoming one of those women who are envied for their taste in everything. Great dress style is almost as good as it gets but great all-round style is the Holy Grail. And, as you get older, it's the *all-round* part that sneaks ahead. The flowers on the table. The cunning arrangement of paintings in the hall. The things she has done with the house in France! 'I love what you've done with this place' is worth ten, maybe twenty times more than 'I love what you're wearing'. And you know you've got it bad when you ask people over and you are still lighting tea lights and hiding cushions and throwing throws and wrestling with the not-quite-right flower arrangement when the doorbell goes and you haven't so much as had a shower (of course a real Show Off would be fabulously turned out too, but some of us can only handle one Show-off project at a time).

This natural progression, from rock stars to reclaimed baths, is nothing new – what's new is the zeal with which we are prepared to pursue our ideal environment. We, being creatures of the modern age, do nothing by halves. We want our homes to have it all, and usual Show-off rules apply – nothing is out of bounds, no reference point is too elitist or ambitious. When the newspapers feature pictures of Cate Blanchett's giant roll-top bath being crane-lifted into her Brighton home, you make a note. When Sheherazade is photographed in front of her salvage fireplace (a Christmas present from Zac, so what do you think, probably not in the £5–600 range?), you make another note. I actually looked into buying a solid limestone fireplace when I lived in a tiny flat the size of Rachel's bedroom in *Friends* and, while that may be extreme Decorexic behaviour, I am not the worst by any means.

Remember the movie *Something's Gotta Give*? Remember the star attraction – the fabulous East Hampton ocean-front house belonging to Diane Keaton's character? In all the big scenes, when we should have been following the relationship between Keaton and Nicholson, Decorexics everywhere were checking out the sofa covers, the lampshades, the layout of the kitchen. But my friend Lily went one step further. She actually rented the DVD, freeze-framed a scene featuring some particularly stunning white brick tiles in the background and then handed it to her builder to get sourcing for her new kitchen. (On second viewing, by the way, Lily pronounced that the house was far from perfect: 'Too many neutrals and the brackets holding up the shelves were ugly. But the flowers were good.')

That's the really significant difference between old-style house tweaking and the Show-off version. We like to think Big.

New entry at Three. You may be decorating; I'm Project Managing

Do you know anyone who isn't having work done on their house? I don't mean getting a loft extension in order to accommodate the ever-expanding family – I mean major, rethinking-the-space work. Digging out the basement kitchen and extending it five yards into the garden; moving the kitchen from the basement to the first floor; converting the downstairs loo into a wet room; knocking through the study and the sitting room and making a mezzanine-level office; replacing all the ugly old spotlights with recessed spotlights as mapped out by a special lighting designer. It's got to the point where, if you aren't having work done, then your neighbours undoubtedly will be, and when they've finished it will be time for you to start again somewhere else. (That's if you can get the basic materials. Ask any builder and they will tell you there is a chronic shortage of everything from timber to tiles because the nation's women have gone house-improvement crazy. Forget runs on the bank. Concrete is harder to come by than white rhino horn since the non doms started digging out their basements to make swimming pools.)

It is a kind of madness. No one buys a house or a flat any more and leaves it as they find it, no matter what condition it's in. That would be to invite the suspicion that you are not up to the job of totally reinventing your living space and doing something much, much cleverer. Estate agents have changed their spiel accordingly. Five years ago the line was 'this is newly renovated – you won't have to touch a thing'; now they dive straight in with their vision of the building's 'potential' before they've so much as shown you the bedroom. The message is: 'You can play God in here. Come on. Let's see if you've got what it takes.' So, if you are anyone, you need to have a team of carpenters and painters and plumbers and electricians permanently filing in and out of your front door, chipping away at that property, getting it just right for . . . Er. Showing off to your friends.

You name it, we're doing it. Wet rooms? A couple of years ago you wouldn't have expected a wet room in a hotel, let alone in a semi-detached in Shepherd's Bush. And what about those long, thin taps specially for rinsing vegetables? And those vast cookers with two ovens and a couple of pig roasting bays that are now pretty much standard requirement? (Who has got a regular four-ring stove any more? You have to have a metre of steel on legs that looks like it's been rolled out of the kitchens of The Wolseley.) Meanwhile one perfect living space is no longer enough, not if you want to compete with the serious Show Offs. For that you will need a place in the country.

I think we all know there wouldn't be quite the same market for weekend country houses if the owners were told they had to make do with the original lino floors and Formica kitchen units. For every well-meaning mum looking for space to plant the giant trampoline, there's a woman whose top drawer is overflowing with swatches of cabbage-rose linens and Cath Kidston catalogues featuring yummy little tents and strawberry-print clothes-peg bags. I, myself, had to be taken in hand by a girlfriend who caught me lusting after a house near Bath and muttering about the possibility of moving. 'Try and think beyond the wooden shutters in the drawing room,' she hissed. 'You wouldn't last a week. You don't even have a car.'

And, of course, she was right. My fantasy was based purely on the decorative possibilities and on a vision of me drifting around the shuttered drawing room, while assembled guests admired my inventive use of John Oliver Winter Sky.* Also,

---

* Note: The incredible proliferation of whites is worth a chapter all on its own, and is a perfect example of how widespread Decorexia has become. When choosing the whites for our house (four in all) I had *ten* testers on the go. I kid you not. And in the end I chose the wrong white because it looks really creamy in bright sunlight. Can you believe it?

I wanted a real log fire and an excuse to wear my Spanish riding boots and possibly one of those ultra-fitted tweed jackets – it's not only Madonna who fancies herself as a chatelaine.

Up from Five to Four. The romantic garden

If you don't have the means to run a second, parallel life in the country, then there's always the option of the lifestyle garden, preferably two (these days rich urban types are buying the house next door so they can extend the fairytale, laterally).

The purpose of this garden is less to showcase flowers and trees than to act as an open-air room set – part boudoir, part Peter Pan nursery – featuring lanterns in trees and on crooks embedded in flower beds, flares and hurricane lamps, bunting made of triangles of faded material, umbrellas with tinkling fringes, and so on. The perfect Show-off garden will have real sofas dragged out on to the lawn, a fire to cook on (a pot bellied stove or an open fire built on bricks – barbecues are just too easy), a teepee and – latest addition to the list of Show-off must-haves – a gipsy caravan. This you will want to convert into an extra spare room, with lace curtains at the windows and plenty of enamel painted jugs and plates. Those who live in smaller properties in town with a couple of yards of decking that smells quite strongly of cat wee (moi), have to make do with lots of tea lights in decorative holders, plus scattered cushions and quilts that aren't meant to be taken outdoors (real outdoors things are too obvious, generally).

At Five. Food

Women have always competed over the quality of their sponge cakes and jam (I knew a woman in the eighties who used to buy homemade jam and decant it into her own jars, to impress her husband) but today's food showing off is of a different calibre. It's your attitude to food that counts now – how much you know, how much you care and whether you understand how to give people what they want.

To be a Show-off cook in the noughties you must:

• *Be organic and packaging aware.* You can ruin your dinner party at a stroke by slamming a brick of Asda vacuum-packed Cheddar down on the cheeseboard. And providing cheesy Wotsits and other e-number loaded treats for your friends' children is a faux pas equivalent to popping on the 18-rated DVD or hiring the children's entertainer who was sacked from the local scout troop.

• *Be rustic and wholesome.* Nigella cooks barefoot, and barefoot with pomegranate-stained fingers is roughly the mood you are going for. Lamb must be hacked off the bone, not elegantly carved. Mozzarella torn not sliced. Herbs are shredded rather than chopped, and food is piled high on dishes for people to help themselves, never served and put in front of them. In the same way that fashion pundits recommend you 'destroy' your look a bit to give it the right air of insouciant chic, food should look thrown together, without being a dog's dinner.

• *Have a conscience.* When Hugh Fearnley-Whittingstall took to the battery-chicken farms and berated us all for buying cheap poultry, it put responsibility on the Show-off foody agenda. Now lazy shopping, whether it's for Fiji mineral water, Turkey Twizzlers or unfair-traded coffee, looks very unreconstructed.

• *Be flexible.* Forget the individual veal escalopes in a creamy sauce, Show-off food needs to be adaptable in order to accommodate everyone's different requirements. If you're having people for supper, a few will turn up an hour late; someone will bring her teenage children; at least one will have a 'food intolerance' and one will be vegetarian or recently AA (so he can't have the wine sauce). It may be that your instinct is to stand on the kitchen table and scream, 'I'm not a sodding magician!' But if you want to score points on the Show Off-ometer you will make like a resourceful provider for whom cooking is an act of relaxation and love.

• *Be prepared to customize.* Special dietary requirements are a mark of Show-off society at its peak, and the higher up the scale you go, the more extreme the requests. In fact, in order to be a genuine contender in Show-off circles, you probably have to have some kind of dietary foible, if only to demonstrate that you, too, are special and worth the added inconvenience. Not being able to eat certain foods – or just preferring not to – is a luxury not everyone can afford, so it follows that you must be pretty big news if you only eat prawns and eggs. (We'll get on to special dietary requirements in the chapter on manners.)

Although food has to taste good, as a matter of principle, it is more of a prop than the focus in an entertaining situation, and the Show-off cook will need to pay at least as much attention to staging the scene. People want to see you've gone to the trouble of skinning the cherry tomatoes and blanching the almonds, but they're more interested in the whole tableau: the people, the plates, the table decoration, the clothes you are wearing. Often the food is just the lure to get the audience for the Show Off's fabulous lifestyle. I hate to mention Nigella again, but, Oh Well. When you tuned in to *Nigella Bites*, did you give a monkey's what she was cooking? Really? I never had a clue. I was looking at her rooms (and they were her rooms back then), her bookshelves, her wallpaper, her splashbacks, the things she was doing with floating candles and holly and sparklers and chrysanthemum heads. Food was just the cover for snooping around Nigella's sun-kissed, west London world and Nigella made food into a top Show-off accessory – the extra element that adds sex appeal and goddess points in a way that cocktails and some Kettle Chips just can't.

Six, up from Eight. Goddess Mothers

You can't put an exact date on it, but at some point, let's say in the dying years of the last millennium, motherhood became central to the Show Off's portfolio of achievements. Previously, raising children was something everybody took more or less for granted. It had always happened: our mothers had done it, and their mothers before them, and so on all the way back to Mrs Australopithecus. It was no big deal. And then a few things happened that changed this:

• Conception became less inevitable and more of an achievement (possibly because women were having babies later), and it began to seem like there was something special about giving birth.

• Because the sacrifice involved in motherhood was perceived – by a generation not that big on sacrifice – to be pretty staggering, and because the psychological dimension of mothering started to be taken a lot more seriously, becoming a mother gave you a newly superior status.

• Women discovered children can make you look good. Not only does a child on your hip tell the world that you are fertile and loved (or at least momentarily fancied), but a cute child is a walking advertisement for your great bone structure and good taste. (So it is that children, having been mostly snotty and dressed in anoraks and washed-out hand-me-downs became extensions of their mothers' aspirations: little hippy boys with flowing blond locks and shell necklaces; glossy fashion girls in skinny cords and mini Ugg boots; proper little misses in velvet collared coats and shiny leather button-over shoes.)

• Last but not least (and this is the biggie) juggling with aplomb became the supreme test of a class-A Show Off, and to achieve advanced-level juggling you need children – four or more if you want to be taken seriously.

This is how we created the cult of the Goddess Mother.

Not all mothers, by any means, have got sucked into the cult of Goddess Motherhood. Many are just quietly getting on with the job as best they can. Many more are struggling like hell with few resources and little support. These mothers, we are all agreed, deserve nothing but respect, admiration and our prayers. But there are plenty of mothers who have identified motherhood as the ultimate opportunity for showing off and sticking it to the competition.

Take Angelina Jolie. Jolie typifies the Goddess Mother – almost to the point of parody – here's why:

• *She's done it, when Jennifer hasn't.* Ugly and unpalatable though it may be, the fact is, that in the super Show-off circles in which Angelina moves, children are *the* big competitive issue. And you don't just score points for having them – the partner-less, childless women with whom you are competing lose points comparatively. This is why, when the *National Enquirer* features pictures of a grim-faced Jennifer, under a headline about her suffering because of Angelina's latest pregnancy, you know that, for once, every word of it is true. Movie deals. Marriage proposals. A mansion on the beach. All of these pale into insignificance compared with the bona fide pregnancy. Angelina's babies have made Jen look *less womanly*. And what goes for celebrities goes for us too. You can't join the club, you can't be the full, rounded, all-options-covered Show-off deal, if you haven't got one of your own.

• *She looked like a goddess even when carrying twins.* In order to be a Goddess Mother you must first be a pregnant goddess: a woman who looks like she's swallowed a basketball, but in every other respect is indistinguishable from the svelte creature she was eight months previously. The celebrities kicked this one off, naturally, and the media have obliged, photographing them from all angles and scoring them out of ten according to how well they are carrying their load. Anyone who looks a bit too big in the lead-up to the birth gets marked down. (Swollen ankles? Strange skin pigmentation? Actual all-over weight gain? *Nasty.*) Anyone who looks fabulous on the red carpet, a few days off her due date, gets bonus points. Naturally, civilian Show-off pregnant women have taken these lessons on board, gritted their teeth and followed suit. Instead of embracing the opportunity to wear sloppy dresses and ankle-support trainers on the one occasion when they could get away with it, they dress for their photo opportunity right up until they swing through the doors of the delivery room. Previously, there was just the pressure to spring back into shape within weeks of giving birth; now you must wear body-con dresses and scary heels and cleavage-revealing tops throughout the pregnancy.

• *She has given birth, thereby confirming her place in the pantheon of real women, and she has adopted too.* This is sublime Show-offery. This woman is a pro.

• *Her children are super cute and they cover all the bases.* If you were in the mood to add up all the messages the Jolie brood is transmitting about their mother, it would be a long and varied list – which is exactly the intention.

• *She has successfully locked out the competition by making sure she has the biggest family in Hollywood.* Who knows how many of them there are now? Too many to fill their specially commissioned rainbow-family double bed, that's for sure.

Had Angelina given birth to the twins 'naturally' that would have been worth another few Goddess points, because the manner in which you give birth is competitive too. The recovery time. The number of weeks it takes to get your figure back. How you manage in the first weeks. How organized you are. What method of baby rearing you are using. Then, a few years down the line, you get to the really competitive stuff, like how they are doing at school. That's all to look forward to.

At Seven. Auto Style

Fashion pundits will tell you that we've never had it so good. There is more fashion at more affordable prices: you can do minis or maxis in the same season, skinny jeans or palazzo pants, flats or wedges. No one is dictating any more. Oh, the relief! The freedom! But what they fail to mention is the terrible tyranny of auto style. Auto style – as in automatic, effortless, unique and individual – is the required level of fashion aware-ness for regular women. You may buy a shirt and jeans from Gap, but then ... then you must do something extraordinary. Twist a vintage scarf round your throat. Sling on a belt that was once used in a Helmut Newton shoot. Put some boots over the jeans, or under them, or cut off the jeans. Create your own look. Anyone can buy clothes, please. It's how you make them your own that counts.

This is all very well if you are a stylist with a size-eight figure and a lot of time to innovate in your lunch hour, otherwise it makes gibbering idiots of us all. Advanced-level fashion awareness requires either a job in the industry, or that thing called 'an eye', or that special gene that tells you it's the right time to get out your old tuxedo. (You can't rely on fashion magazines. Everyone knows those catwalk supplements are the marbles under the skates of the average shopper: chinoiserie; juicy fruit neons; Victoriana with a twist; abstract prints. Fabulous! But you're never going to see the fashion editors or the off-duty models wearing any of this stuff. Are you joking? As a matter of fact, there's only a tiny fraction of the season's new looks that any self-respecting fashionista would dream of buying into. It's probably all about one jacket and a certain pair of shoes – but they're not telling *you* that.)

And the worst of it is the auto part. You would throw yourself on the mercy of some achingly hip sales assistant and just come clean and say, 'Look, I have no bloody idea what to wear with this. A sheer chiffon shirt? Boots? Twelve necklaces? A cummerbund plus some earmuffs? For pity's sake, give me a clue.' But the whole point of auto style is you cannot let on that you need help because that would be like saying, 'Would you stand in for me and have sex with my boyfriend? I'm just no good at it.' What you have to be – in the current climate – is the woman to whom people say, 'Oh, that is so you.' What you are aiming to be is the woman of whom people say, 'Oh, that is so *Her*. It would look terrible on me . . . but it's so Her. Should we call Her and tell Her it's here?'

To summarize. In order to be a contender you used to have to look as good as you could, given your circumstances. Now you have to look as good as Elizabeth Hurley on a swimsuit shoot, *and* have your own inimitable, envy-inducing, fashion-informed signature style. You need to be one of those women who flicks decisively through rails and whips out a few *key pieces* that will *work with* the other pieces in her wardrobe. Preferably you need to have been employed by Anna Wintour at some point.

Note: A useful tip. Keep an eye on the woman flicking decisively through the rail, and if she looks like she knows what she's doing and you like what she's wearing just try on everything she does.

Eight. Job plus sideline

You might think women would show off about their jobs. Weirdly, they don't. The first rule of Show-off culture is to let it be known that you have a serious, challenging job, but it's the stuff you manage to do *on top* of it that counts. Looking great at the party despite leaving the office at seven thirty. Throwing together the dinner within hours of getting back from the business trip. Managing the children and the builders and the various deliveries, as well as heading up a team of twenty. There is no Show-off kudos in having a good job with a law firm if you also have hair that looks like straw and a flat still piled high with packing boxes. No one cares if you're working on some UN peace treaty or brokering a deal that will end whaling by the end of the decade – not unless you also have a whip-toned body, a living room to die for and a brood of decorative children.

There are three types of Show-off working women:

• *Women who work*. These women will run themselves ragged in order to achieve something approximating the non-working woman's lifestyle. Their number one objective is not to be outdone on the cake-baking, flower-arranging front. However successful they are in their chosen field, they choose to measure themselves against stay-at-home mums with two kinds of help.

• *Women who work, and could probably do your job too*. These are the ones who work in the media, but who are also writing a book/film script/on the board of a major charity/doing a landscape-gardening course. Their aim is to cover everything that women in their orbit are achieving, just in case. They look around them and think, if she can do that, why can't I? Psychologist? Why not? Film-maker – that looks interesting. Scriptwriter? Hmm.

• *Women whose partners work, who have a little sideline*. These are the women all Show-off women would love to be. Their business is financed by their husband, which means it can afford to be set up in some style in a converted stable with pink desks, a little kitchen and orchids in every alcove. It's smallish and part time, naturally. The business gives her space, plus a challenge, and it doesn't interfere with their lives, so she is still queen of the fabulous domestic set up.

The fake goddess list of essentials

Mirrors with mottled antique glass
Limed floorboards
Welsh blankets
Tiffany diamond ear studs
Farrow and Ball paint
Cath Kidston (for children's rooms/utility room/garden)
Flowers (from your own garden, ideally)
Heirloom straw hats (on pegs, never worn)
Pippa Small, or other posh ethnic jewellery
BlackBerry, or Smythson diary
White towels
Manolo Blahnik heels (leopard print not beige)
Cashmere (sweaters not throws)
Man's sporty watch
Mulberry bag
Mismatched china plates
Glossy recipe books
Old threadbare Levi's 501s
Spanish riding boots (plain, no fringes)
Turquoise yoga mat

There is bad news. Just when you thought you had it taped, experienced Show Offs have started the breakaway faction known as No Effort Showing Off which – like No Make-up Make-up – still requires plenty of effort, just of a different sort. This time round the challenge is being confidently undone in a way that makes anything more look like lack of sophistication. You twist your hair up rather than getting a blow-dry. You have rough blankets rather than cashmere throws; French supermarket tumblers, as opposed to wine glasses; chipped mismatched plates; cheap specs from the local chemist; rugs from Ikea; and unpainted toenails. The Gaggia has been substituted for a macchinetta. The expensive teak garden furniture has been traded in for some old school chairs. It's one part earthy, one part ethical, one part this-old-thing-it's-just-something-I-inherited, and one part ha-ha-I'm-so-good-at-this-I'm-changing-the-rules.

You can try to chase after this lot if you want, or just stick with attempting to master standard good taste. It's really a question of how much you care.

❀ So, Is Showing Off A Bad Thing?

Yes if:

• Every time you have people to supper it requires a major outlay on new candles, throws, etc. and you spend twice as much time styling your home as getting ready.

• You don't bother about impressing men, but when you're going to see one of the SOs, you splash out on a new pair of shoes and earrings just in case she notices.

• You gauge your appropriate weight not by what registers on the scales, but according to who is going to be on your summer holiday.

• You have stopped shopping for what you want and now shop for what you think other people expect.

• You chose your last two holidays for the social cachet of the place rather than because you really wanted to go there.

• You find yourself segregating friends into degrees of Show Off and trying a lot harder to make the party sparkle when it's the biggest Show Offs' turn.

• A regular family picnic can no longer feature sausages, buns and hard-boiled eggs, but must involve shelled broad bean and pancetta salad and grilled aubergines.

• You honestly don't see anything wrong with spending £70 on a cushion.

• You have been known to travel to Hay-on-Wye just to check out some elk skins that might work for a window seat.

No if:

- You only buy what you love and aim to buy things you have never seen anywhere else.

- You would rather spend the money on a good leg of lamb than some more tea-light containers.

- Your Decorexia is under control (i.e. you've just been to supper in a pink kitchen, and although you were tempted to change everything in your flat to accommodate a new pink kitchen, you have resisted).

- You are perfectly capable of recycling your Show-off clothes for five years or more.

- You think gipsy caravans and teepees and yurts etc. are quite irritating.

- You have a dog and it has a doggy dog basket – not a designer bean bag or something that says more about you than him.

- You have at least a couple of friends who would read this list and have no idea what you were talking about.

5.

Should They Have Written To Thank Me? (or, The New Manners Explained For Anyone Who Is Confused)

This is our manners dilemma in a nutshell. We want to live by a more relaxed code than our parents' generation: we despise the petty codes of conduct that condemn you for not wearing a tie, or reaching for the wrong fork, or speaking out of turn. But here's the flip side of the coin: we also want the civilized security of the world our parents inhabited. And, as we get older and their generation retires to the sidelines leaving us to set the standards, we're more and more aware that without all the trivial niceties (hold the door for the person behind you, think of the neighbours when you turn up the stereo, keep your voice down in public, never use bad language, don't eat in the street) life is a lot less pleasant. We are starting to appreciate this now because it's gradually dawning on us that our manners are the model for the next generation's (and that's a pretty sobering thought) and because manners are getting steadily worse, and I don't just mean out there on the streets. I mean in the lift at the office and in the board meeting. I mean at the wedding of your best friend and by the pool in the nice hotel. I mean in the places where you would expect manners to be at their sharpest and shiniest, when everyone is dressed up and on their best behaviour, and in our very own houses on an average Friday night.

When people talk about bad manners, you think of the extremes: the girl who barges ahead of you in the queue and then, when you protest, tells you what you can do with yourself. The boy cycling down the pavement, forcing old ladies into the road. The fat bloke in the park with the disposable barbecue and the ghetto blaster belching 'Who Let the Dogs Out'. The grapevine is buzzing with horror stories of the unspeakable rudeness that threatens our quality of life. But what about your friends who said they'd come for drinks and then just never turned up? Or the people whose dog trashed your carpet and they never so much as mentioned it? Or the business associate who thought it was okay to tell the waiter that the service was a 'fucking disgrace'? Or the person next to you at dinner who talked across you all night? Or the godchild (so godchild's mum) who has never thanked you for a present in twelve years – never mind with a letter? What about the lack of basic manners among people who are convinced beyond a shadow of doubt that they are polite and thoughtful and pretty damn charming?

Here is a scene that I've witnessed more than once. A woman lurches up to an organic food shop in her 4WD, parks it badly, blocking the street (she's in a hurry!) and rushes into the shop, bruising a display of fruit with her suitcase-sized handbag as she passes. In her wake are two children who follow her example by further disturbing the fruit display and helping themselves to some cherries and a couple of tomatoes. (Their mother acknowledges this with a roll of her eyes, and we, the regular shoppers, are given to understand that this is one of the hazards of having spunky little individuals born of extraordinary parents. What can you do?) Anyway, no time to stop! The woman fills her shopping basket – occasionally knocking things off shelves and failing to replace them – pays at the till while conducting a loud and inappropriate conversation on her mobile ('Oh Jesus, just tell the headmistress we have booked the flights!') and complains, even more loudly, about the speed of the service. Then she flounces out of the shop with her children, still helping themselves to cherries, trailing behind her.

This is Nouveau Rudeness – casual and careless, blithely treading on people's feelings, suiting its own agenda, blissfully unaware of the offence it is causing. It is far more insidious than regular rudeness because it doesn't accept that it is rude, if anything it thinks it's cool and appealing in a hassled, high-achieving kind of way. And it's threatening to become standard, normal behaviour. The more Planet Organic women there are circling the planet the more we get used to them.

❀ Who Are The Nouveau Rude?

The Nouveau Rude are the sort of people who own Lynne Truss's *Talk to the Hand* – educated, well off, nicely dressed people who only cook with olive oil, recycle, give money to charity and who are civilized in every imaginable sense except (and this is where the rudeness comes in) that they consider themselves to be Very Important. Not just important but Very Busy, which gives them the right to put their needs first at all times. Years ago I lived in Norway and, back then, if there was one English speaking person in a room of fifty, then the forty-nine others would all speak English as a courtesy to that one individual. That's always seemed to me to be a perfect example of good manners — being prepared to put yourself out so that a stranger will feel more at ease. Nouveau Rudeness works in almost exactly the opposite way: it's all about expecting other people to work around your individual needs, wherever, whenever, whatever they may be.

For example, a classic piece of Nouveau Rudeness is refusing to move up in the cinema because you have the seats you want, right bang in the middle, even if it means that the incoming group of four have to sit separately. (I have actually witnessed this happening, twice. But don't worry, I spent the duration of the movie popcorn-bombing the NR bastards – a bit rude, but excusable given the context.) Nouveau Rudes always want to be moved on aeroplanes. They have trouble with the air-conditioning in restaurants. They query bills, and the temperature of their espressos, and the position of their hotel rooms and the cost of their dry-cleaning. They treat all employees like servants in bad TV dramatizations of the fall of the Roman Empire and generally behave with an air of entitlement.

You ask yourself, who are these people? Who are their friends? Who puts up with them? But then we all know people whose manners are impeccable; they just happen to stop at the fortress gates of their home. Once they step outside their comfort zone what matters is that they get from A to B in the quickest possible time with the least possible inconvenience and God help anyone who gets in their way (in the 4WD, naturally. Those cars are rude even with no one in them). Of course this also makes them selfish neighbours. Demanding school parents. Hideous people to be around if there's any kind of airport meltdown. Impatient customers. It makes them rude, in fact. It's just that you don't necessarily get to see it.

We are not like this. Good grief no. We are polite most of the time – unless pushed to the limit by a traffic warden, in which case we have been known to lose it a bit. But here is the thing about Nouveau Rudeness, which I expect you've already guessed. It has tainted all of us. We've got used to people behaving less than well and that has gradually compromised all of our standards. I, for example, used to think of myself as quite well mannered, but then, if I cast my mind back over the last month, I have to admit that I've barked at the woman on the end of the phone from Intelligent Finance ('not *that* intelligent, then') and got quite shouty when addressing the foreman of the building site opposite, while wearing a towel and flip flops, at 7.30 a.m. on a Sunday morning. And I am well aware that, without due vigilance, rudeness could become a normal part of my daily life. None of us is safe.

For example, have you ever done any of the following:

• Bawled out a waiter when your food arrives not precisely as ordered (maybe the sauce is on the fish, not on the side. Imagine!).

• Been rude to someone who, on reflection, was only doing their job (the woman on the end of the phone at the bank who asks for your dog's date of birth when you're just trying to get your hands on your own money).

• Arrived at someone's house for supper and instantly announced how tired you are/hungover/full from an enormous lunch.

• Sat next to someone at supper and afterwards realized that you discovered absolutely nothing about them, including their name.

• Repeatedly failed to memorize an acquaintance's name (this could be early onset Alzheimer's but, more likely, you just can't be bothered).

• Made a lunch date with a friend, and then spent the entire hour talking about your problems.

• In traffic, given another driver the finger/cut them up/nicked their parking space/ignored them when they were trying to squeeze in at a tricky junction.

• Deleted pictures of yourself on other people's cameras.

- Worn sunglasses when not strictly necessary, and refused to remove them, even when the sad woman next door was trying to tell you about her husband's illness.

- Cut someone short on the phone who was in the middle of telling you something quite important. (Though this isn't necessarily rude. See the box on new manners rules.)

- Swapped a place card at a wedding in order to avoid sitting next to someone, or in order to sit next to someone you think would suit you better.

- Dropped a friend at a taxi rank, late at night, rather than taking them to their front door. (Note: This is entirely reasonable if driving them home means adding thirty minutes to your journey, but not if they paid for your theatre tickets.)

- Met a doctor and gripped him, all night, about your unexplained bloating/personal theories about how many units of alcohol are damaging.

If you've answered yes to one or more of the above, then you are on the slippery slope to NR, and it's time to take stock of what's rude and what's not without further delay.

Love to; let me get back to you

A few years ago, if you asked someone to supper, they would give you an answer there and then, and after that all you had to worry about was getting the food and drink. Not any more! Nouveau Rudes are commitment phobic. They want to be sure anything they do is worth the effort, and they like plans to be flexible because they aren't sure how they will feel on the night. If you ask the Nouveau Rude to dinner, they may either:

• Let you know their answer when they have sorted a few things out.

• Ask who else is coming.*

• Warn you that they will have to arrive late, or leave early, or both.

• Warn you that they are detoxing.

• Inform you that they aren't talking to so-and-so (in case you wanted to ask them both).

• Ask if they can bring their lover/children.

• Cancel at the last minute. (In less self-centred times the rule was that you could cancel if you were calling from A & E, and a nurse had to dial the number for you. Now you just have to be worn out from the night before to feel justified in staying away.)

Meanwhile the Nouveau Rude host is no better. If you get asked to dinner by an NR they may issue instructions up front

---

* Note: On no account are you obliged to tell them! However, Nouveau Rudeness is so widespread you may feel it's easier to volunteer the information up front so that you can secure some kind of commitment.

about what time you should arrive, precisely, what time you should leave ('we have quite a busy week') and then fail to do any of the following:

• Introduce you to your fellow guests. (This is very Nouveau Rude. We are all supposed to be too cool for names and labels. But, actually, it is only good manners to tell Jack that the reason you have asked him on the same night as Jane, is because they are both astronauts.)

• Fill up your glass. (Neglecting to provide enough wine is as rude as forgetting to buy the main course.)

• Rescue you from the person who appears to be trying to get you to give them a job.

• Rescue you from the two men who are talking across you about share options, and have been for twenty minutes.

• Divert the conversation when it turns to Where do you stand on lesbian mothers, and one of the people present is a lesbian mother.

All of this boils down to four words: responsibility for your guests, something which the Nouveau Rude host is not big on. As a matter of fact, you can always tell the Nouveau Rude hostess because she puts herself next to the two most attractive men and is oblivious to the desert of conversation at the other end of the table. (Nouveau Rude hosts, meanwhile, have been known to switch places on the pretext that they want to mix things up a bit when, clearly, they are gagging to be released from their placement. Everyone spots this a mile off, especially the people who are deselected.)

Note: None of the little stuff counts any more, and that much has changed. Feeding people horribly late. Feeding them burnt food. Greeting them in a towel. Getting them to help chop the vegetables, and load the dishwasher. No one cares, so long as we're made to feel loved by the host, or at least wanted.

Newly rude: Talking about your nanny problems/your financial crisis/your son's prowess at maths/any other subjects that no one but your immediate family could possibly find interesting.

Newly not rude: Asking if you can bring Bjorn who has just flown in from Zurich.

Still bloody rude: Arriving drunk. Producing dope and your own water-cooled pipe and reducing all the guests to catatonic inertia.

Do you have maybe just some salad and goat's cheese?

Food was promoted, some time ago, from fuel for living to lifestyle choice with major health implications – and everyone knows their food rights. Not only are people ordering off-menu in restaurants and getting pretty fierce about it ('I said without the skin. I can't eat this. You'll have to take it back'), but they expect to eat and drink exactly what they want, wherever they are. It is okay to indulge this neurosis, so long as we are all clear that fussing about your food is still bad manners, albeit wrapped up in the guise of responsible, healthy living.

The rule is very simple. Unless you have a life-threatening peanut allergy, in other people's houses you must eat their food. If you are wheat, gluten, dairy intolerant, or even vegetarian, and your host has forgotten (or, quite understandably, pretended to), then eat what you can and don't make a drama out of it. Never say no to sauce/pudding etc. or 'not much for me, thanks' as if eating any of their filthy cooking is a trial; it's not only rudely picky, this kind of behaviour will make your hostess feel as if she is the subject of an Egon Ronay inspection, rather than someone trying to throw a party.

Possibly at this point you are thinking, But it's okay, surely, to point out the white wine isn't properly chilled, and ask if there's anything else? This is because you have three toes on the slippery slope of Nouveau Rudeness. That way lies, 'Would it be okay if we sat down at eight? I get terrible sugar lows,' and, 'Would you mind if I changed the music/turned up the heating/rearranged the table?' (All of which NRs are perfectly capable of.)

If you are in any doubt that exercising your food rights is a form of rudeness, consider this: the only people who eat and drink anything, at any time, in any order, are our parents' generation who all suffer from indigestion, high blood pressure, diabetes and are officially on cholesterol-lowering diets. You don't get them asking, 'Could you tell me what exactly is in this?' as if you're about to slip them polonium 210.

Note: There are always exceptions and, in the following circumstances, you can, legitimately, behave quite rudely.

- If you are fed nouvelle cuisine portions, claim not to have eaten anything all day, and ask if you can have a banana.

- If the chicken is pink, leave it.

- If you have seen the dog licking the food, swap it with your neighbour's when he's not looking.

- Offer any food you can't eat (surreptitiously) to the man next to you. Mostly he will be grateful.

- If you want a coffee, and no one's offering, pretend you need it to stay awake at the wheel.

- If you brought some spectacular Belgian chocolates and you really want to try them, come right out with it (but don't add, 'They cost £40 and I'm buggered if I'm going to miss out.').

Newly rude: Bringing your own food in Tupperware containers.

Newly not rude: Smoking throughout dinner in a smoking household.

Still bloody rude: Snaffling the good drink brought by your guests and bringing out the rough stuff.

Oh. You've dressed up.

Who can forget the scene in the movie *Notes on a Scandal* when the character Barbara (played by Judi Dench) finds herself horribly overdressed for a lunch party with the boho west London crowd? Not me! The day someone decided it was a good idea to rid ourselves of the tyranny of dress codes was the day women were thrown to the wolves. Not only can you never be sure you are wearing the right thing until the moment you walk through the door, but getting it wrong makes you look like some kind of social freak. For example, I am in my forties, reasonably confident, plenty of clothes at my disposal, but what happens when I am asked to dinner by the smart woman I barely know and the invitation sounds casual, but no dress is specified . . . ? I have to get on the phone to my survival pack and canvass their opinion, that's what. Together we have to *guess*.

For this particular occasion, we agree (eventually) that the velvet trousers and semi flashy top strikes the right note, on the basis that the only thing more humiliating than being under-dressed in the houses of the rich is looking like you're expecting valet parking and gold-leaf-embossed martinis. And what happens on the night? Smart woman opens the door, takes one look at me and says (quite loudly as I recall), 'Oh. You've dressed up.' She is wearing a black dress. I happen to think she looks rather more dressed up than I do, but she's wearing no make-up make-up, or possibly no make-up, no jewellery, no stockings and no shoes – that's the clincher. She's unquestionably boho from the knees down. So, before the evening is even underway, I am officially a) overdressed b) wrong footed c) looking like a Try Hard d) excluded from the club e) not boho cool but more Barbara on her big night out. Great.

Dress code uncertainty is a fact of modern life, but rudeness creeps into the equation when those who could throw you a lifeline don't. Why don't you put us out of our misery? Prom dress or no-brand jeans? Should I make an effort, or will I look like a WAG at Glastonbury? It is a kind of rudeness to let your guests sweat when you could just pick up the phone and say, 'You do what you like, but I will be wearing Chanel couture, with a six-foot train.' Rudest of all is to greet them at the door with the words 'you've dressed up', which we all know is the same as saying, 'Oh dear. I thought you were one of us. My mistake.' This is the big problem with no-rules dressing: it favours the socially confident and fashion savvy at the expense of everyone else and has the potential to make Barbaras of us all.

Note: Faux casualness (i.e. deliberately dressing down when it would be appropriate to make a bit of an effort) is a Nouveau Rude habit you generally find among the very well off, for whom it's a game to slum it. We are all agreed that if you are filthy rich you should not deny those who aren't the opportunity to drink champagne (preferably from a fountain of coupe glasses) and dress up a bit. Which is why everyone loves Elton John.

• If in doubt, sharp trousers, great shoes and a piece of knockout jewellery safely straddles the gap between dressed up and dressed down. It's quite hard to under-dress in the noughties if you've got good shoes, a good bag and good hair.

• Consciously under-dressing is for people who think they are just too smart to conform – notably the groovers who turn up at black-tie parties in jeans and velvet jackets, making every other man in the room feel like a waiter.

• Hats for weddings are okay but no longer de rigueur (and keep them small, if at all).

• Funerals are not an appropriate occasion to do the sexy Sicilian number. Modest is still the rule.

• Ultra revealing clothes are rude unless you're a) gorgeous and young, b) safely tucked away in your Ibizan villa.

• It can be quite rude to slosh on the power scent, especially if you are eating in a restaurant and all the neighbouring tables can taste is Opium.

Newly rude: Wearing sunglasses and drinking bottled water in church.

Newly not rude: White trousers for every occasion. Meeting for lunch with cotton wool between your toes, post-pedicure, and wet, post-gym hair.

Still bloody rude: Not bothering to wear fancy dress when your hostess has hand sewn herself into a tomato costume.

What do you mean I'm depressed?

A key element of Nouveau Rudeness is volunteering opinions and information, even if no one wants to hear them. For example, you buy a flat and every NR who walks through the door tells you what you will have to do to make it habitable (quite rude, particularly if you weren't planning to touch it). Or you make a salad dressing and they all have an idea for improving it. ('Got any lemon juice? What about a bit of sugar?') But this is as nothing compared to the modern habit of 'Gordon Browning' your friends – as in remarking on their perceived psychological flaws in the manner of a concerned professional (only without the expertise).

In the twenty-first century you are never more than fifty feet from a psychoanalyst or therapist of some kind. Therapy culture is bigger than the internet or pop music or religion. Even if you aren't in therapy, you will be familiar with the basic principles from watching TV programmes dedicated to analysing dysfunctional parenting or celebrities in enclosed spaces. We all know about anal retentives and compulsive obsessives and separation issues (and that's just from reading the descriptions on the cages in Battersea Dogs Home). The unexpected consequence of this therapy explosion is that suddenly every woman's favourite hobby – dissecting other people – has acquired a pseudo-scientific legitimacy. We don't bitch any more – we analyse. It isn't bullying – it's making people aware of their issues. This is a gift for the naturally rude, who probably would have said it to your face anyway, but can now do it in a faux-caring, just-making-an-observation-based-on-the-clinical-facts kind of way.

Here is a conversation I overheard in a cafe. You might be getting the impression I'm a big eavesdropper; I'm not. It's just that people are getting louder. They are saying Very Important things and they don't want to waste them on one measly lunch partner.) Two friends at a table. A man and a woman:

Her: 'Oh, please.'

Him: 'What?'

Her: 'That was actually quite negative.'

Him: 'Was it? Sorry.'

Her: 'That's the thing with you. There's always this negativity. It's quite hostile. I feel quite attacked.'

Him: 'Oh, come off it.'

Her: 'I'm sorry. I'm just telling you how you come across to other people. You do have a problem.'

Him: 'Fuck off.'

What this woman is really saying is that she is irritated by the man, or just irritated, full stop. But, because she has chosen to criticize him in therapy speak, it gives her observations weight, absolves her of any apparent bitchiness and allows her to say so much more (she could tell him he has a thing for his mother, if she feels like it). The friend can complain, naturally, but bizarrely – even though all she is really saying is 'I want to hurt your feelings' – the woman has the moral high ground. Isn't it brilliant! It's also pretty rude. I'm glad he told her to fuck off.

Mostly this amateur shrinking takes place behind your back, unless you are in a crisis. I have a single friend who had reached a crossroads in her life. She didn't know whether to move, leave her job, take a sabbatical or emigrate. She was unhappy and, frankly, all over the place, so her circle of amateur therapists swung into action and . . . gave her a good kicking. You have to take control of your life. You need to decide what you want. You are frightened of responsibility. You are too passive in your relationships. 'I think they mean well,' she said weakly, 'but it feels like bullying. And, actually, quite rude.' Hmm.

Something else about Nouveau Rudeness: it has no respect for privacy. People are only too happy to ask you how you lost all that weight/facial hair. If X is as good as it is rumoured in bed. When you last had sex. And, likewise, strangers will tell you things you would blush to hear from your closest friend. Fortunately you are not obliged to join in the sharing if you don't feel the inclination. Startlingly graphic honesty does not equate with being well adjusted – as some would have you believe – and you are perfectly within your rights to say, 'Just remembered I need to be somewhere very urgently.'

Newly rude: Making psychological assessments of other people's children using terms such as 'anxious' or 'controlling'.
Newly not rude: Using therapy as an ultimatum, as in: 'I

won't go out with you unless you see someone about your mother complex.'

Still bloody rude: Telling people they look ill.

Who the hell can that be at this time?

Keeping in touch is not the straightforward business it once was. Here are a few things that have changed in the last five years:

• It is no longer okay to drop in. No one drops in. You call to say you are going to drop in, and then you are given your conditions. This is because we are all busy/control freaks and the time you take dropping in, unannounced, might have been allocated for doing the Sainsbury's order online.

• It is newly not okay to ring after ten o'clock. It used to be okay to ring later, but these days your home is your fortress after ten o'clock during the week. If you want to get hold of someone any later, you text.

• It is now considered perfectly acceptable to text or email an invitation and NRs prefer it. That way the invitee has time to work out what suits them, and you're not encroaching on their time.

• Speaking on the telephone has become the rare exception. You speak to your parents on the phone because they still want to have those drifty conversations that begin, 'The roses are out at the front of the house but we're having terrible trouble with the snails . . .' You speak to your best friend, though one of you usually needs to keep it brief. Otherwise, all the people who you used to talk to, for hours on end, you now greet with a low forbidding hello, to which they reply, 'Are you right in the middle of something?' and then you say, 'Um . . . well . . . I am, but I've got a minute.' That's just the routine. Even if you really want to talk, you can't allow yourself the indulgence.

Note: Absence of phone talk is probably bad for your health. If you do talk to the friend you've been emailing all week, you feel your blood pressure drop instantly. Funny how you still can't manage it.

Texting

Nouveau Rudes have given everyone the bad habit of avoiding voice contact and texting or emailing whatever the situation. ('Sorry to hear your marriage has broken up. Between meetings. Speak soon.') Texting is terrific, but not in the following circumstances: dumping. Sacking. Cancelling a dinner date, one hour beforehand. Wishing someone a happy birthday. Commiserating.

As a general rule, all bad news must be dealt with in person, and texting should be reserved for love bombing, flirting, making plans and progress reports ('Stuck in traffic, order me a martini'). You can text an rsvp, but only a thank you in certain circumstances (yes for drinks, not for the weekend).

Also, texting when you are clearly available to speak – as opposed to in a meeting – is quite rude. We all do it without meaning to be insulting, but it's the exercise of control – I will communicate with you, but only on my terms – that makes it suspect.

Texting in the company of others is definitely rude unless it is essential and you have apologized in advance. For some reason it is much more offensive than taking a phone call, probably because you could be saying anything, including 'stuck with total bore at lousy party'.

The trouble with texting is it's contagious, so even the naturally polite can get sucked into the habit of inappropriate texting. We get texted and then we have to text back, because to call at that point would be like pursuing the person in the street who saw you, smiled and then kept on moving. Better you both seem rude and commitment phobic than that one of you looks needy.

Newly rude: Texting in cinemas during the film (we can see the glow!).
Newly not rude: Texting to say, 'Text me to let me know when you can talk.'
Still bloody rude: Texting to say, 'I think I may need some time on my own.'

Emailing

These days an email can stand in for a letter in most circumstances. And emails can be more effective. Whereas texts should be short and to the point, we are so conscious of the possibility of seeming offhand in an email that we tend to beef them up with love yous and miss yous and I can't wait to see yous! In other words, the sort of love bombing you would feel far too inhibited to put in a letter.

Newly rude: Giving your friends viruses.

Newly not rude: Using supposed email glitches as an excuse for not attending the party/meeting the deadline/lending the ski suit on time, etc.

Still bloody rude: Sending the wrong email to the wrong person ('looks like we're going to have to go to this'). Everyone has a misdirected email horror story, but do we ever learn?

Mobile phoning

More has been written about the beastliness of mobile phones and their impact on the environment than on GM foods. It's not the phones, of course, it's the determination of some people to get you to listen to their conversations. That and the things they are prepared to talk about. Here are a few subjects I have overheard being discussed on the bus in the last two weeks: Janet's leaking wound. Someone who slept with someone and he says it was for a bet and she says she doesn't care. Someone else's 'arse operation'. A drug deal. Carly turning up to the wedding even though everyone knows she is not wanted there. My c*** of a boss. There are two kinds of rude mobile-phone users: those who have them permanently attached to their ear (or, alternatively, are always checking for messages from the much more interesting world anywhere but here and now), and people who want to take you down with them into their personal hell.

Newly rude: Photographing celebs on mobile-phone cameras.
Newly not rude: Not saying hello or announcing who you are. It says on their screen.
Still bloody rude: Call screening. We can tell. We know it was switched on before and now you've turned it off. Also: taking social calls from friends when in the company of one other person, and not announcing the need to keep it brief; being on the phone while paying/ordering food, etc.; ring tones that aren't actually nails scraping down a blackboard but might as well be. See, on and on it goes.

Some new manners rules

Smoking. If there are four of you out to dinner, the couple that smokes cannot abandon the other two for a quick fag break – it looks too like half-time analysis. However, in larger groups it is permissible to disappear in groups of two or three provided you make your excuses. There is no doubt that the toing and froing involved in smoking, generally, is rude and disruptive. But somehow the nicotine addiction excuses it.

The new frugality. It was the height of bad manners to talk about money with friends (other than how

much their house cost, and their kitchen refit).
However, post-credit crunch, it is okay to talk about
money all the time – the cost of the holiday, the cost of
the plumber, the cost of fixing the car, the cost
of the food you are eating and the chairs you are
sitting on – and it is newly okay to give everyone very
cheap but thoughtful presents. If you were thinking
of taking vintage champagne, don't – it's just too
pre-CC extravagant.

Emotional dumping. These days few of us know
where to draw the line when it comes to unburdening
ourselves. This means the goodwill of friends is
frequently abused, which in turn leads to them
avoiding phone calls, or becoming brusque and
offhand, in an effort to stem the tide of moaning. The
rule with emotional dumping is, save it up. Don't be
tempted to make every conversation about your
stressy job/lousy love life, or your friends will start to
treat you rudely.

Staring. It's always been rude to stare, but staring is
something we are all guilty of now, as a direct result
of the surge in plastic surgery. Rude or not, stare we
must, because this is new territory and there is so
much we need to check out before we can relax: is it
a facelift, or is it a filler job? Are they fake or is it

❈ The New Minefields

Pregnancy

Ten years ago behaviour towards pregnant women was not something you would have considered including in a guide to good manners, but, as it happens, this area is now a minefield. As ever, it is rude to comment on the size of a pregnant woman ('You must be about to pop any day!') and ruder still to ask probing questions ('So, exactly how long were you trying in the end?'). But now there is a lot more to think about besides. It is no longer safe to make the following assumptions: that the pregnant woman is with the father; that she is under fifty years old; that she became pregnant through having sex; or that she is carrying the baby for herself. As a general rule you should hold off making any judgement calls until the mother-to-be has volunteered some basic clues.

Age, in particular, is a very sensitive area. (I recently had to intervene when I saw a man at a party cross-examining a harassed-looking pregnant journalist, who I happened to know was approaching fifty. 'Exactly how old are you?' he bellowed as I placed myself between them, shaking my head wildly. 'I'm only interested because my wife was an old first-time mother. I might have some tips.')

Note: It is still, and always will be, appallingly rude to ask a woman her age, and if she happens to be a freakish blip on the fertility statistics, then it is worse. The new rule is, always better to assume a grandmother is the mother of a child, rather than the other way round. It's what you call a win-win situation.

Likewise it is newly rude to offer advice to a woman about to give birth without having first established whether she is school of Continuum Concept or more Contented Little Baby (this one divides people along similar lines to those who hate cats and think they are killing all the baby birds, and those who love cats and hate people who don't). Not so long ago, chatting about bringing up baby was pretty safe territory. But now mothers-to-be feel the leaden hand of social pressure weighing down on them – willing them to eat better, sleep more, foreswear drink, cram themselves with folic acid, read up on cranial osteopathy, stop getting anxious (it'll give your child depression in later life) and generally prove themselves to be worthy, perfectly chemically-balanced vessels for the future generation. I have actually seen a stranger approach a mother in a supermarket and challenge her for buying sugary cereal, so you can't blame them for being jumpy.

Then again, new mothers are, themselves, guilty of rudeness in a way they didn't used to be. For years it was understood that stories of episiotomies were strictly for the womenfolk behind closed doors, but now you might easily be given the full technicolour forceps delivery story over coffee. Everyone puts up with these horror stories because we are all cowed by the new status of motherhood (see Show-off chapter), but that doesn't make it any less rude to subject an audience, other than your ante-natal class, to tales from the bloody frontline. For the record: it is perfectly polite to head off any stories involving vaginal sutures or similar with a cheery, 'Oh look! That needs repainting.'

Newly rude: The uncovered 'bump' is delightful if it belongs to Natalia Vodianova, but, on the whole, we can do without it in public. Bugaboo barging in shops.
Newly not rude: Talking openly about your IVF history, including the hilarious sperm-collecting scene.
Still bloody rude: Strangers feeling entitled to pat a pregnant stomach as if it were a prize marrow at a village fête.

Divorce

Divorce is one of those midlife crises that affects us all. Maybe you've been through it yourself, but, even if you haven't, you will have plenty of friends who have and you will have had to face up to the multiple challenges it presents, namely: not taking sides; being supportive at the same time as encouraging them to see sense/get more money/remember that the chances of an affair with an eighteen-year-old lap dancer turning out to be the answer to anything are slim, etc. The potential for handling the newly divorced wrongly is, frankly, off the scale.

First, how to react. It is newly rude to say, on discovering that someone is recently divorced, 'Oh, I'm so sorry.' No, no no. The recently divorced are either a) carried away with the sexiness of their new status and convinced that they are embarking on the life they deserve after years of self-sacrifice and misery, or b) angry, hurt and distressed – either way, they are not in the mood to be pitied. Also, this kind of reaction assumes that divorce is a bad thing, which is insulting to divorcees. The polite way to handle news of divorce is with a rapid raise of the eyebrows and a concerned-stroke-intrigued expression, as this could mean anything from 'I am so not surprised' to 'it's unthinkable that anyone could divorce you'. It goes without saying that it is rude and unhelpful to a) ask for the other party's contact details, especially if you have already let slip that you need a spare man for Saturday night; b) unburden yourself about the time you saw him kissing someone in the park; c) reveal that you sensed trouble brewing two summers ago at that festival (this will be roughly eighteen months before she, or he, was aware that anything was wrong).

Next, there is the question of apportioning loyalty. Ideally, the polite way to handle divorce is by being thoroughly even handed, while paying a bit more attention to the Offendee, i.e. the person who least wanted it to happen. What counts, is that the Offender is going to a better place and the Offendee is going nowhere (or, as my abandoned friend once put it: 'He was going to a warm bed and a fridge full of champagne. I had an empty bed and a fridge full of expressed milk.'). The Offendee needs you more, at least in the short term.

However, despite making perfect sense, this plan doesn't always work. If you know one half of the divorcing couple better than the other, you will inevitably gravitate towards your original friend, Offender or not. That's just the law of friendship. And the harsh truth is that even if you met the divorcing couple on the same day, and you know them equally well, there will come a point when you end up seeing one and not the other. However determined you are to be even handed, and to ask Bill over as often as you've asked Jane, one of them will have a stronger claim, for whatever reason, and the other one will disappear from your life. Don't beat yourself up about this. It does feel rude, but it is one of those natural laws that half a divorced couple must drop clean off your radar. In the meantime, the best you can do is treat them equally until the dust settles and the friendship lines are redrawn. If you are having a party ask both of them separately (with their knowledge) and let them work out between them who comes when. If you are planning a holiday ask the Offendee. The Offender will see the logic, especially (you would hope) if asking them now means asking the Adulterous Couple.

Note: Meeting 'the other person' is the big one as far as the potential to cause offence is concerned. For this reason you must adopt the following strategy at the introductory meeting:

• Meet on neutral territory (somewhere unglamorous. You don't want to have to tell the Offendee that you went to the new King and Corbin restaurant and saw Jake Gyllenhaal).

• Keep the Offendee informed of all plans and promise to call afterwards.

- Avoid talking about the Offendee.

- Avoid talking about money.

- Avoid talking about sex (this may prove tricky, they will be gagging for an excuse).

- Be friendly but not too friendly (it'll make you feel better during the Offendee's debriefing).

- If you're asked, directly, what you think of 'the other person', and you are not ready to give them a rave review say, 'I think you seem very happy.'

That just about covers it.

Divorcees in the immediate aftermath of a separation are, themselves, notoriously prone to rudeness. The most common offence is bad-mouthing the ex in quite specific detail ('Did you ever notice her breath?'), followed by forcing their friends to meet 'the other person' at an uncomfortably early stage, and then expecting them to rejoice in the new order, and accept that the last fifteen years of shared good times were a sham. Then there's the sex talk. Couples never talk about their sex lives but divorcees talk about nothing else: when it started going wrong, exactly how bad it was from then on, how incomparably fantastic it is now, precisely how much more they are getting. Nobody, literally, wants to know.

Note: Talking about sex in graphic detail is also popular among Nouveau Rude men who are single and fancy them-selves to be Gordon Ramsays of the bedroom (i.e. highly energetic and plain speaking). If you are sitting near a man who is telling the assembled company exactly how his last girlfriend liked it and why, it is perfectly okay to lean across and whisper, 'That's not the way she tells it.'

Newly rude: Telling your soon-to-be ex exactly why you are leaving them – in the name of emotional honesty – right down to their unacceptable levels of bikini grooming. (Though, rudest of all – and the most common, if my sources are anything to go by – is the straightforward 'I never loved you').

Newly not rude: The social stagger. It is appropriate to ask both of the ex couple to parties, providing you tell them, so that they can stagger their arrival times.

Still bloody rude: Complaining about your lousy married sex life/banging on about your spectacular post-marriage sex life.

Children

Children provide a whole rich new opportunity for Nouveau Rudeness. Not only does having children increase the Nouveau Rudie's sense of entitlement (see the section on Goddess Mothers), but their children are exempt from the normal rules of behaviour – on account of them being special, and their parents being too interesting to bother with conventional disciplining.

Nouveau Rudie parents consider all that *please, thank you, time for bed, don't eat with your hands* stuff to be for dreary little people with narrow lives, not for interesting, modern individuals like them. They see themselves as liberal, tolerant – cool, basically – and they don't want to compromise this view of themselves by laying down a lot of rules and fighting over whether an eight-year-old should go to bed at nine or eleven p.m. How would that look? And what would their kids think of them? They want to be the kind of parents whose children *talk* to them, not these blimpish symbols of authority. Similarly, NRs believe that their children are too unusual to be subjected to the normal conventions of child-rearing and that what's good for the typical *Supernanny* audience is stifling and spirit crushing for Milo and Minna.

What this means, in practice, is that you (who don't actually have any children, but sometimes have to put up with other people's) get the double whammy of children who are both rude *and* placed centre stage by their adoring parents. The Nouveau Rude are so blinkered to this state of affairs it's almost funny. They are appalled by stories of Asbo toddlers, but don't bat an eyelid when their own feral darlings terrorize the neighbour's dog. They are outraged that sink estate mothers would dare to threaten teachers, but regularly call up to bully the staff at their children's schools. NR children can do no wrong, and if they fall short of expectations it is never their fault, or their parents' (there are no statistics for precisely who queries exam grades, but suffice to say NRs are very, very busy around results time).

The bottom line is we are all a lot less polite than we should be, but we tell ourselves this is inevitable because the world is a busier, harsher, faster-moving place and if we don't look after ourselves everyone will ride roughshod over us, and the NRs will inherit the world. Secretly, however, we know it isn't making us happy.

Not long ago, I found myself in a grim, greasy Cotswold pub – one of the few that hasn't been turned into a temple to organically sourced produce and historic paint finishes. It was lunchtime, so I ordered scampi and chips, the most accident-proof thing on the menu, but what arrived, forty minutes later, was clearly frozen king prawns in sludgy batter. So I complained (actually, I just asked for the bill) and within seconds the elderly lady chef appeared at my elbow, begging to know what could possibly be the problem. She looked crestfallen as she politely pointed out that these were *king* prawns, the ultimate in frozen prawns, but she would be happy to cook me anything else on the menu. And then I found myself saying, 'Look, I am an idiot for not wanting to eat your king prawns. I'm in a hurry is the truth. It is nothing to do with the prawns. I love your pub, and you, and I hope you'll forgive me for ruining your day.' Or words to that effect. It went against every principle of even the most amateur form of Nouveau Rudeness. I was £8 down, and hungry, and every other pub in the area had stopped serving lunch, plus the lady chef was still under the impression that her prawns were a regional delicacy. But the thing is she was happy and so was I – or a lot happier than I would have been had I refused to pay and stalked out into the street rattling my designer handbag.

We had out-polited each other in the manner of old-fashioned black-and-white era Brits, who put up with anything to avoid causing offence or embarrassment. It made no sense whatsoever, but I can recommend the feeling.

6.

Can I Be Single And Happy? (Yes! But only if you listen very closely and do exactly as I say.)

On my fortieth birthday I was on holiday in Brazil with Angry Single. Apart from having an Invisible Man-style bandage wrapped round my head and six stitches in my crown where I had been struck by a flare on a boat in a storm, it was pretty much perfect. We drank a lot of caipirinhas. I opened a letter from my mum in which she assured me that forty was the year when everything fell into place (right again). I spoke to Attractive Available Friend back in London (now not available, but, whatever) and briefly reflected on where I'd got to in my life. In no particular order I had: a good job, a book contract, great friends and a fairly extensive shoe collection. I was financially independent, had my own twinkly office a few yards from the blue front door featured in *Notting Hill*, and the kind of single girl's flat that made my married friends sigh with envy (mainly on account of the pale carpeted bathroom, unviolated by plastic wind-up frogmen and muddy football kit). Life was good, I decided, egged on by AS. None of our non-single girlfriends could just up sticks and head off to South

America for weeks of unscheduled adventure – they were all locked into seven-year plans dictated by school holidays and partner's commitments – whereas we were free! The whole of our lives – or the second half anyway – stretching before us, bristling with promise. But that was Salvador on a hot August night, and AS and I both knew we would probably feel differently come February, after a long cold January when no one goes out, everyone's given up drink and Valentine's Day is just round the corner.

A lot of people are under the impression that the life of the single girl is all Manolos and mocha lattes and riding holidays and getting picked up by interesting strangers in bars. Single girls know better, but, still, it's that gap between the fiction and the reality that causes those occasional feelings of disappointment and frustration. And, just as a marriage is doomed if you expect it to be all hot sex and anniversary dinners, you can never be truly happily single if you don't accept it for what it really is, warts and all.

❀ How It Is For You, Honestly

For a start, you are not having sex

Probably the biggest myth associated with modern singleness is that life is one big pulling opportunity, punctuated with regular bouts of acrobatic sex. According to this post-*Sex and the City* version of the truth, you are either lolling around in boypants, talking on the phone to your girlfriends about your unbelievably complicated love life, or getting ready to go out on a date with someone who makes you go weak at the knees. Well, let's pause right there. Once and for all, single means *manless* – dating, now and then, but otherwise navigating the world on your own. As a rule there is no one in your life to wear special undies for, and nothing to do when you are feeling frisky but crank up the Scissor Sisters and dance, by yourself, on the sofa (because, after the myth of sexed-up single living, the second biggest myth is that you can get away with wooden floors if you have someone living underneath you).

It's important to get straight that not having sex is the normal single experience, otherwise you might be under the impression that you are not only single but the bad, losery, second-division sort. (This kind of false representation of the facts messes with your self-belief, and self-belief is essential to the unattached woman.) So, repeat after me: 'I am single, and I am not having much, if any, sex. I didn't get one non-platonic kiss on New Year's Eve. I sometimes feel over-whelmingly irritated by the sight of loved-up couples. I am really worried about who I am going to go on holiday with this year, now that my holiday single friend has had a baby. I sometimes think I should have just got over the absence of any physical attraction and married my best male friend.' This is normal. You are normal.

You worry about the future (and everything)

Being single is exciting in lots of ways. Who else, these days, gets to cross the threshold of a party thinking, Maybe tonight's the night! I am arriving as single moi, I could be leaving slung over the shoulder of a touring flamenco dancer.

Even so, alongside the hope there is also the niggling worry that you have absolutely no idea where you are going to end up. What's it gonna be: a seafront cabin with laptop and loyal dog? A brief courtship, swiftly followed by fertility treatment and triplets? Or more of the same, until you get too old to walk up the stairs to your flat and have to move to a serviced bungalow? Should you be relocating to the country, or another country altogether? Who the hell knows? It's impossible to call it. Any of it. Your future is one giant question mark.

So, you have not so much a 'bottom drawer' as a stack of pages ripped out of newspapers and magazines relating to things like top-level fertility treatments (that's just a given, if it ever happens); post-natal depression (ditto); cranial oste-opathy for infants (should you have a baby, you are already worrying about how little it is going to sleep); non-surgical and surgical facelifts (everyone tears those out); hair-thinning products (it could be you and, let's face it, you don't need any more problems). You also find yourself drawn to articles about the following women: Susan Sarandon, Geena Davis, Helen Fielding (what do they have in common? Yes, they all conceived over the age of *forty-two*). I once interviewed Susan Sarandon and when I transcribed the tape the entire conversation was about the miracle of late motherhood and how she had pulled it off. (Her secret was a diet rich in fresh Italian tomatoes, and a summer spent hanging out in the sun, having sex. Don't you just love Susan Sarandon?)

All of the above gets filed under 'My possible future life', including recipes for Christmas dinner (one day it could be you doing the cooking!) and manufacturers of garden swing seats (you might live in an Old Rectory) and places to buy tree houses and range cookers and George Sherlock sofas. (This could be because you want to be prepared, just in case, or because women are biologically programmed to fixate about our ultimate sofa at roughly the same time that our ovaries start to wind down. Who knows?) Anyway, there are women out there who would kill for access to your stash of slate suppliers and fireplace specialists and landscape architects – not that you're advertising it. You wouldn't want people to get the wrong idea.

Besides worrying subliminally about what the future holds, you worry that it is far too late for you to catch up with the rest of the female adult population – should The One turn up and your grown-up life begin in earnest. Other women your age know how to do things like look after a guinea pig, plant a geranium, make pancakes, light a barbecue, throw a children's party, etc. The sheer breadth of their capabilities is intimidating for the single female, whose responsibilities stop at feeding and dressing herself. And you are well aware that what is considered charmingly flakey in a twentysome-thing girl about town is straightforward incompetence in a mature woman.

If you do meet The One, what's he going to think? He'll assume – given all the time you've got on your hands – that you'll have some kind of hobby or interest beyond watching

TV and sitting around friends' kitchen tables drinking. (And You Don't.) At the very least he'll expect you to be able to cook, and identify herbs in the ground. What if he wants you to get stuck into the herbaceous border at his love cottage? What if he's got small children who need looking after?

The fact is that in the twenty-first century women are expected to be domestic goddesses, fashion plates, Norland nannies, successful wage earners, happy, depilated, warm, yet capable of project managing their home renovations. It's the norm. And you are not this multi-tasking turbo woman. You are more like her eighteen-year-old daughter, only without the pert body and the optimistic nature.

Performance anxiety

Talking of bodies, remember in *Sleepless in Seattle*, when Tom Hanks is reluctantly getting back into the dating scene after the death of his wife? And his friend takes him out to dinner and suggests he's missing a trick if he's never tried tiramisu, and Tom Hanks assumes tiramisu is some sexual manoeuvre that has become standard practice in the time he's been off the scene? Well, single women know that anxiety only too well. We've all watched those Channel Five late-night sex documentaries featuring the expert with the banana and the condom. We've seen the hardware you're meant to have stashed in your bedside table drawer, never mind the things you're supposed to be able to do with two hands, one big toe and a tub of Vaseline. There was a time when all you needed for sex was a couple of bodies and some mutual lust, but not, apparently, any more. Now you must have Rampant Rabbits and Agent Provocateur lingerie and candles and propping pillows and butt plugs and baby oil. Of course, you tell yourself that good sex does not require a certificate from the House of Erotica, but there is this nagging suspicion that you are way, way out of touch and The One will be expecting some tricks, possibly involving ice.

And performance anxiety doesn't stop at sexual proficiency. Oh no. There's the whole issue of how hairless you are required to be in the modern dating environment: do your forearms need to be as smooth as your neck? Should your lady parts look like a newborn mouse or a clipped privet hedge? If you ask the woman who does your waxing she will tell you that *everyone* is asking for Brazilians or Hollywoods, including Gwyneth Paltrow (so, if you were comforting yourself that it's only the dirty girls who are like Mini-Mes downstairs, forget about it; the classy acts with the shiny ponytails and the ethical wardrobes are hairfree too). In fact, in A-list circles, the naked beaver is practically compulsory.

Here's a true story. Not long ago a certain British actress (who had recently appeared naked on screen) was walking down a street in LA when a passing driver recognized her, leant out of his car window and shouted, 'Get a wax!' Now this actress has a normal amount of pubic hair. Also she is young and lovely, but apparently not so gorgeous that this man was prepared to forgive a perfectly average bush (this was actually *in* Hollywood, but, even so). Fortunately she happens to be happily married to a man who has never complained, so she didn't down a packet of Nurofen and rush off to the wax parlour, right then and there. But, had she been single and dateless, it could have been a very different story. Her confidence would have been undermined in the most fundamental sense. She would have thought what all single women have been thinking since the bikini wax got hardcore: *Is my vagina acceptable?* Never mind *Does my bum look big in this?* Who cares, now we've got our lady parts to worry about.

Ten years ago a woman wouldn't have given her vagina a first thought let alone a second. Bums could be too big, breasts too small, but when it came to the bikini area we were totally complacent. Now it's the new super-grooming zone and expectations are through the roof. Bikini waxes – even if you're not going for the full Mini-Me – are like a cross between an appointment with the gynaecologist and an advanced Ashtanga yoga class (they'll be doing them in teams of three before long – mark my words). The maintenance required (never mind the humiliation) is triple what it was five years ago. No wonder we get a flash of Britney's and Lindsay's every time they exit a limo – they want some credit for all the effort they've gone to.

So now there's a whole new area of our anatomy for us to fixate about. Is it normal? Is it neat enough? Is it what men really want? Do I need surgery? If mine doesn't look like the one on the TV, should I insist on keeping the lights off? Finally, we have our equivalent of penis anxiety. It's equality, but not as we expected it.

Past-it anxiety

There are so many traps laid for single women – so many articles telling you that the reason you're single is because you are not bold enough, too independent, not independent enough. You ignore them all, but the one niggling doubt you can't quite put out of your head is the possibility that you are not attractive in a fundamental, biological sense. You particularly start to worry when you read a story in the press suggesting that women taking the Pill could be turning off the opposite sex.

That's the point when I call my friend A:

Me: 'What if, for the past seven years, I have been giving off a hormone that tells men to keep their distance?'

A: 'Hmm. Not good. But it can't be that simple.'

Me: 'No, but combined with other factors.'

A: 'Such as?'

Me: 'I don't know! Maybe I should have been making a real effort to get through this toxic, anti-man forcefield.'

A: 'Well, why not stop taking it?'

Me: 'I have! Last month. And this weekend I got *a lot* of attention, and now I know what's been going on. I have been repelling all the men with serious intentions. Throughout my *prime.*'

A: 'Oh well. You hang in there. If it wears off that fast, you could be loved up by Christmas.'

The Pill scare was really about the more basic anxiety that women do – even in these age-retardant times – have a sell-by date. Or, rather, that even if the right man is out there looking for you he is conditioned to choose the apple-cheeked, oozingly fertile childwoman before he's even made it across the room to where you are standing. (You're wearing your special hour-glass pulling dress and you've had your hair done and you are radiating good energy, but the right man is helpless in the grip of his Darwinian impulses. It's not his choice to make; it's a matter of the survival of the species.) The bottom line is this: if you are past your reproductive prime, can you expect a man to want you? Wouldn't that be going against nature? Wouldn't you have to be *really something*?

Having to make an effort

This is the big dilemma for single women: do I stick with what I know makes me happy, because time is precious? Or do I step outside my comfort zone and make bold plans in order to meet new people and 'create opportunities'? Obviously all you want to do is hang out with your mates, but there is a voice in the back of your head squeaking, 'That's what you always do! You must find some people you haven't known for twenty years who are unconnected to your regular life. You must break out of this rut.' And the voice is dead right. A week in the sun with some strangers of the opposite sex has to be a more constructive plan than camping in Cornwall with four friends and their families. But, boy, can going off piste result in some truly horrible holidays.

For instance, you may find yourself in a villa in Ibiza,

along with your girlfriend – who knew this banker 'slightly' who was putting together a 'single's holiday' – and you may ask yourself, *What Am I Doing Here?* (Note: In retrospect, knowing the organizer of a holiday 'slightly' isn't good enough. And the concept of a 'single's holiday' might give you cause for concern. You don't necessarily want to be corralled with people whose sole criterion for inclusion is that they are unattached. Trust me.)

You may ask yourself, *What Am I Doing Here?* (or more like, *WHAT AM I DOING HERE?*) when you notice the only reading material the bankers have brought is guides to clubs with foam machines (even though they are all old enough to have children in their teens, and one or two of them actually do). And then you ask the question again when the almost-underage girlfriend of ultra-slime banker starts referring to her thrush and their sex life (and the problems combining the two) and observes that women who have had children (your friend) must be lousy lays. Nice. And then you ask yourself, again, when king banker, scratching his paunch, starts the casual racism. And again when all the big fat bankers are sloping off to snort their fat lines of coke. And then again when the American banker says, 'Play your cards right, girly, and you could be coming to the Republicans Abroad Dinner.' Uh huh.

This is about the point – three days into a week's holiday – when my friend and I escaped in the night to the local hotel where we were met with a brandy and a knowing smile. Had they seen it all before? Single women take a risk in an effort to expand their horizons – only to discover it is not that easy. The world is full of bankers.

If you leave it to other people to pair you up, the results are no better. I give you singles tables at weddings. What is that all about? It's like the end-of-line clearance basket in a wool shop ('everything must go'). You sit down at one of those tables and you are instantly reduced to Nobody Has Chosen Me. Besides, never mind the humiliation, singles tables are totally counterproductive. Once a person knows someone is single (okay, once a man knows a woman is single) it automatically puts them right off. A man wants to think you *could* be free, but, for all he knows, you're living with a film director who is currently on location/on a break from a long-term relationship/half involved with Hugh Grant. He likes to think he has plucked you from right under the nose of the most eligible man in the room, preferably his oldest friend. What he never, ever thinks is, 'Wow. She's single. How convenient is that!'

❀ How Other People See You

If you are single, you are obliged to live out the fantasies of all your friends who used to be single and now can only get 'me' time if they lock the bathroom door and pretend to have gastric flu. You must be spontaneous, hedonistic, always hopping on a plane to Marrakech at the last minute. (You've got no kids! No ties! All that spare cash . . . you have no idea how lucky you are!) Your married friends call you up on Sunday morning and shout down the phone, 'Well? Come on. I want to know *all* the details!' And if, by some chance, you didn't end up going to a Rolling Stones' secret, last-minute gig, followed by the after party and the after-after party, then they might easily say: 'You are a disappointment to us, do you know that? You are all we've got.'

This burden of responsibility is a nightmare. Most of the time you just want to go to work, come home and eat packet risotto in front of *Property Ladder* because that's all you feel like doing. After all, it's not like you're on a different biological trajectory to the rest of womankind. Just because you're single doesn't mean you're permanently up for a party, including ones in Hoxton that start at 11 p.m. You are boring and tired, like everyone else, and mostly your plans for the weekend extend to sourcing a lampshade. (Come to that, you don't get home from work and change into lovely cashmere sweat pants and fine-layered T-shirts, and put your hair up in a sexy firework ponytail, because why would you bother when there is *no one there to see*?) However, you must collude in the myth of glamorous singleness – up to a point – because otherwise your situation is not special. It is exactly the same as everyone else's, only without a man.

Men who can't/don't want to see you

There is a cut-off age – let's call it thirty-eight for the sake of argument – after which some men think single women should be supplied with grey uniforms and kept in camps on the outskirts of towns so that they don't interfere with normal, healthy interaction between the sexes. These women aren't merely ignored by this lot, they are pitied for their false hope and their refusal to retire from the scene gracefully. Even some quite intelligent men find it incomprehensible that they are still bothering to wash their hair and change their undies when, clearly, it's all over for them.

This is the actual conversation I had with M (himself forty-something and single). You need to know that the Lucy in the conversation is unbelievably pretty. Any woman of any age would kill to look like her, and I'm not joking. She does, however, happen to be forty-two.

Me: 'Doesn't Lucy look sexy?'

M: [*Looking everywhere but at Lucy*] 'Mmm.'

Me: 'Don't you think so? That dress, that hat!'

M: 'Mmm.'

Me: 'What? You don't like the hat?'

M: 'No no. I just . . . Don't get me wrong. But why bother to go to so much effort?'

Me: 'Sorry, you've lost me.'

M: 'Well, it's not like anyone is going to actually . . . take her up on it.'

Me: 'Hang on . . . because?'

M: 'She's great, but she's [*mouths the appalling number*].'

Me: [*Icy death stare*] 'So, let me get this straight. Anyone would stand a better chance than Lucy, providing she was ten years younger.'

M: 'Er. Well. Yes.'

This man is not illiterate. He is not a pitbull-owning publican or the leader of a polygamous sect. He doesn't dress up in gimp suits and live in a cellar. He is not a narcissistic celebrity. He is simply one of the millions who doesn't register women much over thirty-five on his radar. There is a worse category of offender than this: the ones who think like M *and* are under the impression that they are permanently being stalked by women over thirty-five who would stop at nothing to get their hooks into them.

You know these men, instantly, because they will avoid direct eye contact, lest you should get your hopes up, and advise you of the fact that they have a girlfriend before they get around to asking your name. They have an 'off' face (that's the one you get) and an 'on' face that's reserved for babes and consists of wide eyes, a leer and a gaze that keeps slipping back to those breasts. If, for some reason, they cannot avoid talking to you, then the conversation will be strained – like the rare attempts at small talk between rich men and their domestic staff – and they will be barely able to restrain themselves from saying, 'Look, no offence. But, obviously, I am just being polite here. Do not get any ideas.'

Here's an example of one of these conversations (to get the picture you really have to be able to see that expression – but never mind):

Man (who thinks he is doing you a favour by not ignoring you): 'Hmm.'

Me: 'You look a bit restless.'

Man: 'I'm meeting my girlfriend.'

Me: 'And you are?'

Man: [*Long pause*] 'Jeff.'

Me: 'So, you're Jack's friend. The one with the boat.'

Man: [*Thinking*, She's mentioned the boat. Jesus, she doesn't waste any time.] 'Yuh.'

You: 'Do you want to know my name, or not, because you've got a girlfriend?'

Man: 'Sure. I just need to . . . (*keep you at arm's length. I get this all the time.*)'

Me: 'Doesn't matter. I'm married, by the way.'

Man: 'Oh. Okay. [*Visibly relaxes*] 'So, I saw you arriving. Is that your car?'

Me: 'Sorry, got to go and meet someone, anyone . . . byee.'

If you are going to be happy and single, you will need a sense of humour, and you will need it most when the plainest, dullest, paunchiest man at the party assumes you are hitting on him.

Unhappily married women

Women, too, can test your patience – specifically unhappily married women. Some married women are suspicious of single women because they think you might be after their husbands, but unhappily married women *hate* single women because you are a reminder of the courage they lacked. Sorry, but it's true. They look at you and they feel threatened: the fact that you didn't rush into marrying Deadly Roger, just because you were pushing thirty-five, and broke, and all your friends were getting married, seems to them to be a veiled criticism of their entire modus operandi. These women do not welcome your presence and they don't bother to disguise it. They will frown on your lifestyle, question your motives and misinterpret everything you say:

You: 'Oh, I love Milly's new short haircut; it's like a little choirboy's.'

UMW: 'You think she looks like a boy? Roger! Did you hear that? She says our daughter looks Exactly Like A Boy.'

Needless to say, you have known the husband forever (see How to stay friends with married men) which is why you put up with this nonsense in the first place.

Vastly superior women

Fortunately there aren't many of these about, but a VSW can seriously undermine the single woman's joie de vivre, just when you least expect it. Take the day I visited a girlfriend in hospital who had just given birth. As I hovered by the bed in the maternity unit, cooing over the baby, idly scoffing the grapes, one of the other visitors (a mother with a toddler in tow) leant across and whispered, 'This must be very hard for you.' Ha! Don't you love that? The woman who had brought forth life could celebrate this happy moment, but I, the childless single girl, could only feel regret and failure. It's moments like this that perfectly illustrate why single women originally rose up and created a mocha latte, yoga and fairy-lights culture for themselves, because there will always be those die-hard cases who treat the unattached and childless like life's rejects. (You will note that Kylie Minogue survived cancer, but still what the press preferred to pity her for was her single state. Maybe that even *gave* her cancer – all that self-determination. All that success. Hmm.)

The picky Issue

No one would ever say this to your face, but some of your married girlfriends aren't sure if you are really marriage material. They love you to bits, but they are frankly amazed that you are still losing your front-door keys, getting two-day hangovers and eating cereal for supper. Sometimes even the people who wouldn't change you for the world wonder if you don't need to change, quite dramatically, in order to find a man. And it's a short step from there to concluding that you are Too Picky.

This is something you have considered yourself. You are only human and there will have been times when you've looked back over your life so far and thought, Yikes! Was I concentrating? Have I been floating along in a bubble? Were there men I didn't bother with who would have been kind and caring and wheeled me around in my old age? Should I have just got on with it years ago and married one of my mates? (Not that anyone asked you. But there have probably been men in your life who you could have persuaded to take you on, if you'd really put your mind to it.) And sometimes, when you go to their nice, warm houses and watch them putting their children to bed and you get shown the new kitchen extension and hear about the second-honeymoon safari, your self-doubt taps you on the shoulder and whispers: 'This could have been you if you hadn't been so . . . you know what.'

But here's the thing: Too Picky is a concept that only rears its head when other people decide you are running out of time. For years it is a healthy sign of your self-respect that you refuse to contemplate getting together with the rich bloke you just don't fancy or the fanciable bloke you don't much like. But then, one day, it will be suggested to you that you are, in fact, too critical. Your standards are inappropriately high and you need to give these men – or anyone who has the generosity to pay you some attention – a chance. No one would dream of suggesting you buy the dress that doesn't fit under the arms in case there are no other dresses out there. No friend of yours would advise you to invest in the north-facing flat with the crack den in the basement, so that at least you'll have a roof over your head. Yet – once you get past that stage of life when you are going to a wedding every weekend – apparently you should be prepared to hook up with the man who doesn't feel right. He's bright and interesting, they say. He knows so many people. He is loaded and he is fond of you – the least you should do is give him a break. What does it matter if he spits his food – dear God. What's a bit of biscuit in your eye compared to an old age spent all alone? (Note: A lot of people, mainly women, who have not experienced living alone, will fear it the way men fear sharks. Once you have lived alone you know that Spitting Man is a compromise you definitely don't need to make. These people are projecting, so do not be unsettled by their anxiety.)

Once and for all, there is no such thing as a compromise bar that starts to slowly descend, from the age of thirty-five, until, by the time you reach the forty-five mark, you must be ready to consider men with lofts converted for model-train sets. (Don't ask what the appropriate compromise level is once you hit fifty. Oh, okay, then, I'll tell you: it's men who don't like women but need someone to look after the house now that their mother has died.)

So. To summarize. Single culture has done wonders for the single woman's morale: there is nothing sad or pitiable about the single state any more and, particularly in these control-conscious times, singledom has a lot going for it. But the fact remains that if you are single by the time you turn forty you will have:

• A mother who blames herself.

• A father who blames men.

• The odd friend who thinks you should probably see 'someone'.

• And then there's everyone you have ever met of the opposite sex – single or not single – who at some point has looked at you and thought: Come on. There Has To Be A Reason.

People will love you, like you, some may even envy you. But

you would be hard pressed to find anyone who thinks you are *accidentally* single. It is important to accept that There Has To Be A Reason and to have your own theories clear in your mind. That way, the next time someone asks you why on earth you're still on your own, you'll be prepared.

The inevitable self-pity crisis

Maybe the trigger is some well-meaning older person announcing, 'So, you never married.' ('But I'm not finished yet,' you want to tell them. 'No need to be so definite.') Or it could be your single friend calling to say, yes, they are back together! And they are going to the Caribbean for Christmas. My own self-pity crisis happened at a reunion party given by an ex-boyfriend's sister. Not just any ex-boyfriend, but the one I went out with for nearly five years – the one with whom I was joined at the hip from the age of eighteen to twenty-two. He was there, but he wasn't the cause of my undoing – it was his father. (It's always the older generation who rattle your armour, in my experience.)

Egging me on to slip away from the party, he took me round the family house, opening the doors of rooms that took me straight back into long wet summers listening to Bob Marley, the dress with ribbons, the too-tight jeans, the kitchen where we congregated after parties bleary-eyed and carrying our shoes, the creaking floorboards in the corridor, the tiny single bed where I never slept. Then he walked me round to the outbuildings to show me the frog-eyed Sprite I learnt to drive on, and the rusty motorbikes that used to carry us whipping along the lanes, my skirt flapping up behind. I hadn't been back to the house in seventeen years, but nothing had really changed – other than that the family had all moved on and were now raising their own children in their own houses. Almost everyone I knew from those days had been married for years, except for me. So, when my ex-boyfriend's father said, 'I never thought you of all people . . . I just don't understand why you're on your own,' it hit me like bad news I hadn't been expecting and I very nearly cried. It wasn't that I had any regrets. It wasn't that I thought it should have worked out differently. It was just that sometimes (you know this feeling), looking back over your history, you think, But we were all in the same boat – how come everyone else found the right person and not me?

This is self-pity pure and simple. It's also alcohol and nostalgia, and too many late nights. And it's old men. Old men are terrible for unintentionally stoking your sense of injustice. They would never have let a lovely thing like you go to waste. It's a crying shame and a mystery and an indictment of their sex. A woman like you all on her own! Coping with the leaky boiler. Struggling out with the rubbish. Walking home on dark and windy nights. You can feel quite sorry for yourself by the time they've finished. But this is just old men doing what they do. You are not a heroine in an Edith Wharton novel – you are a single woman. It's okay.

A Note About Self-pity: You would never give in to self-pity if left to your own devices, but others may encourage this 'why me?' feeling. All it takes is some well-meaning girlfriend you haven't seen for a while to give you the speech ('Isn't there anyone, at all? I can't believe it!') and, the next thing you know, you are having the 'Where are all the bloody decent men?' conversation. This is allowed, providing there are no witnesses, but, as a rule, you should try to avoid it. For one thing, no one *cares*, not unless they are in an identical position. For another, it is a mistake to keep blaming the opposite sex for your singleness. They are all you've got.

Maybe now is a suitable point at which to recap on your boyfriend history to date.

❀ A Brief Going-out History

Up to this point the men in your life have been great, just never quite right. And, naturally, that's led you to think there may be no right man out there for you. This is because you have a typical long-term single-woman's relationship history. You imagine it's unique, but it's really not. Here's how it goes:

The Inappropriate Boyfriend

Some women restrict their Inappropriate Boyfriends (i.e. boyfriends no woman would consider ending up with) to the experimental years between the ages of, say, seventeen and twenty-four. These are the same women who look at a packet of cigarettes, see the warnings emblazoned in bold type, and are entirely perplexed as to how anyone could ignore the message, reach into the packet and spark up a match. You are not one of these women.

The Inappropriate Boyfriend takes many forms. He might be mad for hard drugs. He might be a foreign correspondent who is never in the country, or a charismatic artist with a penchant for his sitters, or an unreliable drunk, or a married man. Or he may just be emotionally unavailable. (They're all equally inappropriate if the goal is to find someone to live happily ever after with.) You, however – who count yourself to be a pretty good judge of character are in denial about the built-in expiry date that comes with every IB. It's not that you think you might end up settling down and having his children, or that you know for sure you never will. You just sort of dodge the whole issue because it's easier not to think about it. The Inappropriate Boyfriend is a phase that's gone on for far too long – it's as simple as that.

The last date I had with the most inappropriate, in a long line of Inappropriate Boyfriends, ended up with me spread-eagled, face down, underneath his parked car (he was under the one next to it, face up). The idea was that the police – who were combing the area with flashlights searching for the driver of the car – would not think of this hiding place, get bored and go away. Only they didn't get bored, because they thought we were terrorists on the basis that, when flashed by a squad car, the IB had put his foot down and set off at high speed through the streets of Victoria with them in hot pursuit. (He was over the limit and already had a load of points on his licence, so, being an IB, this seemed like a reasonable response.) From our hiding places on the tarmac, we could hear the officers on their radios summoning back up, and blocking off all access streets in the area. I'm not sure they weren't already scrambling a helicopter when one of them crouched down next to the car, looked me straight in the eye and said, 'Hello. What have we got here?' (Apparently the hem of my new coat had given the game away.) The good-girl coat acted like a character reference and I was let off with a caution. Meanwhile IB was in the van, down the station, yet again. And that was, more or less, the end of another inappropriate relationship.

This particular IB may have been extreme. But all long-term singles share a taste for this sort of self-flagellation, which you like to think is normal, even though you're thirtysomething and paying a mortgage.

The Going Nowhere Boyfriend

The point about this boyfriend is it could, conceivably, go somewhere. A lot of stuff fits: you have friends and interests in common; maybe you've known him for a while and had time to observe his character in various situations. Either way, it's progress for you because a) he does not have a police record, b) he has not recently attended The Priory, c) he lives in the same city, d) everyone you know likes him and/or fancies him and e) you have consciously chosen him. (Note: The long-term single is in the habit of waiting for men to pick her, which is why she has such an impressive list of Inappropriate Boyfriends.)

However, what you fail to notice about the Going Nowhere Boyfriend is that, right from a few weeks in, it is going nowhere. You should be able to tell this because:

• When redecorating his house he gets his best girlfriend to advise him and doesn't so much as mention it to you.

• He only uses the first person singular, never 'we' or 'us'.

• He doesn't automatically take you to parties.

• He doesn't automatically meet up with you after said parties.

• He has special girlfriends whose opinions he quotes at you.

• He thinks your best friend is too loud.

• He doesn't know your first boyfriend's name.

• He has never asked you to help him shop for his flat/his sister/his mother.

• He appears to think Christmas is an automatic relationship holiday for the duration.

• He gets tight lipped and defensive when you are rude about his past conquests (as in, 'Was that Fat Ankles or Toilet Duck?').

• He does not have a photograph of you, and shows no interest in getting one.

- He is not remotely interested in your work.

- He asked you what you wanted for your birthday.

- On Valentine's Day he bought you yellow roses not red, which everyone knows are half the price.

- On Valentine's Day you sent him an extra anonymous card, and you caught him checking the postcode, more than once.

- He gets sulky if he thinks he is going to be required to see your family, even though it's only happened once in five months.

Incredibly, despite all of the above, you go out with the Going Nowhere Boyfriend for months and months and then, when it's over, you are shocked when his best friend says:

BF: 'The thing about Going Nowhere is he never commits.'

You: 'But we went on holidays. We made plans.'

BF: 'But he never committed. Hold on a minute. Don't you know the difference?'

You: 'YES!'

Only the thing is, you didn't. Even if you have known serious commitment, you are perfectly capable of ignoring its absence if you just don't want to face the alternative.

The Figment Of Your Imagination Boyfriend

This is the one you imagine will become a full-blown relationship just as soon as he returns from America, at some unspecified date. He hasn't exactly given you reason to think this, but you think it anyway. You think it for roughly a year, until the moment when you say to your friend, A (sotto voce): 'You know we had a thing.' And A says, 'Me too! And so did she. And Anna. And Charlotte. And Hannah. And see that woman over there, the one in the red? She was with him last week in New York. Isn't that funny!'

The Floating Ex-boyfriend

Oh dear. Something else that separates you from the average attached woman – you have a tendency to romanticize all your relationships, including the ones that have been over for quite a while. You don't say, 'Ho hum. He has dumped me. Better move on.' You don't even say, 'There we go. I've dumped him. Time to look around for someone I want to be with.' Instead you say, 'But we were together for *three years*. Maybe I'll spend the next three vaguely wondering if he'll ever find someone better than me.' You don't consciously indulge this thinking. But the part of your brain devoted to self-preservation (this is apricot-sized in most women, and invisible to the naked eye in long-term single women) is not doing its work properly. So you are deluded.

Just because the Floating Ex ends up coming back to your place – if you're both there at the lights-on stage of the party – does not mean you are destined to end up together. Likewise, he doesn't think about you every time he hears 'Venus in Furs', or get the urge to call you when he sees a miniature penguin on the TV. And there is no way he remembers your anniversary, or talks about you with his friends, or wonders if you might be at so-and-so's party, and buys something sexy to wear, just in case. Should you happen to have a Floating Ex in your life, just ask yourself the following:

• If you are destined to be together, then why do you only get together at 3 a.m. on Saturdays in months that end in r?

• If you are destined to be together, then how come he's had three girlfriends since you broke up, while in the same period you have mostly been checking his horoscope for auspicious signs?

• If you are destined to be together, then when was the last time he made you feel really good?

• If you are destined to be together, then why, in fact, aren't you?

The I Want This To Be Right Relationship

This one feels like it could be right. Except for, every so often, when something gives you that lurch of dread. Maybe you meet a woman at a party and he thinks she is a great human being, when it is blindingly obvious that she is a Grade A piece of work. Maybe he recommends a film and it's the most pretentious piece of waffle you've ever had to sit through. Maybe you are making an observation about something that really matters to you – like the fabulousness of Alison

Goldfrapp – and he smiles indulgently because he can't imagine you could really expect him to care about Alison Goldfrapp. Or he makes a cat clawing action when you're just being normally, hilariously perceptive about a colleague's short-comings. None of this stuff seems like a big enough reason to end a relationship, and it might not be for lots of people. But you are looking for a soulmate, nothing less. It's not you being weird and asking for the moon – this is not the right man.

Back to the drawing board.

What to say if asked why you are single

If you are asked why you are single (as you will be every now and again, namely at extended family gatherings) do not hiss: 'Can you believe it? *She* is married, and *her*. What's that all about?' Even if you devoted the best years of your life to a man who ran off with his physio, it is not a good idea to offer this cruel injustice as the explanation for your current situation. Single women must own their singleness and be at ease with it. You should say something like: 'Oh, I am just hopeless at picking men!' This strikes just the right note of breezy self-awareness and optimism, and there's some truth in it too. Alternatively, go for one of the following:

- Why do you think? (You have to know the person slightly for this to work. And be prepared for the answer.)
- Who says I am single?
- Why is Kylie single?
- Well, it could be that I shouldn't have spent the nineties on Easter Island.
- I'm having laser treatment for excessive body hair. When that's done, look out!
- I haven't met The One. (They won't settle for this, but what do you care.)

Do not say:
- Why shouldn't I be? Arsehole.
- Mind your own business.
- I don't know! I have tried everything! Pray for me.
- I fucked up. I should have married my first boyfriend. Do you want to know the whole story . . . ?

Some practical disadvantages of being single

- If a bird flies into your flat, there is no one to get it out (and you have to call your friend's ex-husband who lives nearby).
- You need to get your hostess to do up the zip of your dress on the doorstep at the party.

- On holiday you always get the maid's room that overlooks the internal courtyard.
- You can't store suitcases in the top cupboard because you'd never get them down.
- There is no one else to blame for not turning up at the party.

❀ Being Successfully Single

Look. Meeting a man is not your only goal in life. It doesn't keep you awake at night (although it has been known to). But the key to being successfully single is keeping an open mind. You want to exude contentment and confidence, but also avoid giving the impression that you are so pleased with your single life you wouldn't give it up for anything – including the right man. It's all about presentation.

Some double standards to be aware of

There are plenty of double standards when it comes to what is acceptable for single women and what is appropriate for their attached sisters. For example: married woman sobbing at a wedding: aaah; single woman sobbing at a wedding: eeew. Married woman with dead plants in her window boxes: busy; single woman with dead plants in window boxes: unnatural. Married woman with slightly straggly eyebrows: not a problem; single woman with slightly straggly eyebrows: given up and lost the plot. Married woman with new puppy: normal; single woman with new puppy: oooh, child substitute. Like it or not, singles are judged differently. That's just the way it is and you need to be aware of it.

Tricky behaviour

You can be as tricky as you like, so long as you're involved with a man. You can flounce and pout and sulk and sob and rage and stamp and throw car keys out of windows and lock yourself in the bathroom. None of these options is available to the single woman, because no one would put up with it.

Sometimes the single woman will witness a married woman giving her husband grief, for example:

MW: 'I look fat.'

H: 'No, you don't.'

MW: 'I do. And you made me rush. So I look even worse now.'

H: 'Well, I think you look lovely.'

MW: 'Why did you make me rush? Now I've forgotten my earrings!'

H: 'Because you said we had to be there for eight, that's why.'

MW: 'We could have been five minutes late! Because of you I look absolutely *hideous*.'

At about this point the single woman will think to herself, Honestly! I'm the one who looks fat! Maybe *I'll* just throw a small huff. I really feel like it, as it happens, and I am tired of being reasonable, and jolly, and always ready on time. I too will get tricky.

Unfortunately, this can never happen because a huff without someone to manage it is a burden for the people around you, and, if there is one thing the single woman cannot afford to be, it's a burden. You must be sunny and amenable, the best guest, the most reliable friend, the tonic at the party and the one who blends in on the family holiday. Precisely because you are not part of a couple, you need to give out the message, loud and clear, that you are no trouble, and guaranteed life-enhancing. Being successfully single means having lots of different options and knowing plenty of people who might think, Yes, bring her along! rather than, Maybe not. You know how she gets sometimes.

Enjoying a drink

One of the hangovers from BSC (Before Single was Cool) is the suspicion that single women are drinking themselves into a stupor out of a combination of loneliness and frustration. What this means is that people *notice* single women getting drunk more than they would notice any other demographic, with the exception of small children. They are waiting for you to get swervy and take to the dance floor, on your own, clutching a bottle of champagne, and then collapse sobbing on the shoulder of some man who has long since married your best friend. Even if you stick firmly at the swaying stage, you've already triggered that connection (drunk, sad, desperate for a man, poor thing) in the minds of all those who have no idea how much fun you are having being single, and how little you care.

Maybe these people don't matter. Maybe you're cute enough to get away with solo swaying to the Scissor Sisters (though don't try it to 'Saturday Night's Alright (For Fighting)'). But bear in mind that all men over the age of thirty-five have pretty fixed views about women and drink – not women in general, you understand, but women they could be interested in. They *love* women who drink. They're crazy about wild party girls. They think it's terrifically sexy if you get floppy and giggly and don't care what time it is or where you are. But they are all, to a man, petrified of a genuinely drunk woman – even if they helped to get her that way. Uninhibited is good. Determined to dance is good. Singing is good. Stumbling is less good. Slurring is worse. Shouty and argumentative is not good. Legs buckling is bad. Weepy is bad. Sick on floor is really bad. He decided not to call you, by the way, at slurring.

Maintenance

Spending all your hard-earned cash on smooth legs that never get stroked and bare armpits that never get nuzzled is discouraging. It's not unlike cleaning your flat every morning in the expectation that the estate agent will show someone around – and then they don't even bother to turn up. Nevertheless, the single woman must be prepared at all times. Even if you know that the chance of your freshly waxed areas getting man exposure is roughly zero, there is a certain confidence that comes from being good to go at a moment's notice. Plus there's the issue of interpretation. What is scruffy for Ms Attached is evidence of Single Woman's low self-esteem. She hasn't got round to it; you don't love yourself.

Anyway, grooming (don't you hate that word?) works in mysterious ways. I have a friend who is living with a man she first slept with solely because, that same day, she had shelled out for a very expensive seaweed wrap. The seaweed wrap made her a) more confident on account of her baby-soft skin, and b) absolutely determined not to waste her investment. So there's a possible double incentive for grooming.

Note: There is no point having a Brazilian if you are home alone every night. Why would you tolerate the pain? A high bikini is what the single woman should aim for. That way no one can criticize your maintenance values and no one could accuse you of being presumptuous.

What not to wear

A woman who has a boyfriend can turn up to a party wearing a holey jumper, a ripped skirt and trodden-down ballet pumps, and this woman will look bohemian and sexy. The boyfriend doesn't even have to be in the country, just the fact of his existence excuses her shambolic appearance and invests it with overtones of sensuality. A single woman wearing exactly the same, on the same night, will look scruffy, grubby and, possibly, a bit unstable. People will look at her and think, Poor Susie. She really has given up, hasn't she?

Similarly, only women with boyfriends can wear really slutty, take-me-to-bed clothes because they are protected by their spoken-for status. Those plunging necklines, visible knickers and ankle-challenging heels are all so many advertisements for their boyfriend's sexual prowess, nothing to do with them looking for trouble. They can wear anything they like, pretty much, and still not seem half as desperate for attention as the single girl in the bustier top.

This rule (Having A Man Gives You Licence To Wear What The Hell You Want) applies across the board. A woman who has a boyfriend can wear a suit and tie, or dungarees, or a Bo Peep dress. She can cut her hair short using the kitchen scissors and pluck her eyebrows away to nothing. She can wear heels that make her six foot seven and orange lipstick and bunches. This is something you have to look forward to. For now you need to follow some simple rules.

There is one unavoidable truth about clothes that many of us are still determinedly avoiding: if you want sex, then you need to dress with sex in mind. You must factor sex into the equation when you fling open your wardrobe as opposed to thinking: a) that's black, no one will notice it's a bit past it; b) that's easy, and I can't be bothered to look on the other hangers; c) Oh! God! I spent £300 on you! I must wear you before the Cossack look goes tits up, or has it already?

Dressing with sex in mind does not, repeat not, mean second guessing men's fantasies. That could work, but it will not work nearly as effectively as you wearing whatever *you* think is blindingly sexy, for two reasons:

A) A woman in slit satin skirt, fishnet tights, clingy top or similar will look like the reluctant deputy headmistress in the school charity performance if she simply isn't that kind of girl. Put Kate Hudson in pvc and you kill the magic. Put Scarlett Johansson in sloppy boy jeans and beanie and pfffff – the pussycat siren is snuffed out. You have to do sexy your way.

B) Who knows what men find sexy? It's different for all of them, and just when you think you have a handle on what they like, they'll remind you it isn't that simple. There you are, trying on the mistake dress one last time before taking it to the Oxfam shop, and he gets that look.

'You can't be serious! It makes me look like an extra from *Tenko*.'

'I know, or a worker in a munitions factory . . .'

Some of them like a woman in a fresh sprig of a poplin dress, others like Zeppelin breasts varnished with silk jersey slashed to the navel, and most of them continue to surprise themselves every day (culottes . . . hmm . . . strangely saucy, or is it the shoe boots?). So, don't try to work out what works for them. They know not what they like, until they see it on you.

That said, there is no harm in pausing for thirty seconds to reflect on some things we do know about how men react to the way we dress.

Clothes confidence

The right kind of men don't like Too Safe: they see a girl in tight jeans and a sparkly top with blonde highlights and they think, *Zzzzz.* The modern male requires that extra bit of flair and style. He couldn't say exactly what it is that makes a lukewarm outfit cool, but he knows it when he sees it, and being in close proximity to it flatters his self-image almost as much as a great pair of legs in a miniskirt. Working a look, as we might say (if he starts saying it, you may have a problem) is a skill that men get almost as much as we do, and they respect a woman who refuses to compromise. If you clip into the bar wearing your zebra print Manolo Blahnik sandals with bare legs and a flippy skirt, even though it's snowing outside, it makes the man you're meeting feel like a contender. (There's nothing average about My Girl! *We* are way more interesting than that!) Men don't necessarily notice what you wear, but they like it if you look like you know what you're doing. They like clothes confidence and they like unusual.

That said, unless you move in architects' circles, or on the very cutting edge of the video art movement, you must never confuse a man's definition of 'unusual' with an appetite for the genuinely unconventional. Cloven-toed boots, pleated stuff by Japanese designers, asymmetric hairdos, dresses over shorts over leggings with stripey socks, anything that Tilda Swinton wears, almost everything that Sarah Jessica Parker wears, anything cobalt blue, or bright yellow is guaranteed to chill them to the bone. Think pretty with an edge, and you'll be on the right lines. Green handbag. Red shoes with an ankle strap. Leopard print coat. Nifty straw trilby.

The look you really want to avoid (apart from goth) is

what your mother might describe as 'lovely'. Lovely is a bias-cut floral dress and kitten-heel slingbacks, wrap dresses worn with cashmere cardigans, and pastel ballerina tops over slinky skirts. It is perfectly flattering and beyond criticism and it ticks all the Trinny and Susannah boxes but you won't get noticed in this stuff (put some outrageous heels on the bottom of the dress, and add a fur tippet and it's a different story). Once, a long time ago, the brilliant Isabella Blow told me I must wear a hat if I wanted to find The One. 'You have to stand out in a crowd. You have to let them see you,' she said. 'And men love a hat! They see the hat and they want to meet the girl.' I never got around to wearing a hat Isabella-style (shaped like a galleon, blocking out the sun) but I should have taken the point. You don't have to put a ship on your head to get men to notice you, but, if you spend a decade wearing black trouser suits to parties, don't be surprised if they walk right past you to get to the girl with the parrot on her shoulder.

What men think about clothes

All men are different, but just as most women are a little squeamish about hairy backs, so you can make one or two generalizations. Here goes.

Simplicity. Women admire nothing more than a woman who can put a Ganesh T-shirt with a tartan miniskirt with ankle boots and two kinds of wrap, toss a leather jacket on top and look like a million dollars. Men would describe this inspirational eclecticism as bag lady. Give them a chic LBD any day. (Note: Sometimes you may have got the impression that men like black clothes on women. It's not the black they like – it's the lack of complication.)

Heels. Unless they are miniature, all men adore heels and not many would get out of bed for a loafer. (That said, there are heels and there are threatening weapons of emasculation. Go easy on the Godzilla numbers.)

Underwear. They like it to match. It's a bummer, but they do. And they think flesh-coloured underwear is the pits, even though you have explained, a million times, that it is a necessary accompaniment to sheerish clothing. And they hate white underwear that has gone grey in the wash and bras that declare brazenly, 'We are here for support. Period.' Annoyingly, they actually notice your underwear and there is no getting round this.

Unfitted. Men expect to see the shape you are, up to a point. You can't hope to get them interested in the sloppy wool dress worn with boots, even if it is Marc

Jacobs. (This is probably to do with the possibility of other men looking over and thinking, 'Could be a big lass, hard to tell.')

Unisex. I mean the dark polo neck and the dark trousers and the dark jacket with the dark boots. I once had a Joseph grey trouser suit that attracted more compliments from women than any article of clothing I've ever owned. One day a man was trying to describe where he'd seen me: 'You know, you were wearing the bus conductor suit,' he said. I didn't actually look like a bus conductor, honestly, but men just don't get clothes that have no desire to be sexy.

Here's another story about trousers. I once knew a man who ignored me for months until the night I wore a dress in his presence. 'You're wearing a dress,' he said, before proceeding to try to seduce me. What he meant was, 'You're a woman. You didn't tell me.'

Polo necks with anything. I have never met a man who gets a polo neck, even on the ski slopes.

Kindergirl. Anything with bows or faux buttons or ribbons or pom poms. This may work for some men, but not the ones you want to know.

Mother stuff. Second only to men's fear of extreme fashion is their fear of the women around them turning into their mothers. Loafers. Navy. Blazers. You know it's Luella, he doesn't.

The Right Space

Everyone is looking at your flat, let me tell you. Even if you're not that bothered about your surroundings, you need to be aware that your home is the public statement of your single state of mind. If it's a bit down at heel and short on evidence of self-love, by extension you will seem like one of life's losers as opposed to what you are, which is delightfully free! Sexily single! Totally embracing your single woman opportunities! Alternatively, if it could easily double as a shop called Coco Bonbon, and all the light fittings are tinkling drop chandeliers, and all the pictures are embroidered hearts or fifties fashion photographs, then you will be taken for a Professional Single (which is to say someone who is loving her testosterone-free existence and would not necessarily welcome any manly interference).

Your living space should be somewhere that is inviting to everyone, including children and dogs (i.e. not murkily lit, with banks of devotional candles, or a study in shades of white and taupe). It may be that no children, or animals, will ever cross your threshold, but that's not the point. This place needs to give off the signal that you are a happy, well-adjusted, red-blooded woman who just happens to be living on her own, not someone who is isolated from the normal, messy routines of life. It must be somewhere a man could feel comfortable (so forget the four-poster bed covered in collector's dolls and the flimsy French cane chairs). And it has to be clean and reasonably tidy. Men in particular are very judgemental about mess. They like to be able to make it, but they rely on women to know where to draw the line. If you look like Béatrice Dalle – remember her? – you might get away with lipstick-smeared sheets, coffee cups in the sink and cigarette ash on the rug, but only *sexy* grubbiness, and only if you are under twenty-five. After that men are thinking, No. This is tipping over into unhygienic and I don't know how to get stains out. Who is going to get the stains out?

Don't recreate your parents' home

There is one decorative option that the single girl should go out of her way to avoid: recreating her parents' home. Naturally you would never do this intentionally, but then your mother wants you to have a set of occasional tables, and a painting that used to hang in the hall, and some ornaments you once admired, and a gilt mirror, and the next thing you know your sexy single-girl flat looks like the stage set for a one-act play called *The Daughter Who Never Married*. Beware silver-framed photographs charting all your solo adventures; heavy curtains with matching pelmets; oatmeal fitted carpets; Chinese silk lampshades; cork noticeboards criss-crossed with tartan ribbon; a lavatory furnished with books and prints. See where this is leading? Your flat looks like you wish you were living the life of a steady married woman, so you're going to do the next best thing, and pretend.

Things that count in a single flat

• *Your book collection.* Should The One come round, he will look on your shelves and you don't necessarily want him to find a full set of *Grazia* and two copies of *Women Who Love Too Much.*

• *Your CD collection.* He will go straight to this and start rummaging around looking for clues, so if Ziggy Stardust is the most important cultural influence on your life to date, and you've mislaid your copy, hurry up and replace it. Alternatively, feel free to fake it and buy in some Billie Holiday and *Getz/Gilberto* if all you have is *Now That's What I Call Music*, volumes 5 and 6.

The fridge. Must contain decent wine and a few beers plus a bit of food for emergencies, and make sure it's organic. Drink and nothing but drink looks mean and alcoholic. Drink plus some battery-farmed, pre-sliced chicken thighs looks worse.

The bathroom. The shower/lavatory must be spotless, obviously, and your toothbrush shouldn't be too manky and squashed. Also, don't leave out nasal hair pluckers or other things he would prefer to imagine you don't need (however, tampons should be prominently on display if you happen to be near the age when you might not need them any more).

Flowers. Flowers suggest that you are leading the life. Ditto expensive tapas from the Spanish deli. Fairy lights draped around pictures. Fat, quality candles.

The kitchen. Besides the well-stocked fridge you will need some good-looking appliances: a Dualit toaster; a granite pestle and mortar; a stainless-steel cocktail shaker. Maybe even a mini espresso machine. It doesn't really matter so long as your kitchen looks like it might get used and doesn't begin to hint at the amount of packet risotto that gets consumed on the premises.

The bedroom, we'll get on to.

How to make your flat look like you're having sex

I'm not talking about installing a love swing à la Samantha in *Sex and the City,* or leaving boxes of tissues by the bed – this is about creating an atmosphere. The key words here are warm and glamorous – a wet room works for some, a beaten-up leather sofa for others – but you know what to steer well clear of. Beige. Repro antiques. Eighties paint effects, especially stippled peach. Pine, if possible. Those indoor plants that can survive a nuclear strike. Curtains in a print featuring mustard, caramel and three shades of terracotta. Heavy ethnic drapes. Your place should evoke a Parisian love nest in a leafy square, or a shag pad in *Austin Powers* (this doesn't have to cost money

– it's all about priorities). Even if you don't possess any satin French knickers, or a pair of black patent knee boots, it's important to think like the woman who does rather than give in to thoughts such as *Will it show the dirt?*

Note: It is important that none of us succumb to the tyranny of sensible, but the single woman in particular must Just Say No to practical and manageable and low maintenance and comfy and all those concepts that are designed to make sheep out of women. One of the many perks of being single is there's only one pair of feet to monitor, so you can have the eau de Nil stair runner, and the white bedspread, and the stone linen chair covers, if that's what you fancy.

Some useful additions

• Throws (providing they aren't beige), Welsh blankets (providing they aren't moth-eaten), sheepskins, etc. cultivate a snowed-in-up-at-the-mountain-lodge atmosphere.

• Plants. You are a sensual creature, a nurturer. You love nature (for which read sex).

• A gas log fire. It's so obvious. One flick of the switch and suddenly you are in *From Russia With Love*.

• Dimmer switches.

• A lot of candles, but not enough to make an MTV video.

• Glasses on display (the more twinkling the better).

- A cocktail cabinet (well, you can only dream).

- Abandoned shoes.

- Hats on hooks – or maybe that's just me.

Now for ...

The bedroom

On no account should your bedroom look like it belongs to the world's greatest living seductress, but nor do you want it to look like the box room. In my starter single flat the bedroom was the last job on the decorating list and, for quite a while, it was furnished with a queen-size bed with single duvet (I lost the double), a clothes rail and an anglepoise lamp. One night a nosey actor friend poked his head round the door as he was leaving, sighed and said, 'No sex, then.' And of course he had a point. You can have sex anywhere, but if your own bedroom is totally unprepared for visitors you have to ask – are you?

You will need

- A bed big enough for two.

- White sheets (not, please, the floral-sprigged hand-me-downs).

- A bedcover, maybe furry.

- Some proper lights, not a naked bulb dangling from the ceiling.

- A rug.

- Some books (we are not aiming for the love-trap look).

- A radio (men love radios, and you can get a Roberts in a colour to match your wallpaper!).

- A mini fridge (why not! You might as well look as if you've had some fun in here).

You will not need

- Family-sized containers of baby oil/Vaseline.

- Photographs of your parents and godchildren.

- Ted the teddy bear.

- Full ashtrays.

- A television.

- Slippers/pool slides.

- Your teeth-whitening moulds.

- A large framed artistic photograph of a naked man.

Now for the men who might make it back to this flat.

❋ Dating

Dates (i.e. getting to know people before you sleep with them) are the number-one drawback of being single. Most are a sophisticated form of self-flagellation, which leave you thinking things out there in man world are even worse than you had imagined. You get home from ninety per cent of these dates, open a bottle of wine and pray for God to make you a lesbian. Nevertheless, dating has got to be done. You must date when the opportunity arises in the same way that you are obliged to vote in elections, because a) otherwise you are not in a position to complain about your lot, and b) there is always the fractional possibility that it might bring about some positive change in your life.

Also, it's good to practise, or that's the theory. The men who ask you on dates are thinking pretty much the same thing, although the ones who are recently signed up to AA or recovering from some emotional crisis are *literally* just practising, and you may even be an allocated exercise on a confidence-building programme.

You would think that dating, now that you are grown up and independent and have had several serious boyfriends and a couple of one-night stands, would be a piece of cake. But, no, it is as nerve-wracking as it ever was.

(Well, maybe not quite. On my first proper date I got into the waiting sports car wearing a borrowed long Rumak and Sample dress, which I then closed in the passenger door. I know what you're thinking. It's a sports car not a Lear jet. If you trap your dress in the passenger door, you just open the door and tug it right back in. Well, clearly you don't remember being seventeen and about as confident as Carrie on prom night. I was *too nervous* to open the door because I thought admitting that the hem was trapped would somehow compromise the perfect moment. So the skirt stayed where it was. And when I emerged from the car, one hour later, I was wearing a dress that from the right looked pretty good, but from the left looked like it had been dragged along a road for forty miles. Which, indeed, it had.)

Anyway, why wouldn't you be nervous going on a date? A date is an interview for sex. It is two people pretending to talk, or watch a film, or eat food, while they decide if they want to see each other naked in the nearish future. Even if you are ninety-nine per cent sure it's not going to work out, you still want your date to fancy you, which means you still worry about what you're going to wear, and wonder if it's your fault that the conversation is so sticky, and feel less than good about yourself when he bolts at the end of the evening (and if you bolt it doesn't feel that much better).

If anything, you are *more* likely to be nervous at this stage of the game, because the chances are you're taking a gamble. Dating when you're young is at least pure: you go out with a boy because he is sexy, or funny – because you want to, not because one of your friends has said, 'Come on, what have you got to lose? If he seems a bit low key that's only because he's had a bit of a bad time what with the redundancy, and the divorce. Look, I've sort of said you would, okay?' The trouble with dating now is you feel obliged to give it a whirl, even if you're not convinced, because to turn down the opportunity looks like SIC (that's Safe In my Cocoon) behaviour.

There are, however, some circumstances in which you can just say no.

Some reasons not to go on a date with a man, even if everyone says you should

• When he calls you up, you have nothing to say to each other or, what little you manage to say, he doesn't understand. He says, 'Er, okay. I *think* I get that. You're joking, right?'

• He was cruel to a woman you know.

• He wears sweaters with nothing underneath. (Later on we'll get on to discarding these superficial deal breakers, but sweaters with nothing underneath cannot be overlooked. This is guaranteed slimeball territory.)

• He wants you to make the plan.

• He is squeezing you in between a movie preview and a late-night party. (Even if he ends up taking you on to the party, this is rude, self-obsessed behaviour and you want no part of it.)

• He is an addict.

• He is two weeks out of a serious relationship.

- He is a friend of friends of your parents, allegedly very good-looking, terminally single. (Yup. They're always the last to know.)

Even if you make these exceptions, you will end up going on some terrible dates.

The totally out-of-character date

There comes a time in the life of even the most contented single woman when she asks herself, 'Should I pretend to be more interesting than I am, on the off-chance that it will open up a whole new world of opportunities?' You are not the sort who spends every Saturday visiting art galleries or watching obscure art house movies. You don't paint, or garden, or take photographs, or cook, or have any hobbies to speak of. (God knows what you do with your time, but that's not the issue.) The point is you could, with a bit of manoeuvring, go out with a certain man who speaks four languages, has a career in the arts and used to be married to a feminist writer. (This man has shown a bit of interest, but you have so far dodged it on account of not understanding much of what he says.) Still, if you apply yourself, anything is possible, and he has a house in Venice.

This is how the date goes:

Him: 'You know Venice, of course.'

Me: 'Yes!'

Him: 'Do you speak Italian?'

Me: 'No.'

Him: 'You prefer French?'

Me: 'No . . .' [*Clearing throat*]

Him: 'What, then?'

Me: 'Well. I do have some How to Learn Spanish tapes.'

Him: 'Ha Ha Ha. Your favourite Italian church. Come on.'

Me: 'Oh . . .'

Him: 'Come on. Favourite Venetian painting, then. You studied history of art, didn't you?'

Me: 'Pfff. Well . . . Um.'

Him: 'What are you reading? I'd love to know what's beside your bed. Let me guess.' [*Runs through a list of eight or ten books, one of which I have read, three of which I have never heard of*]

Me: [*Enigmatic smile, nodding as if I have read them all*]

Him: 'You tell me what you'd like.'

Me: 'From the reading list?'

Him: 'What about Barolo?'

Me: 'Er . . . is that the one with the flowery cover that's a bit like . . .'

Him: 'The wine.'

Me: 'Yes. A litre. Please.'

You leave this date and spend the next two hours trying to speed read all the books on your shelves that you haven't actually read and for the next month you have mild panic attacks when reading the arts reviews.

Self-esteem score: -10

Pros: There is a world of men out there which you are not

tapping into, but now you know for sure that you are just not up to it.

The man-who-hates-women date

This one is similar to the out-of-character date in that it happens when you decide a shift to the other end of the spectrum – as far away as possible from your usual type – might unlock a new world of possibility. In this phase you can, believe it or not, mistake the man who hates women for a tough character who knows his own mind – especially if you've only met once. Here's how this date goes:

Him: 'You don't need any more peanuts.' [*Moving peanuts out of reach*]

Me: [*Trying to reach peanuts*] 'Well, I'd like another cocktail, then.'

Him: 'You don't need another. We're about to have dinner.'

Me: 'I really *do*.'

Him: 'Look at how dressed up these people are. It's pathetic.'

Me: 'I like it.'

Him: 'It's so bourgeois. The women dressing up for the men. The men paying for the women. Jesus. My ex-wife spends obscene amounts of money on clothes.'

Me: 'Oh?'

Him: 'That's how women are. They want to fucking rip men's guts out.'

Me: 'Hmm.'

Him: 'See those two. At the corner table. It's obvious what stage they're at.'

Me: 'What stage is that?'

Him: 'The same stage as us. We both know where this is leading.'

Me: 'We do?'

Him: 'To bed, of course.'

Me: 'Chopoojkk.' [*Me choking*]

Him: 'Oh please. For fuck's sake. Women always want to play games. We are both *adults*, aren't we?'

It is now officially okay to exit this date.

This date makes you wonder why the friend who accidentally introduced you didn't call you up and say: 'Sweet Jesus, don't even think about going on a date with that guy! He is wreaking revenge on the entire female race! He won't even pay for your dinner!'

Self-esteem score: 2

Pros: Next time a man makes you feel nervous and idiotic and overdressed you will know it's entirely his problem.

The might-like-you-for-a-sister-in-law date

So you meet a couple and you get on like a house on fire. She gets that slightly predatory look towards the end of the evening and suggests you all get together again – plus her older brother who is fabulous, and happens to be single – and naturally you jump at the idea. The following week you all meet at the cinema as planned. The brother arrives, late, looking moth-eaten and reluctant – like a nocturnal creature that has been forced out of its burrow in order to mate. At a rough estimate you would say he is fifteen years older than you. He then proceeds to sleep right through the film, and snores.

This date bothers you because it came about via New Friends who assessed the situation and decided moth-eaten sleeper was roughly your entry level.

Self-esteem score: 2

Pros: None

The your-friends-all-love-him date

Of course it would be terrific if you clicked with your friends' eligible friends – Roger ('think of that house!') or George ('he's so funny and charming') – but, try as you might, you can't work up so much as a crumb of attraction for Roger or George. Even so, some of your friends think that attraction is a discipline – there are times when it comes easily, other times you just have to concentrate and make it happen – which is how you end up going on this particular date. For a split second you are persuaded that not remotely fancying someone is no different to not feeling like getting up for the early flight that will wing you off to the holiday of a lifetime.

Note: Being able to fancy someone because of his general, all-round suitability is a gift. You either have it or you don't, and long-term single girls rarely do. Anyway.

I have been on a couple of these dates, and it's like going out with your brother, only going out with your brother is more fun and doesn't make you feel like a paid escort. Also, you invariably end up offending the date, because you're on edge and bound to drink too much, and whatever it is that you particularly didn't fancy about him in the first place is liable to become an obsession. (For example, you may find yourself shouting, 'Your arms aren't that short!')

Self-esteem score: 3

Pros: Maybe he's having a party in six months' time and he's really nice so he knows lots of people.

The sexy date

You go on the sexy date and you have sex. This is what the sexy date is for. He might as well be a gigolo except that he knows a lot of people you know and they're all going to rally round in the morning and say, 'Oh well. He is gorgeous. Why not?' The trouble with the sexy date is he's wanted in six postcodes and never dates twice. It's not so much a date as a hit and run. Not that you weren't in possession of most of the facts before you rushed home with him (although who ever thinks it's going to be the same deal for her as for all the other girls? That's how the sexy date racks up his numbers; every woman is convinced that with her it will be different). He takes your phone number, which is sweet, and gives you a courtesy call the next day (he actually says 'this is a courtesy call'). It is incredible that this is happening more than twenty years after your eighteenth birthday.

Self-esteem score: -6

Pros: At least you have had sex.

Basic dating rules for the experienced woman

- Let him pay; it's a date.
- Don't wear the shoes you can't walk in. You don't want to be dependent.
- If you feel an unwelcome kiss brewing, dive into your handbag. (Note: Giant It bags, as well as being quite silly, are very useful mini minders. You can put them on your knee/next to you on the banquette/ between you walking down the street, and it's like having a small, sharp-cornered chaperone.)
- If you think it could work out, don't go some-where where you are bound to bump into friends (see next chapter).
- If you think it probably won't, suggest you go to see a play that you've been dying to see. That way you'll feel you've achieved something.
- Don't talk about your sexual history, or lack of it.
- Don't ask about his ex.
- If a coffee arrives on the table before you've even sat down, don't summon the waiter to take it away. Your date is AA and he is on a drip of double espressos. He will have at least seven before the night is out.*
- Don't cry.
- Don't get so drunk you have to lie on the floor of the Ladies.

- If the date has gone well, and he's had a good time, you will know because you'll get a text on the way home.

A word about internet dating. We all know people who know people who have met their partners via the internet. There are niche organizations out there that can hook you up exclusively with men who have first-class degrees, small dogs and river-view apartments. The possibilities are endless and clearly the potential is not to be sniffed at. However, in spite of all this good news, I am not the one to sing the praises of internet dating because a) I have never done it and b) I have a very good friend who has done it, a lot, and it hasn't got her far (although she could now walk into a room full of strangers and break into a tap-dance routine). That said I am able to pass on some of her internet dating tips, for those of you who want to give it a try:

* One of my top ten most horrendous dates (and the competition is tough) was with a bloke who had recently foresworn alcohol. The level of tension at our table was such that the people to our left and right started to stare. He was shouting and chucking back double espressos and stabbing the table with a knife. I was ordering half bottles of wine (his idea, not mine) every twenty minutes, just to numb the noise. By the end of it I was lolling helplessly in my seat and he looked like he was plugged into the national grid. My advice, if dating an alcoholic for the first time, is wait until they are past the early caffeine-overdose days, and then maybe go to the zoo.

• Do not sleep with them on the first date. Or the second. The third is about right.

• Analyse the prospective date's photograph in forensic detail. You are looking for clues in the background, such as golf trophies on the mantelpiece; gilt-framed picture of him on his graduation day; gun cabinet; statue of the Virgin in a candle-lit alcove. These will tell you a lot more about your would-be date than his smile and the positioning of his parting. (Obviously a shell suit or wife beater is worthy of note too.) Likewise check for clues as to his actual height – door handles, counter tops in kitchens, etc. (There is a height description included in the profile but men are prone to over-estimate in the region of three inches.)

• Beware the ones who don't specify weight. And if, under status, it says 'not specified' (hello?) or 'in a relationship' (hmm) or 'engaged' (blimey) or even 'not so happily married', you might want to steer clear.

• If he's ticked the 'more than one or two pieces' in the jewellery category, what d'you think?

• Check his newspapers of choice. Crucial.

• If you make phone contact and he has a comedy voice, make your excuses.

• If you have to postpone a first date and he says something like: 'Oh, I was so looking forward to seeing you; my whole week has been gearing up to this,' ditto.

• Meet him for coffee before you plan a proper date, that way you haven't wasted an evening if it's a disaster.

• Get him to text. You can tell a lot from a text. Like can he be funny and flirty without tipping over into obscenity? Pictures of his erect penis might be too much (it happens).

In general, I don't have a good word to say about dates (unless you've already had sex, you're falling in love, and then they're not dates but celebrations of your fabulousness). So let's turn the page and see if we can make that happen . . .

7.

How To Meet (The Right) Man After Forty

Before we get started, you need to know that the man you fall in love with will bear absolutely no resemblance to the man you were planning to fall in love with. He will live an hour away from where you live, minimum. He will be wearing a shiny suit and, possibly, a brown shirt. He will be an enthusiastic smoker, drinker and risk taker, three things you have cut down on, if not given up altogether. And he'll have the sort of baggage that requires its own baggage handler. On closer analysis there will be not one, but roughly twenty aspects of this man that you would qualify as non-negotiable deal breakers. You never know when and where you are going to meet The One, but this much you can guarantee.

Because one of the reasons why you are single (and this is the only one that is strictly your fault) is that you have written off every kind of man who might conceivably cross your path. You have built a fortress out of your preconditions, and you are glowering down from the battlements, slightly baffled as to why no one is attempting to storm the gates. Men do approach from time to time. But then they see the vats of boiling oil teetering on the ramparts, and think better of it.

As far as you are concerned, this fortress is a normal precaution for vetting prospective partners, and so it was, initially. But then time passed, you settled into a routine and now you are mistress of the You Won't Get Past Me Checklist. No one can blame you for this – there are a lot of arseholes out there and you need to be vigilant – but, nonetheless, the List is the number-one cause of long-term singleness.

❀ The List

Did I mention that I was set up with The One, at a lunch, three years before the party at which we officially 'met'? The reason the lunch doesn't count as the first meeting is because we barely spoke, and the reason we didn't speak is because I ran his details through the List database and, in nought point two seconds, it came up with a You Cannot Be Serious rating. Of course it did! The One was very recently divorced (not for me, thanks). He had three children in tow (uh oh). I think he'd had a savage £5 haircut and I'm almost certain he was wearing the brown shirt.

Okay, forget the haircut and the shirt. The truth is I couldn't get past the suburban postcode, and the messy divorcee's life. I wasn't even looking at the man in front of me: I was seeing barbecues in the miniature garden of the start-again home. Commuting on the overland train (at least an hour door to door). Family holidays in resorts with wave machines and all-you-can-eat buffet bars. Swapping my light 'n' airy lateral conversion in the heart of London's leafy Notting Hill for the suburban life in Acacia Grove (this really did turn out to be his address). So, at that first meeting, I summoned the List and the List gave me permission to do nothing. It said, 'Why volunteer for trouble, sweetie? You're happy as you are, aren't you? Exactly. And, even if you weren't, why would you swap the lovely life you have for such an *untidy* one. No, no. We can find you something much more suitable.'

You imagine the List is there to prevent you from wasting your precious time. You think it is the product of years of observation and experience, tempered with that sixth sense that saves the long-term singleton from making the bad mistakes and regrettable marriages of younger, less experienced women. So far so true: the List does protect you, and prevent you from taking some wrong turns, no doubt about that. But it also allows you not to take the risk. You curl up on your own with your List, on your pillowy white bed, and you'll be fine.

And this List, let's be clear, is not made up of sensible broad guidelines such as, Must not be married, or, Should live on same continent; it is extremely specific. Here are some edited highlights from my List and I'm not making a word of it up:

• *Must have hair*. Hair is good but what if top of his List was must have large breasts? That puts a rather different complexion on it, doesn't it?

- *Must not have ex-wife or children, ideally*. Like the pool isn't small enough as it is.

- *Must not wear fleeces*. The bulky navy ones. I'm not going to budge on this one. Fleeces say you're the kind of man who takes his wife to the pub for their anniversary dinner.

- *Must not wear short sleeved shirts*. See above. Add golf/cricket/rugby club to anniversary venue.

- *Must not wear jewellery*. Although you *can* tell a lot from jewellery. Any man wearing a leather-thong-based necklace is certainly a narcissist who still imagines he could have been in the Rolling Stones. Pierced earrings past the age of forty equal midlife-crisis man. Gold chains on a mahogany chest are the equivalent of the long little fingernail (just plain sleezy). Ethnic bracelets: 'always remember I went to Goa before the dream turned sour'. I could go on.

- *Must have a good job* but not one that requires him to get up at five thirty and take a laptop on holiday.

- *Must not wear hoodies with nothing underneath, or V-neck sweaters*. Hoodies are for boys. And 'nothing underneath' is another I Love Myself sign, only this time there's also the suggestion of And I Am Hot in Bed.

- *Must not own sweaters in pistachio or pale pink*. Please. You're too grubby to wear pale pink sweaters.

- *Must not sing flat*. (This, too, I stand by.)

- *Should play sports to fairly high standard.* No excuse for this. It's probably a hangover from school and the pre-sex checklist of a boy's fanciability.

When you think about it, this List would be more appropriate for an eighteen-year-old girl. And that's part of the problem: you don't edit the List over time, taking into consideration your changing circumstances, men's changing circumstances and the greater understanding and tolerance that you have learnt during your twentysomething years of interacting with the opposite sex. You would think that you might go back over the List and scratch 'must have hair', but no. The List has everything you have ever thought about boys from the age of fourteen, right up to the present day, and you are still adding to it. Must not have beard. Must not say 'babe'. Must not have greying chest hair on show. Must not have designer specs or lemon-yellow socks.

So. Right now, and without any further ado, you need to abandon the List. Come on, there is nothing on your List that is genuinely non-negotiable. So you hate goatees – get him to shave it off. So you're allergic to three-quarter trousers – tell him. Liberate yourself. Start over. Not your type? Right, and that's been such a success for you to date.

By the way, in case you thought it was just us, single men have Lists too. And, like yours, they consist of big stuff and small, and then some idiosyncratic, unfathomable stuff. You need to be aware of this because it may help to put your own Listitis into perspective.

A typical man's List:

- Must have big breasts, or biggish. Not small anyway.

- Must not be hard work, as in clever. Should have heard of Martin Scorsese, Armando Iannucci, Barack Obama, Bill Gates, but not be really up to speed on interest rates.

- Must be fit.

- Must be very attractive.

- Must not have very short hair.

- Must not wear sticky make-up.

- Must not be funny, as in Catherine Tate.

- Must not care about things too much (i.e. must keep it light).

- Must not be mad about football (sounds like it would be a bonus; in practice, irritating).

- Must be sexy but not so sexy that has slept with more than one man of their acquaintance.

- Must not be embarrassing, i.e. opinionated or too loud, but must be interesting and capable of holding own.

- Must not have much body hair, especially not moustache.

- Must not wear knee socks.

- Must not be too old, certainly not older than thirty-six.

- Must work in a sexy job, earning less than he does.

If men were as wedded to their Lists as we are, then the survival of the species could not be guaranteed. Fortunately, most of them are prepared to leave the List at home and see where inspiration or alcohol leads them. (Look at the way they shop. They go into the supermarket looking for rice and eggs, and come out with a garlic press, three sets of boxer shorts and some ballpoint pens.) The point is, if he's the right man, then he won't care if you don't tick all of his boxes, so why should he tick all of yours?

It may interest you to know that when I met The One (properly, for the second time) he was determinedly seeing several women. He had famously never been attracted to – let alone gone out with – a blonde, natural or otherwise. He had reason to believe that I was tricky and hard work, on the basis of that first meeting over lunch. I told him my age (way over his preferred cut off, at least ten years older than his previous girlfriend). In short, Heather Mills McCartney would have rated better against his personal checklist, but the juggernaut was already rolling and not even a few slurred words over the third margarita (mine, not his) could stop it in its tracks. (Note: There is almost nothing you can do that would put off the right man once you have made that connection. We will deal with the almost nothings a bit later.)

The new, edited list

After much deliberation, these are the only up-front non-negotiables:

• *Must be kind.* If you have heard him be vile about anyone (including Heather Mills McCartney); seen him be cruel to animals, children, or boring hostesses; caught him casually crushing the arrogant teenager or the drunk buffoon with a few well-chosen words, then this man is not kind. You want a man who is so kind that when you pour water over his head in bed (as punishment for some transgression you dreamt up after the second brandy) he says, 'I should kick you out, but I forgive you. Now go to sleep.'

• *Must like women.* You think this goes without saying. *Of course* every man you've ever been out with has loved women. But are you absolutely sure? Did they like it if you contradicted them in public? Were there many women they found attractive who were a) over fifty b) large c) noisy? Were you conscious that they preferred you post-Sydney-flu thin, i.e. half a stone underweight? Did they sometimes express admiration for women who were famously man-pleasing saps? Thought so.

• *Must adore you* (see Am I Turning Into My Mother?).

- *Must be smarter than you*, or at least as smart. Smarter, probably, or you will keep looking for that Achilles' heel.
- *Must have bigger feet than you*. Obviously. And must be hairier.
- *Must be able to make you laugh* in all situations, including when you get to the airport and discover he has no passport.
- *You must fancy him unconditionally.*

If you cannot put a tick next to all of the above, then I would seriously consider calling it off right now. (Note: Some people will tell you that a lovely personality can compensate for a lack of a sense of humour. They are wrong, but if you are determined to settle for someone who doesn't make you laugh, then you'd better be sure you have a big house, lots of money and loads of funny friends.)

So you've dumped the List, or at least made a concerted effort to put aside your prejudices. Now what? First a small pep talk: you need to *be ready* for this to happen. I mean you need to be prepared and willing for your unfinished story to have a happy ending. Otherwise there is a chance that you will meet The One and think, 'Oh, I don't know. Is he perfect? Is it perfect? Maybe I should look around a bit more. I've waited this long – I don't want to screw up now.' Long-term single women have been known to get hooked on keeping their options open. You secretly like the feeling that something life changing and extraordinary could be just round the corner. It's not commitment phobia (nooo) more like a fear of certainty, or normality, or – just possibly – growing up. You can't quite bring yourself to admit that the future starts here. (Yikes. What, *now*? Hold on . . . haven't decided whether I want to live on the top of a hill or break into TV or train as a naturopath . . .). And the reason you, who travels solo, and makes friends easily, and never says no to an adventure, need to rethink your game is because you may be ready to try everything and risk everything but your heart.

❀ So What Might You Be Doing Differently?

When I got engaged, a man I have known slightly for years said something that stopped me in my tracks and made me break out in a cold sweat. 'You're getting married?' he asked, peering at me intently. 'Really? I honestly thought you weren't interested in all that.' Whoa! Let's pause to dwell on that phrase for a moment: Not Interested In All That. So self-sufficient and content that I had gone beyond men and love and cohabiting and children? *Where did he get all that from?* Of Course I Was Interested. Of course I wanted to meet the right man and fall in love and live happily ever after – doesn't everyone? In the meantime – mindful of the possibility that it might never happen – I was getting on with my single life and making the most of it. Interesting, though, no? My Happy Yet Obviously Open To Offers was his Don't Bother Trying Here. Well, it got me thinking. So much of being successfully single is not about how you feel, but about how other people perceive you: it's all about striking the right note.

Naturally you think it goes without saying that you are available (just not desperate) and open to new opportunities (just not gagging for them), but, trust me, from the outside it might look as if you've made a commitment to the single life and not even The One could tempt you away from it.

You are intimidating, face it

There are zillions of wonderful, attractive, warm, sexy single women and all their friends are amazed that they could be on their own for so much as a long weekend. But, here is the thing: single women are intimidating. The fact that they have jobs, cars, proper music systems, can travel alone, negotiate their own pay rises and instruct builders, is problematic for a lot of men. If you have been single for more than six months, then someone will certainly have said to you 'men probably find you intimidating', which makes you want to punch them – however, it happens to be true. You are officially out there on your own and loving it, and this makes men feel a little nervous.

You would have thought the opposite would be the turn off – the vulnerable, mascara-stained divorcee with three kids under ten, a bulging overdraft and an incontinent dog. But no! This woman is snapped up before the other side of the bed is cold. No sooner has she settled the custody arrangements than her solicitor/one of the fathers on the school run/the organic-vegetable-delivery man, are all queuing up to take her to dinner and marry her. (As a matter of fact, they would skip the dinner and cut straight to the nuptials if they could.)

And why? Because men know what they are getting with a divorcee. She's man-tested and domestic-life approved and there aren't going to be any nasty surprises in store. Whereas you – who knows what sort of partner you'll make after so many years of paying for your own dinners and blowing up your own bicycle tyres? You are an unknown quantity, which boils down to three words: 'potentially hard work'.

It is deeply unfair. You are not actually intimidating and you would much rather hand over the bicycle-tyre duties. However, there's no point saying, 'Screw them if they can't handle it!' tempting though that may be. You know that you are a pussycat – and a chaotic pussycat at that – but, unfortunately, you're going to have to prove it.

Here's another story: I once went to a wedding at which I was seated at dinner next to a famously eligible single man. I was delighted, of course, though mainly petrified. But I wasn't going to show it. Oh no. I'd been given an opportunity some single girls would have locked their best friend in the Ladies for. I was determined to rise to the occasion and be sparky and witty and dazzling. So, as we took our places at the table, I said to the glamorous single man – a bit flirtily, not quite looking him in the eye – 'What a lousy draw.' (As in, NOT! Obviously! Ha ha! Lucky, lucky me! Getting yooooohooo!) He glanced at me, but didn't reply. Minutes passed. He talked to the girl on his other side. He talked to the girl opposite. More minutes passed. Pretty soon the dinner was finished and we'd barely spoken a word to each other. I couldn't work out what had gone wrong. Maybe I'd been too forward? Maybe he thought, Oh God, she's a fan. I can do without this.

Except the truth was – as I discovered, weeks later – the exact opposite. 'He was crushed,' reported my source. 'The fact that you actually *complained* to him about the seating plan. He couldn't believe it. And he'd been looking forward to sitting next to you.' Aaargh!

Too much irony, you see. The deadpan delivery without the flash of a smile, the encouraging elbow squeeze, the reassuring giggle, the teasing wink. Dear God, he actually thought *I meant it*. Me, the one who was overawed. Me, the least scary person in the entire room, if you were looking at it from my perspective. How could he not have known? Which is precisely the point. This encounter clearly demonstrates something women forget at our peril – that you can never be too charming or encouraging to members of the opposite sex, because they are rarely as confident as they seem. Also, it is a mistake to assume people automatically know when you are being ironic; even the driest of the species needs a little nudge.

How to be unintimidating (in a good way)

• You may be frowning more than you think. Why wouldn't you? You have a mortgage to pay, babies to have ...

• Forget your work. The man you're with thinks he has a pretty stressful lifestyle. If you're taking calls all night on your mobile/sinking glasses of wine while muttering about the day you've had, he will see this as competition.

• Don't take control, at least not all the time. You are just trying to be helpful, but grabbing the wine list, suggesting the club and then leaping out into the street to hail a taxi, will make him feel like your son on a day out from school.

• Don't tower. If you are taller than him in your heels, make a joke of it, or take them off.

• Keep it light. If you are very, very exercised by your company's recycling policy, by all means let him know, but don't harangue the poor guy. There is a time and a place. You don't want to remind him of Daniel Day Lewis during the 'I've Abandoned My Child' speech, throbbing vein in forehead and all.

• Don't always be huddled in a gang of women at parties. Women in gangs look conspiratorial rather than cute. You will scare men away.

• Don't sound like you've done it all. So you saw

Led Zeppelin's reunion concert and you've swum with dolphins and danced with penguins blah blah. What if he wants to take you to Brighton for a dirty weekend? He isn't going to dare suggest it now, that's what.

- Easy on the irony (as we have established, you may just come across as nasty).

You have Try Hard paranoia – get over it

The trouble with being single for more than a year is you start to get Try Hard paranoia. You think, I am perfectly happy with my life and, what's more, I am extremely keen that no one should mistake me for a sad single person on the pull. That is my first priority. On no account do I want anyone at the party/in the restaurant/on the street/the taxi driver/a passing satellite, to think I am trying to get a man. Spot the girl in the corner in the Dolce & Gabbana bustier dress with clutch bag and done hair and no one paying her any attention – not falling into that trap, thanks. Not me!

Here is the actual conversation I had with Angry Single friend before my first official date with The One:

AS: 'You have to wear one of your dresses.'

Me: 'You're joking! *A dress*. I'm wearing jeans.'

AS: 'Why?'

Me: 'Because I don't want him to think I'm making some *huge* effort.'

AS: 'Why?'

Me: 'Because. I don't want to look like I think this dinner is a really big deal.'

AS: 'Oh For God's Sake! Just because you're wearing a dress he's not going to think you're desperate. He's not going to think, How Sad. Look at that! She's trying to trap me. He's going to think you look lovely.'

Me: [*To myself*] Or, alternatively, he might think: *Uh oh, she's really pushing the boat out . . . I've got a fortysomething who thinks she's in with a chance on my hands.* 'Listen. It's a fashion thing. I want to look cool, not keen.'

AS: 'Oh, wear the bloody jeans!'

Me: 'Really? Okay! I'll find a really nice top, I promise.'

The Not Try Hard thing is dangerous because it doesn't just affect the clothes you wear on dates. If you get sucked into Not Try Hard world you will hold back from letting men know you like them. You will say, 'Okay. Why not?' when they ask you out, not, 'I'd love to!' You will curb your natural enthusiasm, and wait for them to be nice before you are nice back. This 'you first' attitude is not just unhealthy, it makes you seem offhand and will give men the impression that you want to be left alone. Of course a man should know, instinctively, that you're only playing it cool because you'd rather die than come across as the clingy, needy sort. Of course he should be able to tell, by your choppy haircut and your bitten nails and the really nice smile you gave him at the beginning of the evening, that you are a friendly, man-loving type. But I guarantee he won't. Instead he will think: She's stroppy. Or, more likely, he just won't register you. All that men have to go on is your Tryometer, and if yours is idling in the red zone, because you are determined that no one should mistake you for a woman who *might be looking for a man*, well, then, don't be surprised if no one comes looking for you.

There is a variation on this theme, known as blokey-girl behaviour. A little bit of boyishness is cute: wearing men's sweaters, providing you aren't mansize; downing shorts like Karen Allen in *Raiders of the Lost Ark*; taking a power drill to the dodgy shelves while wearing nothing but a T-shirt and sports socks. This stuff will enhance your chances with the opposite sex, but there is another level of boyish behaviour, which is confusing to men. Blokey Girl matches the men drink for drink, joins in the jokes about Dolly Parton and wears the kind of clothes (leather jackets, flannel shirts, parkas) that all the men would like to own (rather than remove, one piece at a time). Every once in a while, one of the gang gets drunk and makes a pass at Blokey Girl. But then the day comes when he turns up with a petite blonde wearing a pencil skirt, lip liner and a hair band (all the things Blokey Girl knows he really hates) and Blokey Girl will be introduced as his old mate and end up getting the bus home alone.

This girl isn't you, naturally. Though maybe you recognize the temptation to blend in with the boys rather than ask for special treatment. Men might see past this (take off your glasses, shake out your hair, my God but you're beautiful), but the chances are they'll assume you are opting out of the game and forget you have different sex organs.

The importance of flirting

I know, I know. There is nothing quite so dispiriting as lavishing forty minutes of your class-A, top-level, full-mat-sequence flirting on a man, only to discover he is married, or gay. We have all been there. You've just established that you both lived in Florence. He's said, 'You know that place too? That is uncanny,' and then he's said, 'That's exactly how I feel,' and then, 'I'm so glad I came to this party!' And you are honestly expecting the next words out of his mouth to be, 'Look. I know it's a long shot, but I've got the day off next Friday and I was wondering . . .' When, out of the blue, My Wife Anne gets her first mention of the evening and THWACK! Those tiny, green shoots of romantic possibility that were just breaking the surface, quivering in the light, are buried under a ton of slurry. (What did he think you were doing tossing your hair like a maniac and laughing at everything he said? Bloody Selfish Bastard.)

Whatever you do, never let this sort of disappointment visibly phase you. Even if you were in the middle of figuring out what your children might look like, on no account show your irritation. (You are joking! Why didn't you mention this earlier? I missed my fucking lift home because of you! What part of 'If you're staying, I'm staying' did you not understand?) Because there is one thing worse than wasted flirting, and that is no flirting at all.

Note: Not long ago, seated at a dinner table in LA, I watched a woman tear into a man for not declaring he was married. They weren't on a date, they weren't even sitting next to each other, but still the woman felt she had been cheated and was not afraid to make her displeasure known. Here's how the confusion arose. The man was flirting with her. No more than he was flirting with any of the other women at the table, but nonetheless – rather unusually for an Englishman – definitely putting some effort into making the assembled womenfolk feel good about themselves. That, plus the fact that he wasn't wearing a ring, led her to believe that she was in with a chance.

'You are *married*?'

'Yup.'

'You are not serious.'

'Yes I am.'

'You don't have a ring.'

'I'm English. Some of us don't.'

Open-mouthed display of shock. 'And so you think that's just fine?'

'Er . . . Yes.'

'Really. Well, *I don't*.'

Now, we all know where Cheated Woman was coming from. It was a big party and, had she picked a different target and sat at a different table, she might have been halfway to bagging an eligible producer. But, by advertising her outrage, not only did Cheated Woman look very sad (she might as well have leant across the table and roared, 'I spent three hours at the hairdresser for this! I bet your wife isn't as hot as me. Jesus, this is so unfair!'), but she was doing a great disservice to her single sisters. Never mind the fact that Married Flirting Man may never flirt in public again – there were unattached men present, and they got the message, loud and clear (oh boy, did they) that it is safer to act like a cold fish than to give a woman the smallest cause for hope. Bad Cheated Woman. Single men are wary enough – what with the stories of women with ticking clocks sticking pins in condoms, and not being able to tell how old a woman is to the nearest decade until they get their hands on her passport. They're already confused, so it's a mistake to criticize a man for flirting.

Above all, never let these sorts of setbacks turn you into the kind of selective flirt who only bothers to shift into gear if she has the nod from the hostess, plus back-up confirmation from the barman. Flirting is about radiating the right stuff, regardless of where it is directed. In other words, it doesn't matter if the person you are flirting with is a genuine romantic prospect – the guy over by the rubber plant, the one you aren't even aware of yet, could be catching the ripples. Or, later on, the man you charmed might be talking to his single friend and happen to mention this hottie he met (you) who is going to be at so-and-so's on Saturday . . . That's how flirting works: if you save it for the chosen few, you are missing the point. Also, you will notice that the girls who have no sliding scale of appropriate flirting, and are barely conscious of doing it, are very rarely single.

The right social life

You don't have to have straggling chin hairs to give off the message that you aren't really looking. There are many other just as effective ways of ensuring that you never bump into The One. For example:

- Hanging out with girls at parties. It is well known that girls are fun to talk to at parties, but it's also the easy, minimum investment option.

- Spending weekends with your safe couple friends who have moved to the country, or your gay friends with the fabulous garden.

- Planning holidays with girlfriends months in advance, no men included.

- Spending all your time with couples, and thinking nothing of it.

There is a reason why your social life has become virtually man-proofed: you have single woman's social dilemma. You are caught between the social life that suits your attached friends – i.e. most of the people you know – and the one that might actually get you somewhere.

The key for long-term singles is choosing what *not* to go to. A significant proportion of your friends are married and struggling with several young children. The problem is they are still, determinedly, issuing the invitations: Sunday lunch with a forest of high chairs; drinks with the parents of their children's school friends; the occasional dinner party at which you are seated in between your exhausted host and Serena, whose husband is on a business trip. These experiences can really drain the single woman's supply of positive energy (your number-one asset after a healthy bank account) and you have a duty to protect this at all costs. There is nothing so dispiriting as getting all waxed and tweezed and shelling out £20 on tights and £40 on taxis and another £50 on a blow-dry (well, you get what you pay for) in order to spend the evening with people who are actually talking about the stalls at the school Christmas Fair, and who is providing the mulled wine. You need, in other words, to get ruthless.

The secret is to view your social life in four categories, from A to D. A is Real Friends time. You go to As whatever, including when you are on your knees and have to catch a plane at 8 a.m. the following morning, because these friends are a tonic and they have the donkey-stroking factor. Category Bs are killing-time invitations (i.e. social situations with no chance of meeting new people or anyone you particularly want to see). They invariably result in unwanted hangovers (you have to drink a lot to get through them) and the feeling that life is passing you by: avoid them unless you really need to leave the house. Cs are a good-chance-of-meeting-men occasions: these you don't turn down, even if you are in a full body cast. Ds are dates. (We've dealt with these. You know the deal.)

Embracing the right to say no to invitations is a very

important step for the single woman because it relieves all that guilt you feel for not getting out there and making the most of every opportunity (i.e. more than six bodies gathered in a room). The un-single are allowed to exercise their right to pick and choose from the social smorgasbord, but singles feel obliged not to pass on any invitation, however dodgy. You don't want to go. You have a strong suspicion it will be them, plus the weird brother who is over from Australia, but your single's conscience says, 'Is it really okay to stay in and watch *Britain's Got Talent*, when My Future Husband could, just possibly, be there?'

The answer is most definitely yes, because your instinct is invariably right. Also, if you skip all the B occasions, you will have that much more enthusiasm and energy to channel into the Cs – namely the night when you will meet The One.

Should you be moving to the country? (No!)

Moving to the country (possibly via a weekend rental cottage) is a rite of passage for a lot of attached women who want to get out of the smoke, grow their own vegetables and generally feel like they are enjoying a better quality of life. Naturally there comes a point when the single woman wonders if she, too, shouldn't be seeking a rejuvenating change of scene. The country represents new, wholesome opportunities: there are views, and walks, and gardening, and animals, and village life, and, last but not least, a whole fresh source of men. Your thinking – and I've been here, fleetingly – goes something like this: I will raise chickens and grow peonies, wearing floaty dresses and a big hat. I'll have a whole new wardrobe built around the Toast catalogue, and a roaring log fire and a devoted dog. The main reason nothing much is happening in my life is because it's not *Real*. The country is real. It's full of people with real values – real men, who never think about their hair or have smart/casual crises. Anything could happen if I moved to the country. And what you are really thinking, underneath all this, is, Imagine the decorating opportunities.

What no one tells you, however, is that the country is strictly couples only, unless you ride, or you're the Duchess of Devonshire. Here's why. Ask yourself, what are you going to do when you've fed the chickens and dug the garden and laid the fire? Watch TV and finish the second bottle of red, is what. That's what they all do, but if you're part of a couple at least one can keep the other in check. Not only will you become a lush within a matter of weeks, but you'll be forced to settle for local Linda's highlights, and you will develop chapped hands, broken-veined cheeks, slightly yellow teeth (mysterious but true) and then, every so often, you won't bother to change your knickers and just wear them inside out. As for waxing in winter – why would you? You need the extra warmth. And if you think your social life now is patchy and a little short on opportunities for sex, just you wait. Once ensconced in Little Upplington, you may be invited to dinner with some neighbours who have specially asked Geoffrey, who hasn't been quite the same since his quad bike tipped over on the farm last Easter. Until that glorious day, you will be socializing with the estate agent who sold you the cottage, the solicitor who did the conveyancing and the woman who ran up your curtains, plus someone you went to school with who you never liked, but who happens to live in the next-door village.

Okay it might not be that bad, but it will be close. And if (and it's a big if) there does happen to be some Sam Shepard single-vet type, waiting for a sexy out of towner to share his life with, you won't be able to get near him. He will probably travel to and from work in an armoured vehicle. (That's another thing they don't tell you about the country: the women are hardcore. You with your silly shoes and romantic ideals will be trampled into the mud before you can say, 'Excuse me, but in the pictures everyone eats in orchards with bunting in the trees and none of the men have hairy cheeks.')

Calling all matchmakers

You may think no one matchmakes any more, although I have been told by several people, since meeting The One, that *they* considered introducing us, but ultimately couldn't quite face it, on account of the List. (What they actually said was, 'You are soooo critical. In the end we didn't think it was worth the risk.') If you do have this reputation, your matchmaking-inclined friends (and they are a dying breed) will find the idea of setting you up about as appealing as a cross-Channel swim. Surprisingly enough, these well-meaning people don't want to be tested on how effectively they have revised your likes and dislikes. If they think there is a possibility that you are going to grip them in the kitchen after the first course and hiss, 'Are you *joking*? Me? Him? How in God's name did you see that ever happening? Do me a favour. Just take me through your thought process, step by step,' they probably won't bother in the first place. And this is a very great pity because a steer in the right direction, from someone who knows you, who knows him, someone you like and respect and trust, is not to be sniffed at. Of course your friends will get it wrong sometimes. Of course it might not work out. But what have you got to lose?

So encourage anyone who can to help you out. Say, 'Look. You know that quite nice bloke you work with at the BBC? Why not ask him over on your birthday? Would you? I'll bring the champagne.' And when they say (because people are bored of your situation and lazy, let's be honest), 'Oh, um. I'm not really celebrating my birthday this year,' then say, 'I need you to do this for me. Come on. I'll throw in tickets to the opera.'

Note: You can try the internet if you choose. You can see someone in the distance, find out his name and call him up. You can advertise in the post office or approach strangers in the street. All of the above are possible. But there is no substitute for the natural supply that your social/work contacts provides, if only you can get the right people to put in some effort.

Not all matchmaking has to involve a stagey dinner party. Sometimes a friend can push you in the right direction from a discreet distance. Here is the email exchange that I had with the hostess of the party at which I met The One.

S: Are you coming to my party?

Me: Oh God! I'm meant to be going to stay with some friends in Suffolk that weekend. Maybe I can get out of it.

S: Please come. Weekend in Suffolk some other time. I have asked brother-in-law to provide an array of recently bereaved millionaire lawyers or bankers for our inspection.

Me: Okay. I'll get out of it. [Thinks: It is a category C! I must definitely go if it's category C. Even if it would be easier to go to the category A weekend and lie in the garden making no effort and meeting no one and eating.]

S: Hurrah! I think you might like [The One]. Do you know him?

Me: You Are Joking! People are always trying to set us up. [This is a slight exaggeration. There was that lunch, that I've already mentioned. And the time we were put next to each other at a work dinner. And a drinks party, way back, when his boss tried to push us together. But he had come up in conversation more than once, as in 'what about him, he's great . . .'] Not a runner, I think. Anyway he's got a girlfriend.

S: They've just broken up. So he is single now . . .

Me: I actually know he's not The One. Thanks for the thought, though. [Meanwhile sit back, stare at computer and pause to reflect: But *She* obviously rates him. She bothered to mention him, specifically. Never, in the fifteen or so years since I have known her, has S suggested 'I might like' a particular man. Why now? And what if she emails some other girlfriend and suggests him as a possibility? Maybe I'm missing something here?]

Lightbulb moment: I need to go to this party and I need to take a long, hard look at this man because a) others have seen his potential, and b) if I don't, there is a very good chance someone else will, right under my nose.

Ping goes the email. It's S again:

S: Well if you're not interested maybe he'll do for me.

Yup. I definitely have to focus. S is gorgeous. She has given me a steer and now she's saying, 'Wake up, sister, or the big girls will clean up.'

So I had a helping nudge, but you don't need an email matchmaker to get you into This Could Be It Mode (aka the ideal state for approaching the opposite sex).

Getting in the zone

• *Assume that you are going to be having sex in the very near future.* It generates that mixture of adrenalin and pheromones that people have been trying to bottle since the beginning of time.

• *Make the extra effort.* If you go to the party wearing your second-hottest dress, because you are saving your number-one dress and you've already decided that you'll only stay for an hour, then you might as well not bother. You will not exude the right anything-is-possible glow and The One will look in your direction and think 'downer'.

• *Do something differently*. Wear heels instead of flats, put on a slithery dress instead of jeans, do something unexpected with your hair (though obviously not involving an Alice band). You won't necessarily look any better, but you will *feel* like you've changed up a gear. Part of the game (after a period of being overlooked) is believing you are definitely worth some attention, rather than passable in a low-lit environment, and that means surprising yourself. For example, on The Night I deliberately didn't go for the standard summer fallback (white jeans, wedges, nice top) and wore a bright, slinky dress and flat gold sandals. It didn't get the fashion vote, and my legs didn't look as long as they would have in the wedges, and the sandals really didn't work with the dress, and my arms looked a bit hammy, but the change made me behave differently. In the flat sandals, which I almost never wear, I felt flighty, and the dress was flapping its eyelashes before I was. Had I worn the wedges and jeans, I'd have stalked about imperiously, crushing canapés underfoot and towering over half the men – and that's a look I return to regularly – but on The Night the dress forced me to be more feminine and flirty. More approachable (particularly for those of Sarkozy stature).

• *Don't fall into the perfect party preparation trap*. The theory is that confidence is being buffed and tweaked all over, but if you believe you have to be the perfect ten before anything can happen, it almost certainly won't. The girl who has just spent a week's salary on ultra groomage and accessories is liable to be thinking, Someone Bloody Well Better Make All This Effort Worthwhile. Out of my way! I need to find a man to admire my shiny hair and glossy shins. I have had my fucking teeth whitened, thank you. You don't want to be this girl; she is in breach of the rules of attraction. Besides, if you tot up the times you've got lucky, versus the times you have not, I guarantee you will discover that undyed roots and bitten fingernails are no obstacle to lust in a well-adjusted man.

• *Lose your friends.* I know, this sounds like madness. Who has the single woman got if not her loyal girlfriends? Who else is going to hang with you at the bar until the party fills out, and rescue you from the leering uncle? Who is going to bung you in the cab at the end of the night and then ring to check you haven't fallen asleep in the stairwell? Nonetheless, as much as you love them and need them, your friends will cramp your style. You need to be able to flirt outrageously and reinvent yourself slightly if you are to attract The One, and friends are not the ideal audience for this. Like your family, they have a pretty fixed idea of who you are, and whoever that happens to be – clown, cynic, crazy extrovert, unworldly innocent – they don't appreciate any deviation from the script. What you don't need is MF rolling her eyes as you nibble provocatively on the rim of your champagne glass or AS bellowing, 'Go on, do your Hoffmeister Bear impersonation!'

Plus, if something should happen to develop when your friends are in the vicinity, you can expect them to react in one of the following ways:

- Gawping, followed by circling at a not-discreet-enough distance, texting all your other mutual friends with updates on your progress.
- Giving the double thumbs up immediately behind his head.
- Leaping in to 'help things along' ('Isn't she just gorgeous. I just love her! Doesn't she look amazing tonight? Isn't this brilliant?')
- Hovering, followed by proprietorial vetting ('Who's this, then? You two seem to be getting on raaather well. Is this the first time you've met, or what?').
- Alternatively, if drunk enough, they may start popping up behind sofas, sniggering.

This stuff doesn't change the older you get – if anything it gets worse because the stakes are higher and your friends have more invested in you getting it right. (Friends have Lists too.) So, don't automatically arrange to go to the party with a couple of girls, or, once you get there, rush to find the people you've known all your life. The fact that I went unchaperoned on The Night meant I was free of all responsibilities (good), I was forced to make an effort (good), I was in need of a lift home (good) and, best of all, no one was watching. Also, when it came to leaving, there were just two of us making onward plans, not six including three saying, 'Let's go to your flat and drink the fridge.' Think about it.

• *Then, pick your man*. Don't wait for him to find you (and don't settle for talking to the first person who catches your eye because this could be The Night and you are in control). The One says he saw me steaming across the room, nostrils flared, elbowing women out of my path, but this is not true. I did spot him in the distance and then sort of worked my way across the room in his direction. I did get into a conversation with a man standing right behind him and then spun round and pretended to be surprised to find him there. (As it happens, I very nearly overdid this. It is only *so* incredible to meet someone with whom you have friends in common at a large party given by one of them.) But it's true that I made it happen. And then – drum roll, please – I did that thing that happily single women so often forget to do. I set about making him like *me* (as opposed to waiting for *him* to prove to me that he was worth the trouble).

• *Flirt and then some*. However much you think you are flirting, double it. What the hell, quadruple it. Barely there flirting will register as average civility if it registers at all. We have already established that singledom makes a girl cautious. She is pre-occupied with not looking like a mad, sad, ticking man huntress. But trust me – you need to be flirting at a level where you think, Blimey. Steady on. He'll think you're a Pro! before you can be confident that he has twigged you might quite like him. I flirted so badly with The One on The Night it was borderline offensive. Had I been watching me from the wings I would have made me gag. (I actually commented on his impressive height. I actually said, several times, 'It is sooo good to see you!') But it was no more than was absolutely necessary because, to this day, he claims he didn't notice. He can't remember the height comment, or the lingering eye contact, or me gazing up at him adoringly in the manner of Cherie Blair on the few occasions when he said something serious. (He *did* notice, obviously, he just didn't *know* he noticed. Men are all Helen Kellers in the context of flirting.)

Some rules of flirting

(They're the same as they were when you were eighteen, but you need to really work them now that you can't rely on nubile flesh and hot pants to reel them in.)

• Laugh a lot, like a mad person. You cannot smile enough or laugh enough.
• Be intensely interested in everything he says (casting your eyes around is counter productive, especially if you're hunting the canapés).
• Maintain eye contact for long enough that you are both in no doubt it is not accidental.
• Be very impressed.
• Tease, a bit, but not about any of the no-go

areas – height, hair, lisp, mothers, his level of inebriation/sweating.

- Flatter, but only lightly, in passing, and not more than once. (Don't push it. Don't for example say, 'Oooh, you are muscly,' and grip his biceps. That would be odd.)

- Don't talk about yourself, unless pushed, and then keep it brief. If you hear yourself saying 'The other project I am really pleased with . . .' then for God's sake stop right there, slam into reverse and quickly add, 'But that's boring. I want to hear all about you.'

- Get conspiratorial. When you are joined by the man who starts going on about *The Da Vinci Code* tour, give him your special look.

- Don't touch. You could lightly touch his forearm, maybe. But better not.

- Disappear at some point. For roughly ten minutes. You want him to have the chance to miss you.

- Some say fiddle with your hair, your cleavage, your earrings. I say don't risk looking like you have fleas. Don't lick your lips/teeth under any circum- stances. He may think you are chasing canapé particles.

- Be extravagantly open about everything (bar medical stuff). Honesty is disarming.

- Make him responsible for you. Say 'would you get me another drink', 'would you let me lean on you while I do up my shoe', 'would you tell me what you think about buying property when the subprime market is in collapse'. (No, obviously you don't want to overdo it. But a man likes to be singled out of the crowd. Providing it's not to replace your tyre.)

- Flirt with other men. You can work this one of two ways. Either flirt extravagantly with everyone in the hope that it will make him a bit jealous, or flirt a lot with other men, but make it obvious that you are reserving your booster flirting for him. Who knows which is more effective? But charming other men is crucial . . . it introduces that all-important frisson of competition.

While you're doing all this flirting, The One, (or the Could Be One, it is early days, after all) has decided you are definitely worth the effort because you are making him feel good (aha!) and so he is flirting right back. He is dazzlingly attractive and attentive and funny and clever and sexy! He is GORGEOUS. You cannot believe you didn't see it before. But then the last time you gave him zero encouragement (he would say it wasn't even that good). You remember being perfectly friendly and approachable but *he* remembers arrows raining down from battlements and trying to keep up a charm assault from under his shield and then thinking, Oh fuck this. I'll talk to my neighbour.

In other words, the only difference between him at that lunch, and him right now, is the way you are behaving towards him. (And his hair has grown a lot. And he doesn't have a small boy sitting on his shoulders, but anyway.)

Now you've established that you have time for each other you are ready for compatibility testing. The higher your compatibility score the more you will both feel like you have a genuine connection, and the more likely this is to continue beyond the party (if you don't agree on much, that's useful to know at this stage too). If you mention Philip Seymour Hoffman, Fiona Bruce's eyebrow, Elton John's 'Tiny Dancer', the importance of tortoises in your childhood, as well as Caramac, and he looks blank more than once, you are in trouble. Then again, if he was glued to *Curb Your Enthusiasm*, once owned a lurcher and now owns a bichon frise, is reading *Stalingrad* but is happy to admit he loves Neil Diamond, you will get the reassuring feeling that it's not just the champagne making you want to kiss him urgently. Halfway through playing marriage exams with The One we discovered that both our fathers ended their careers as major generals. Can you believe that? Are you remotely surprised that two hours into the party I was already thinking, That is too much of a coincidence. Obviously we are going to get married.

❀ What Happens Next?

Do you leave the party with him? Yes. Do you go on somewhere else? Yes. A bar and then a karaoke booth, ideally. (Don't stop to eat; that's a downer. If you think there's a risk you may be sick, grab some nuts.) Do you go back to his place? No. You go back to yours. Obviously. Then you are in control and he can see your single-girl flat, which will give him the strong impression you are cool and have had sex this century (good work!). And he'll get to see your CD collection and you will discover that you both have *Madman Across the Water* (freaky) not to mention early Fleetwood Mac, rarish Neil Young and most of David Bowie's oeuvre pre-*Tin Machine*. And he'll notice the photograph of you and The Famous Actor (no harm in hinting there could have been something there). And he'll spot your lovingly tended window boxes (maybe not, but you get the picture). Do you sleep with him? That depends.

As a rule it is not a good idea to sleep with a man on the first date unless:

• He lives in a foreign country. He's flying back the next day and you think, What the heck.

• You have history (i.e. you have met more than twice and been the subject of an attempted matchmake, or two).

• It is 4.30 a.m. and you have been in each other's company for the equivalent of two long dates, or three short ones, and to call it a night now would look a little like playing by Swiss finishing school rules.

• You suddenly feel like you can't bear to waste all that grooming (see the seaweed-wrap story).

• It seems totally inevitable, so why play games? If it's meant to be . . . and there is quite a lot stacking up that suggests it could be . . . Hold this thought.

The One is having a delightful time. If he thought about it – which he hasn't – he can see this progressing to date two. But there is no way that he is any further down the road than that. He has several other women in his diary and has made a solemn pledge to himself not to get involved with anyone for at least a year. From here on in – despite the inevitability of you being together – you need to keep a cool head.

Sleep with him, by all means, but on no account assume that you can play a totally straight game just yet.

The early days
You are in the grip of a form of madness: not sleeping, not eating (but still living in restaurants), always dancing and kissing and behaving like a tourist, taking boats and taxis and ordering cream teas in hidden-away hotels, and shopping.

All serious relationships begin with a major consumer binge and this one is no exception. You are blowing silly money on patch waxing (i.e. topping up every four days) and pedicures and leg oil, not to mention clothes that you wouldn't have considered trying on a month ago (the ones that reveal more cleavage, quite a lot of arm and plenty of leg, in colours like pink and lilac, or even a blend of both. Quite possibly you will buy clothes during this phase that are *so not you* that you will open your wardrobe a year later and finally understand what is meant by 'losing your mind').

Never mind the clothes. You pick up new cushions and candle holders every other day; you buy Prosecco like it was Pepsi and vast bunches of lilies and decorative-looking fruit to arrange in bowls and rare olive oil and *more* beauty products. Meanwhile you stop buying Solgar vitamins the size of horse pills and visiting the woman with the inflatable boots who magnetized your water and convinced you to wear purple while working at your computer – so it all evens out in the end. (Note: This is when you officially say goodbye to all the habits and hobbies that we can now – without risk of offending anybody – loosely group under the title Sex Substitutes. These include: long, ritualistic beauty therapies; excessive yoga; hoarding vitamins; carrying 1.5 litre bottles of water at all times; body brushing; semi-precious ring buying; devoting hours of leisure time to obsessively sourcing the perfect shade of strawberries-and-cream fabric for the window-seat cushion, etc.)

There is no doubt that this is serious. But even so. The first two to three months is the probationary period of any relationship, including ones that are obviously meant to be. During this time you will need a committee of girlfriends on speed dial, available round the clock, to keep you on the straight and narrow and prevent you from doing anything stupid. Your team should ideally consist of your Angry Single (with lots of recent romantic experience); your Wise Married Friend and your Mentor Friend. Your committee's advice is invaluable because they have something you lack – perspective – and they are not surviving on four hours' sleep a night.

Late Love is such a miracle you will assume that, now you have found it, nothing could possibly get in the way. The committee is there to remind you that the Early Days rules never change.

Here is the conversation I had with MF ten days (three dates) into my relationship with The One:

Me: 'He is sending me weird texts!'

MF: 'Like what?'

Me: 'Like commitment-phobic texts. Like, "I'll call you later on in the week and *maybe* we'll see each other at the weekend."'

MF: 'He's busy, poor guy.'

Me: 'And that's not all. He said "my life is all over the place at the moment". And "it's a bad time for me to be getting involved".'

MF: 'Well, it is. And it is. He's being honest.'

Me: 'I want to know what's going on. I'm going to ring and have it out with him.'

MF: 'Right. And what are you going to say, exactly? "Do You Love Me?"'

Me: 'Well . . .'

MF: 'It's been ten days. On no account call him.'

(I don't call him.)

Here is the conversation I had with WMF:

Me: 'He is sending me weird texts!'

WMF: 'Oh, not *texting*. We don't like texting.'

Me: 'Yes, texting and nothing but texting and he's saying weird things.'

WMF: 'Never mind what he's saying. Texting is emotional distancing. You have to nip the texting in the bud right now.'

Me: 'But I need to send something back, surely? Just one text.'

WMF: 'If he wants to talk, he has to ring you. That is the rule. Nil by text.'

(I don't text him.)

Here is the conversation I had with AS:

Me: 'He is sending me weird texts!'

AS: 'Oh fuck.'

Me: 'I think it's all going wrong. He's behaving really oddly.'

AS: 'Oh God. How oddly?'

Me: 'He's being vague about when we're going to see each other next. He said *maybe* we'd see each other at the weekend.'

AS: 'Well, fuck that. Tell him you're not going to be around anyway.'

Me: 'What, you mean lie?'

AS: 'Yes! Send him a nice, friendly text saying, no problem, because you're away for the weekend. And if he asks for details make it sound sexy.'

Me: 'But what if I bump into him?'

AS: 'He lives in the suburbs. As if we could forget.'

Me: 'Okay, then.'

(He calls me straight back asking to see me on Monday. Ha!)

Note: These women are all coming from different places, but together they have averted an escalation of Early Days jitters, which might have resulted in me going round to his house in the middle of the night (*not* . . . too far! But, hypothetically) and shouting through the letter box, 'We are meant for each other. This is a miracle. Can't you see? Helloooo.' Their purpose is to remind you that total transparency is for stage two, after he's admitted he loves you.

First-base rules

Listen. He is hooked. The rational, critical part of his brain has been disabled and you don't have to bite your tongue or hold in your stomach or pretend you like *CSI* ever again. It turns out that there are no scary new sexual gymnastics required (at least none that you couldn't tell your girlfriends about). A Brazilian is definitely optional. The waxing is probably appreciated, but you can afford to ease up a bit. And he couldn't care less that you're old enough to remember *Z-cars* (he likes it). In short – the chemistry has done its work and there is nothing you can do to put him off. That said, there's no harm in avoiding the kind of behaviour that triggers negative thoughts in the average male brain. Namely:

She's a Mess

Don't drink and dial. The right man expects to have to pull you out of a hedge once in a while, and check that your knickers aren't showing. However, this does not mean he will react well if you decide to call him from the taxi at 3 a.m. after the night out with the girls from work. Naturally you will think your behaviour is spontaneous and funny and sexy and uninhibited, and more or less exactly like Goldie Hawn in *There's a Girl in My Soup*. But it will sound something like this to him: 'Mad messy, bit scary. No self-respect. Love me, Love me, LOVE ME, I don't love me! I am a Mess.' It's so unfair. Especially when all you wanted to do was tell him about the really funny thing that happened in the Ladies at the restaurant. But that is what he will hear.

She's making assumptions

You are not. Jesus. You really aren't. You are just behaving as you would normally: planning ahead, getting twenty or so friends over, asking your parents to lunch, thinking vaguely about where you might be for Christmas. However, The One is a modern man and fully cognizant of the predicament of the woman with the ticking biological clock. He knows that while the ultimate sin a boyfriend could commit used to be getting a girl knocked up, at this time of life it's *not* getting her knocked up and wasting her childbearing potential ... or just wasting her time full stop. One of the very few disadvantages of Late Love is that, however relaxed you may be about your future, The One could be forgiven for perceiving pressure all around. For this reason, you must:

- Keep friends and family out of the picture for a couple of months. There is always the risk that one of your male friends will get sloshed and emotional and start telling The One that you are very, very special and he had better treat you well or else blah blah. Also, there is every chance that your mother will say, 'We'd given up actually.'

- Have a life. Note: You have several advantages over the youthful you, and first among them is you have a million things to do before you can begin to think about what happens at the weekend. Men love not being responsible for a woman's happiness. Since *Prime Suspect* and *Silent Witness* they have all longed for someone who has a passion in life besides them. If your work is a dead end, and the fact is you have been at home getting ready to go out since 3.30, don't let that stop you from spinning through the doors of the restaurant in a 'done the deal, now I'm ready to play' sort of way.

- Not get domestic on him. By all means cook for him when he is at your place, but don't even think of reorganizing his spice rack, cleaning his oven, throwing out his nasty cheap pans and replacing them with top-of-the-range Le Creuset. Even if this is just second nature (in which case, lucky you) it looks like nesting. We don't want any hint of nesting.

She's trying to change me

You are not! You just happen to have seen a jacket in Gap that would be perfect for him and some lamps that would really improve his living room and it makes perfect sense that he should see your hairdresser because your hairdresser does a lot of men's hair, and wavy is his speciality. No no no. You will be making sweeping alterations in due course, but it is tactless and counter productive to start now. (As WMF says: 'Never buy a man clothes; it's like dressing your dolly.')

She's high maintenance

Of course you don't want to be mistaken for *low* maintenance. It's important that he picks you up from the station, even if it's only a five-minute walk from his house, and frets if your hotel room overlooks the air-conditioning unit, and worries if you are left standing outside the cinema in the rain. But, equally, he needs to be sure that you would happily get out and push the car at midnight in a muddy lane, and deal with the wheel splash. Note: In earlier life, many men are under the impression that high-maintenance, tricky women are sexy. They quite like a decorative girl who takes three hours to get ready and then is rude to their friends. Just in case you were one of those girls, and you are under the impression that there is still no better way of driving a man wild than behaving like a diva with toothache – all men get over this stage (with the notable exception of actors) and, from midlife onwards, their trouble radar is set on low tolerance. From this point on, high-maintenance behaviour includes: always making them late; not making an effort with friends/colleagues; sulking in the company of relatives; expecting every Saturday night to be gala anniversary night; insisting on his undivided attention, even when visiting his mother, in the home.

She's stuck in Professional Single mode

You are not this woman, but there may be elements of your life that border on PS. For example: those jumbo toile de Jouy pillows on your bed. The cafetière for one that you sometimes absentmindedly reach for in the morning. The white floors that really aren't football-boot friendly. The decorative plates propped up alongside the bath where he might have hoped for a shaving mirror. The salad-with-a-bit-of-chargrilled-chicken suppers. The absence of anything in the kitchen like bread or biscuits. The miniature suitcase (no room for his wash bag). The Polaroided shoeboxes (no room for his shoes). The Baies candles that give him hay fever. The tiny TV that doesn't get Sky Sport. All this is fine providing you welcome his mess and don't make him feel like a bear in a doll's house when he is on your turf. If you find yourself saying, 'Oh, sorry. I seem to have just poured myself a glass of wine,' or, 'Would you mind removing your shoes and clothes before you enter the bathroom,' then for pity's sake get a grip.

Some other things to avoid when you have found The One

• Dissecting his sexual history. There are times, generally around 4 a.m.-ish, when you feel inspired to talk about his previous relationships in some detail (in other words you require him to come up with one story, per ex-girlfriend, that begins something like, 'She was a nice enough person, but that cellulite . . .'). He is never up for these conversations because he knows no good will come of it. And he knows you will remember every word, which may not matter now, in the first flush of confessional love, but will come back to haunt him later.

• Sharing your history. It's very simple. He doesn't want to know. If your previous boyfriend was impotent and liked to dress up as a clown, he couldn't care less. All of it makes his extremities shrivel.

• Too much information. The boils you've had. The hairs you've dealt with. The time you had dysentery and how it went, exactly. You can get so carried away with having found your soulmate that you may mistake him for the person who wants to hear your warts-and-all stories. He doesn't want to hear about the warts.

• Calling him by your last boyfriend's name. We've all been there. You can laugh it off once, or even twice. But don't let it happen a third time.

• Getting really bossy. You've been running your own show for a while and you may find it frustrating to relinquish any control. Please do. Let him book the flights, even if you would have got the slightly later one, with the better connection, that cost £100 less.

- Talking about your incredible age and withering ovaries. There is almost nothing you cannot discuss with this man. But this is one thing you would do well to avoid, until phase two. He knows!

Second-base rules

So, it's been ten weeks and everything is going swimmingly. Now you are into stage two. You are actually officially dating: people expect you to turn up together; friends are pressing for the formal introduction. You have unleashed the love word and simultaneously stopped talking openly about your other relationships (one door opens, another one closes). The cocktails and clubs routine, five nights a week, has slowed down a bit and you have crossed the 'let's not presume too much' boundary and he is keeping shirts and shaving kit at your place. Now we've all got to Second Base before, so how do you know this time is any different?

When he's The One, you will know because your being together forever will feel completely inevitable. You might think you've had this feeling before – which is why you don't altogether trust it – but you really haven't. What you have had before is an entirely different feeling, which is 'I *want this* to be the right man'. Remember him? You willed it to work, but there was always something missing, which – now you know – boiled down to you not speaking the same language.

But the right man will be absolutely on your wavelength. He will lean across during *There Will Be Blood* and murmur, 'I'm so bored I want to kill myself,' just at the point when you were dozing off. He'll remember the odd things you remember – bad TV ads, lines from songs, sinister waiters. You will never again have to preface an observation with 'you probably won't know what I'm talking about, but . . .' or 'I don't want to sound mad/critical/weird but . . .' because he'll be right there with you. Don't get me wrong. You'll still disagree on all the important issues and fight like jackals. But the fact is *he gets you*. Simple as that. And not only is this feeling very appealing (I am known *and* loved, not just loved providing I don't reveal too much of the real me), it makes you realize how lonely the alternative must have been. People think they break up because they fall out of love. It isn't that. They break up because they can no longer ignore that empty feeling you get when reminded that the person who is supposed to be your soulmate is really just your mate.

Maybe that's the definition of love – not just teenage love, not just lust, not just we-went-on-the-same-skiing-holiday-and-look-what-happened, but proper Love – when the need to explain, or the feeling that it might just be better to keep quiet, stops.

Some other signs that he is The One

• He makes you feel like the undisputed most attractive woman in the world. There is a brief period at the beginning of every relationship when you are fairly smug and confident. But this is different. You feel omnipotent. He could go on a peace-keeping minibreak with Scarlett Johansson and you would sleep like a baby.

• You have a sense of forward velocity – plans being made, people being met – and he is setting a brisk pace. (You always know you are in the relationship that is going nowhere when he's reluctant to commit to some family event. The right man is actually eager to get the family do under his belt. He wants their approval. He has a plan.)

• He doesn't want you to change. You know when you can feel them flinching, because they don't want you to be you, or not right here, right now, in front of their friends? That never happens. He is actually proud of you.

• Both of you are equally keen. Equally anxious. He is terrified meeting your best male friend for the first time, and gets a haircut to meet your parents (anything less and he's probably not that bothered).

• He likes it when you come back from the shops with a ton of clothes and always insists you try them on.

• He drives stupid distances to spend the night with you.

• He finds your ugly moods entertaining-stroke-absurd rather than exasperating.

• He listens to your stories when even you are getting bored.

- He can give a really proper, tension-diffusing hug.

- You can happily sit on his knee without trying to take the weight.

- Nothing you do together, including searching for mothballs in Homebase, seems boring.

- He has held your head over the lavatory bowl when you've been sick from eating a dodgy oyster (ahem). (If you are French this might not qualify as an essential rite of passage, but if you are British you will know that it counts for a lot. There may not be a direct connection, but the man who holds your head over the lavatory bowl without complaint will probably be okay when you get early onset Alzheimer's.)

- The sex is the best yet (obviously).

- You can talk about sex and not just in a satnav kind of way.

- None of those things that routinely embarrass new couples are, in fact, embarrassing. People drunkenly saying, 'You're going to get married, aren't you?' Conversations about your previous partners. Talk of babies. None of it makes him nervous.

- For the first time in the history of your relationships, you will not feel the slightest urge to discuss him with anyone. Your girlfriends will say to you, 'What's it like? How's it going? Tell me,' and it will feel like there is nothing to say. Imagine that, no dramas. No, 'Well . . . I think it's okay, but we haven't seen each other a lot this month.' No, 'I don't know, it's a bit difficult now that I'm working and he's not.' You have some fairly challenging stuff going on in your lives. There are work crises and domestic dramas and wisdom-tooth abscesses and dog disappearances and car write-offs, but none of it has made the slightest dent in your happiness bubble. You are sleeping like the Nytol ad because, as we have already established, You Just Know.

Stage two can last anywhere between six and eighteen months, but not indefinitely because at some point it has to end in one of the M words (marriage or moving in).

In my case it ended in marriage. I'm not going to bore you with the details of the proposal. I can tell you that it was in Cortina, in the snow, at Christmas, and that I was covered in chill-induced eczema that made me look like I'd had an accident with the fondue oil. I can tell you that I was struck dumb when it happened and – though my whole life didn't flash before me – I was conscious that one long chapter was at an end and the next one was going to be very different. I can tell you that the ring was from Argos and we toasted the deal with Prosecco. But all I need to tell you, really, is that it happened. It turned out I wasn't too old or too unfit or too stuck in my single rut. I didn't have to compromise or visit a plastic surgeon or join an internet dating site. And I can honestly say – with absolute certainty – that I found the right man at the right time (He's employed! He has hair! He makes me laugh!) albeit unconventionally late in the day. And, if it could happen to me, it can *definitely* happen to you.

While we're on the subject of late love . . .

Are you having the right amount of sex?

This is a question that preoccupies all of us. Or rather, the question that we want answered is: Are we having as much sex as other women in the same situation as us? I have to tell you that I had prepared a chart outlining the right amount of sex according to relationship status (i.e. single, together for five years, ten years, etc.) but when I road tested it on the survival pack they went nuts.

WMF: 'I think you'll find this is pretty optimistic. You're going to make everyone feel inadequate.'

MF: 'Is this a joke? You've got us on pensioners' rations. We may have been together for longer than you but we're not finished yet, thanks.'

AS: 'I don't fit any of these categories. I had sex about seven times last week, but last month I don't think I had any. What did everyone else say?'

There is, it seems, no consensus as to the right amount of sex, but we all have our own ideas of what is reasonable, based on conversations with our friends, gossip, TV programmes, news stories and anecdotal evidence such as the rumours about Brad and Angelina waking up the wild animals on that safari. This is the thing about the right amount of sex – we think it's dictated by libido, age, etc., but it's mainly to do with expectation.

I will have you know that I complained to The One on our honeymoon that we weren't having the right amount of sex. We *were* having a lot of sex, we just weren't nipping back to our room at every available opportunity, and sometimes we were sleeping during the siesta, and we hadn't once done it in the bathroom, or under the piano in the bar. This was troubling me because it didn't match up to my idea of the right amount of sex for a honeymoon (which is indecent amounts, accessorized with Sienna Miller in *Layer Cake*-style undies, which, to be fair, I do not own). I broached the subject with my new husband who was suitably chastened, but did look a bit surprised. We had, he reminded me, already had sex once that day, and it was only 1 p.m., and we'd had sex the night before, and the afternoon before that. Did I want more sex or was I just getting antsy because I had finished my book and he was only halfway through *The Insider*?

Well, he had a point! I didn't actually feel short-changed, yet the expectation of honeymoon-scale sex weighed heavily upon me. When you have beds the size of badminton courts – looming accusingly – and no reason to wear any clothes, and long, hot days with nothing to do but order daiquiris, you feel disappointed in yourself if you aren't taking advantage of the space. The privacy. The endless uninterrupted twenty-four/seven opportunity. You panic. You think you are letting the side down and not having the right amount of sex, given your particular situation. But here's the thing about having the right amount of sex. It doesn't work the way you think it does.

How to have the right amount of sex

Make time (and make it possible). Right at the start of a relationship you always have time for sex because your real life is on hold. But life kicks in again and then you have to try a bit harder to make it happen. For example:

• Stop watching that extra late-night TV programme.

• Say goodnight to the dog. (When I met The One, the dog had to be banished from the bed because he would lie there taking up all the room and then turn his head disapprovingly to the wall if we so much as looked at each other. After that he hurled himself against the door, night after night, but it was an improvement.)

• Get away from your routine. Paying the bills in bed, checking your emails. No no no.

• Don't talk about stuff in bed that will not only put you off sex, but quite possibly cause an argument (money, work, families . . .).

• Dress up. Go out. And when you get back don't sit at the kitchen table and have another bottle of wine.

• Have a crisis. If the kitchen ceiling comes down, if you've been up half the night waiting for the flood-alarm man, if you are both at your wits' end, but being quite heroic, that is much more conducive to sex than the candelit dinner at Maurice's.

• Have a laugh. Don't get out the box set of *Curb Your*

Enthusiasm because that will compete with your plan, but don't choose a guaranteed sex night to talk about your negative equity.

• Break out the sexy undies. They demonstrate a certain willingness (and he might not be able to tell by your expression alone).

• See other people. It's good to be alone, but sometimes it's nice to watch each other show off.

• Don't be a good girl. Forget taking supper out of the freezer. Forget switching off and tidying up and making sure your earrings are back in their box. Don't say, 'Just have to quickly wring out my hand washing.' This may not actually kill the moment, but it will deliver a sharp kick where it hurts.

• Plan it. As in I want it, right now, or in an hour when the football has finished. That way there can be no misunderstandings.

Some myths about the right amount of sex

• You will have sex if you go to a fabulous hotel. Nope. You will go to a fabulous hotel, drink too much and then you might get hotel-room performance anxiety.

• A bedroom furnished with candles and aromatherapy oils is the first step to great sex. Nope. These have connotations of sex therapy and the last thing you want is to feel like you are embarking on step three of a programme to get your relationship back on track. Being alone in the house is the first step.

• You can't have sex if you're tired. Yes you can! Waiting for you to be less tired, him to be less tired, both of you to be bang up for it is a recipe for no sex ever again.

• You should be doing something different. Like what?

• You should be having sex like the people in *Lust, Caution*. Well, by all means try, but have the number of NHS Direct close at hand.

And finally, if you can talk about the right amount of sex, then you are probably getting it.

❊ Aren't You Glad You Waited (or, Why Late Love Is Better)

There are some downsides to meeting The One lateish in life, namely: the baggage of two adult lifetimes; the vexing issue of what to wear on your wedding day (I will just say, there can be no veil, not of any description); and, last but not least, the gasping ovaries. You can't dodge the fact that, if you want a family, your chances are slim to zero if you don't find the right man until you are in your forties – and that is a great pity. But, in the words of my GP (who also married late and never had children), 'There isn't just the one way to be happy. And wouldn't life be dull if we all took the same path.'

Meanwhile, there are numerous advantages to Late Love. For example:

What you see is what you get

If you plight your troth at the expected time, you are, whichever way you look at it, taking a hell of a gamble. The man standing in front of you is not the man who will be standing in front of you (possibly stooping) on your twentieth anniversary. Will the intervening years treat him kindly or will his weight balloon and his eyebrows mutate? (Well, who has got over what happened to David Hemmings?) Will his midlife crisis involve a sports car and a Tag Heuer watch or, alternatively, sleeping with your close friends in rotation? Might his appetite for parties turn into a full-blown drink problem? Will his occasional golf habit eventually require a timeshare in Sotogrande? What if he decides to chuck it all in when he hits forty and make you sail around the world with three children and a home-tutoring manual? See? Suddenly marrying at the right time looks almost reckless. If, on the other hand, circumstances conspire to make you wait ten years longer than is recommended, you minimize the chance of nasty surprises down the line. Fall in love any time around the age of forty and you can see exactly what you're getting, from pattern of hair loss to optimum earning potential. If he has aspirations to country life, or politics, they'll have surfaced by now. If he's mean, he won't be able to hide behind the excuse of outstanding student debt. You will know where he is going and you'll know where he's been. Even if you're only a little bit of a control freak, you cannot fail to see the advantages.

He's seen it all before

Okay. So it wasn't your life's plan to marry a divorcee. You'd rather have married someone with no previous experience, so it was all an adventure for both of you, and you could learn together. Then again, are you nuts? Who would you rather travel through the desert with: the seasoned tour operator who knows all the pitfalls or the rookie who's never been away from home before? A man who has already been married knows that the monster argument you've just had is easily resolvable (when you were assuming you were breaking up). He has done compromise and negotiation. He has lived with hormonal fluctuations. He is absolutely up to speed on what drives women crazy in a relationship, and he knows what gets to him and how to avoid it. Not only has he seen it all, but he knows the flashpoints, the mistakes you can make, the stuff you can take for granted and he really, really doesn't want to Go There again. It's sort of like having your own in-house Relate counsellor.

What they see is what they get

He likes you, as you are, right now. This means you feel fabulously, unprecedentedly secure, and makes him sexier than any man you have ever met (what a guy for scrambling over the

Russian girls to get to you!). And think of it: you will never have to have the 'Do you fancy me as much as when we met?' conversation. Or not until you're in your seventies.

Men get better with age

You don't believe this when you are younger: you think it's propaganda put about by women who are looking for father substitutes and fat bank accounts. But, of course, it is absolutely true. They've come through their ruthless selfish years, their hard-partying years and their career-establishing years. They've had the midlife crisis if they were going to have it. They are kinder. Calmer. More confident. Inevitably they are better practised at sex and basic food shopping, and they don't have so much to prove. They don't feel threatened by your independence, in fact they are relieved. Their friends have been edited down to the few who really count, and they no longer need to socialize in gangs (you could happily stay in, on your own, on New Year's Eve, and it wouldn't feel to them like failure). They don't mind you being funny (young men love that too until they start going out with you, at which point they think you are undermining them). They don't mind you being argumentative (young men love that too, until you start going out, at which point they think you're strident and opinionated). They don't mind you dressing a bit weirdly. (They like it. They aren't interested in blending in any more.) They are big enough, in short, to let you be exactly who you are and to love you for it.

We get better with age

The big advantage of Late Love is it comes at the very best time in a woman's life – when we have finally taken delivery of our full ration of self-esteem. Some girls are lucky and get regular visits from the self-esteem fairy throughout their twenties and early thirties, but most of us have to wait for the big booster that arrives on the cusp of your fortieth birthday (and not a moment too soon). That's the point after which you care more about what you think and want, than what other people think and want of you. Which is a real advantage if you're planning a serious relationship. Finally you can say, 'I want him, because . . .' instead of, 'I think I like him, but does he like me? That's the real question.'

You are ready to appreciate this is as good as it gets

The trouble with finding your life partner at the obvious time is you never know what would have been round the corner had you waited. The divorce courts are groaning with couples, one or both of whom never quite got over the suspicion that their lives could have been truly something had they only had the guts to look around for longer. Not us! Late Lovers have one very important advantage over those who marry at the normal time: we have seen enough to be absolutely sure this is as good as it gets. All the options have been covered, one way or another: pretty boys and city boys and artists and speed freaks and guys who blow-dry their hair and ones who don't wash, and, lo! We have proved, conclusively, that the world is not one big melting pot of potential partners. We will never take Late Love for granted, or squander it, or abuse it because we know just how hard it is to come by. Plus we have the advantage of having witnessed our friends' marriages and the stuff that happens once you start pursuing separate interests and leaving parties at different times. (And, let's be honest, this is the perfect time to put together a wedding list. You've got over your Shaker phase and your chilli-lights-in-the-kitchen phase and your cover-the-world-in-cowhide phase and finally you have arrived at something like your own taste. Imagine if you'd got married fifteen years ago? The stuff you'd have been landed with. What a waste that would have been.)

Your parents are not mildly disappointed

In order for parents to be unreservedly delighted about your choice of partner, they must be staring into the abyss with the big flashing sign that reads UNMARRIED DAUGHTER. Fear is the key. It works on their List of Things They Could Not Tolerate, over time, and it gradually erodes every one of them until the point where they would be grateful if you brought home Hugh Hefner in a gimp mask. (My mother once passed a motorcycle messenger on the stairs leading up to my flat – that's a man encased in biker leathers, wearing a black helmet with tinted visor – and announced that 'he seemed rather nice'. Anything with a pulse, and that was six years ago.)

Naturally parental approval is not the first thing on your mind when you are looking for The One. Still, there are so few ways in which we can reward them for all their efforts over the years it is comforting to know you can make your parents very, very happy by announcing your engagement after they have given up all hope.

And last, but certainly not least, you get to be a sometime mother to three teenage children.

8.

Now You Are A Stepmother

Let's cut straight to the chase here. No one ever says, 'You have three stepchildren? How fabulous!' Once in a while someone will react to the news with an encouraging smile. Once, literally, a friend said to me, 'I'd love to have some teenagers in my life. That must be fun!' But, on the whole, the woman who inherits other people's children is viewed with a mixture of awe, pity and incredulity. This is good. If you are not one of those selfless, unassuming people who go about their lives without need of fanfare or an audience (in other words, the average mother) then you should really be a stepmother.

Stepmothers get all the credit. You are a hero just for turning up at a school rugby match. A superhero for taking a day or two off work because your stepchild is sick. A super superhero for letting his friends sleep over and giving them pizza in front of the TV. Mothers are expected to do all this stuff automatically. It would be unthinkable for a mother to get on the phone to her friend and wail, 'I've got five twelve-year-olds turning up this afternoon! What do I do with them?' But a stepmother can do this, and be openly resentful, and mutter things like, 'Bloody hell, this isn't how I imagined spending my Saturday afternoon,' and anyone listening will chuckle and marvel at how she's taken on so much with such good grace.

And there is more! If we get it wrong, it is funny, charming, forgivable! The chaotic, flakey stepmother is a long-suffering character. (She is trying! Give her a break . . . God, they aren't even her children.) But the mother who messes up, who fails to send her child to school with the right sports kit, two weeks in a row, that mother is an embarrassment. I haven't even got to the best bit yet. Here it comes. However the children turn out *It Is Not Your Fault*. Or, rather, if they turn out to be Amy Winehouse, it is *All Her Fault*, but, should they be quite nice and presentable, then it is a credit to your stabilizing influence. Isn't that great?

No one ever mentions this about step-mothering. It is 'thankless', it is 'the worst of both worlds', you get all the hard work without the thrill of seeing your genes reconstituted and the knowledge that you are loved unconditionally. Well, maybe. But you also get to play at the most rewarding job there is without risk of being held to account, and your guilt levels are really very low compared with those of regular parents. Not that it's all a walk in the park by any means.

❀ Some common fears

You are not equipped to look after minors
The first big difference between mothering and stepmothering is that the children/teenagers (in my case, twelve- and

sixteen-year-old boys and an eighteen-year-old girl) know the rules better than you do. The second difference is that they are expecting someone to take control, and you, too, will be waiting for someone to take control, until you realize there isn't anyone, apart from you.

The truth is, there are vast, yawning gaps in your experience. For example, you have never done one of those supermarket shops that involves driving your car round to the pick-up point and filling the half-acre boot to the ceiling with carrier bags. You have never made macaroni cheese, or a birthday cake, or bought oven chips. Or hosted a children's party. Or made conversation with a mother on the touch line of a rugby match. Or dealt with head lice. Or 'aged' some history homework with a teabag. Or packed a holiday suitcase for a twelve-year-old. Or made sure someone other than yourself was wearing a hat and suncream. Or kept a diary for five people. And the prospect of becoming one of these women, who takes all this in her stride, on a daily basis, is really quite . . . daunting.

There have always been women like this in your life, Carolines mainly, whose sheer breadth of competence blows you away. These are the women you hold in awe above all others. Sometimes, when one of them says, 'Oh, I put a couple of fish pies in the freezer before I went to drop off the children and walk the dogs, and then I realized I had to pick up the trestle tables and put the tent up in the garden, which didn't take as long as I thought, so I still had time to do the accounts before I made the children's costumes . . .' you want to curl up on her knee and ask her to take your life in hand. You want to say, 'You lost me at the fish pies! Please Come And Live With Us. I Am Not Competent.' Obviously all the Carolines say to you, 'Oh, you'll be fine; it's just common sense, really,' and that's what everyone says. But they don't realize the true extent of the problem.

For the most part you can muddle by. Your stepchild will say, 'Don't you usually dilute Dettol?' just at the crucial moment. Or, 'I swear you're meant to put the birthday candle holders in the other way round.' Or, 'Don't we need towels if we're going swimming?' But, at some point, you will be exposed. When this happens – for example, you put ice, rather than a plaster, on Younger Stepson's burn and it falls to a real mother to point out your mistake (when did air become the big enemy? We've only just moved on from the butter remedy) you must not panic and think This Is Just The Tip Of The Iceberg. I Cannot Cope. The fact is, if the children in your care are relatively bright, and alert to the possibility of screw ups, it's not nearly as scary as you think. Often they are just studying blood loss in biology, or gas leaks in geography, and will be able to chip in with relevant information such as: 'The tourniquet needs to go above the wound, not below.' It's called teamwork, and it's the future.

You will become the kind of woman who wears stripey jumpers and spectacles on a chain and lose your identity

This is ridiculous! You're acquiring stepchildren not moving to a pig farm on Exmoor! However, there is certain stuff that goes with families that represents – to the fevered mind of the new stepmother – the death knell of civilization and the first step on the slippery slope that leads to wearing sleeveless fleeces and forgetting to wax your moustache. It's the little, apparently insignificant things, for example, the cereal packets ranged along the back of your kitchen units. Where, in your single girl's kitchen, there used to be a gleaming cafetière, a small selection of glossy covered cookbooks, a granite pestle and mortar and a bowl of fresh garlic bulbs (Marisa Tomei might live in such a kitchen, I think you'll agree), there is now three feet of dusty cardboard boxes, too big to store in any of the cupboards. (Some say Tupperware containers are the lesser evil in this situation, but I say if Tupperware containers feel like the last straw, and it's a personal thing, then don't go there.)

Your fear is that these on-show cereal packets are a fore-warning of what lies ahead. They will lead, inexorably, to the convenience cutlery with the coloured handles, the child-friendly chair covers (anything that doesn't show the dirt) and then the easy option social life (better stay local, too knackered to go anywhere nice anyway). Next thing you know you'll be keeping a pair of comfy car shoes by the front door and using your Bag for Life as a handbag. 'You have to be practical in your new role after all,' says the Stepmother Guilt Fairy. 'You're planning on cooking Bolognese wearing a cashmere sweater? Oh dear me.' 'You really want to take them to that grown-up noodle bar when there's a Nando's just down the road? Well, well.' 'You're thinking of painting the floors *white*? Oh, don't let me stop you. It's just that these days you have a family and rather different priorities, wouldn't you say?'

You will come across the Guilt Fairy now and then, and sometimes she's right, but never when it comes to resisting the kid-friendly, wipe-clean makeover. In general, your personal Guardian Fairy is the one you want to trust with the minutiae of your life and she says, 'Screw her. Go for the chippable pottery plates. Keep the white sofa covers – you can wash 'em. Take them to the sushi bar for Chrissake (they love it!). Do not, on any account, give in to the primary-coloured wall chart detailing each member of the family's movements or the oil-cloth table cover. There is no law that says a family home has to look like a Play-Doh advertisement.' What this Guardian Fairy means is you will get depressed if you don't do it your way, and then you will get twisted and paranoid and accuse your husband of turning you into a style-free blob who never has her roots retouched on time and has missed out on the last two jeans styles. And it's simply not worth it.

Note: When you talk to men who have children from a previous marriage, this is the message you invariably get: 'Don't make the mistake of thinking you can change your stepchildren. My (new) wife thinks she can turn them into the kind of kids who wash their hands before lunch. It just isn't going to happen!' Ignore these men, whatever you do. They don't get that the only way to make the whole stepmothering experience manageable, let alone pleasurable, is by sticking to your standards. Hand washing before lunch may be a goal too far, but, if you happen to feel strongly about hand washing before lunch, then go for it. What matters is that you feel comfortable and vaguely in control. Your stepchildren do not care if they have to leap through a few hoops in order to get left alone. They don't really mind if you have a thing about when they can and can't wear their tracksuit bottoms, or when they can and can't eat the humous out of the plastic container – they get the underlying point (you must be kept sane). And, guess what? The sooner you start to lay out your rules, the sooner your house will feel like your home.

They will not do what you say

It will take a while for you to get to the point where you are ready to put this to the test. As a novice stepmother, your instinct tells you what needs doing, but self-preservation tells you that it is better to make your husband deal with it. This means there will be a lot of conversations like this:

Older Stepson: 'I'm going out and I might be back in time for school on Monday.'

Husband: 'Hmm.'

You: [*Waggle eyebrows, nudge, summon husband to space behind the kitchen door*] 'Tell him he isn't going anywhere.'

Husband: 'Okay.'

You: 'Tell him he can't go and if he doesn't know why then . . .'

Husband: 'Okay.'

You: 'LISTEN. This is what you say: "If you think it is reasonable for you, during your exams . . ."'

Husband: [*Now back in the kitchen*] 'Right. If you think it is reasonable, etc., etc.'

Older Stepson: 'Dad? Why have you gone all weird?'

The whispers-off phase of step-parenting is a necessary adjustment stage and it does postpone direct confrontation between stepchildren and stepmother. But there will come a day – maybe six months in, maybe longer – when you will hear yourself roaring, 'Get upstairs to your room Right Now,' and that will be it – the start of your life as a hands on, real life, no holds barred stepmother.

It is quite a shock to discover that you come pre-programmed with a whole lexicon of Mum phrases like 'because I say so' and 'there will be big trouble' and 'I'm going to count to five' but they're all in there, waiting to be used liberally. What's more – despite all your worst fears – your stepchildren will, more often than not, do exactly as you say. This has nothing, whatsoever, to do with your natural authority, or their intense respect for you. It's simply because they are used to being bossed around. 'Take them off,' 'Turn that off,' 'Clear that up,' 'Stop that now,' is the backing soundtrack to their lives and, as far as they are concerned, it doesn't make much difference which adult is doing the nagging. Also, they are not that bothered. You think that every instruction you issue is a test of your authority, and you are white-knuckling it waiting for the one that gets met with the 'so make me' look. Fortunately, most children are not that interested in confrontation, and it is usually more comfortable for them to comply than to take a stand. The exception to this rule is hormonal teenagers.

Now I have been incredibly lucky with my stepchildren. They have not invented a secret language or snipped my wedding dress into a million pieces. But there have been moments and there will be moments. These are some of the things you might remember when those moments arise:

• You must not swear. This will happen in the heat of the moment, but when it does don't take the giving-up-smoking approach and think, I've slipped up once, might as well get stuck in. Your stepchildren will excuse the occasional stream of filth but it does you no favours in the long term.

• You do not have to engage. Teenagers long to be ignored by wise and even-tempered adults. When they say, 'I am going to burn my bedroom down – just try to stop me,' don't start yelling and threatening to call the cops. If you simply walk away, it will be much more effective. (Often, if you remind them of some idly offensive remark, long after the event, they will say, 'But I was just being an idiot then,' as if you should know better than to dignify that stuff.)

• You don't have to sort it out now. Think of a punishment later. If you think of one on the spot, nothing will seem big enough and you will go straight to 'no privileges for the rest of your natural life', which will be hard to enforce.

• You don't have to put this in context. There is a temptation, with teenagers, to use the opportunity of a flare-up to put them straight on the wider issue of their disappointing behaviour in stark contrast to the staggering amount of effort you put in to making their lives easy and comfortable. They are costing you as much as running Elton John. They never think of anyone but themselves. You bend over backwards for them and they can't be arsed to so much as put a plate in the sink in return. They have no idea how lucky they are compared with you at their age, or how long a leash you give them, or how, frankly, gobsmacked they are going to be when they get out into the real world and discover that Ben & Jerry's does not grow on trees and HD TV is not a basic human right. This, however, can only end badly. You will never get them to agree with you and you'll only end up tempting them to say something really provocative, which you will be unable to ignore.

• Removing them or you from the scene is always a good way of defusing a crisis. Go for a walk. Kick them out to the park. Space is a great healer.

• If they have been really vile, don't cook. There is nothing like a weekend of Babybel sandwiches to remind a teenage boy where he is going wrong.

They will think you are weird

They really won't. If you are a bit weird, they will get used to it and, besides, children appreciate mild eccentricity (hence the bond with their grandparents). But *they* are not the ones you need to worry about, it's their friends.

It is imperative that you do not announce, in front of a group of twelve-year-olds, that you love your cleaner (even if Younger Stepson knows what you really mean is, 'I am so happy she got the wax out of the carpet,' his friends will be alarmed). Also you should refrain from talking in a Russian accent; singing loudly in the kitchen; talking to the oven; admonishing the fridge, computer, etc.; loitering in the background, wincing, when they are playing Call of Duty Three; offering them fruit (as if). And never, ever, say anything that could be construed as excessively posh, such as, 'Would anyone like a biccy?' Any of the above is incredibly embarrassing behaviour and sufficient grounds for being labelled weird. The rule is, when their peers are present, limit the chat to, 'Would you like another sausage? How about some more Coca-Cola?' This way you will not let the side down.

They will think you are hideous

It is well known that all females older than Keira Knightley are considered to be physically repulsive by the younger generation, and this lot are going to be seeing you first thing in the morning, on the beach, sweaty in a tracksuit after a run (just kidding with that one). It's not that you're necessarily that bad, but you're not a blood relative, and therefore you will be judged as a random, older, decaying person. You can clearly remember having to sunbathe alongside your mother's friends when you were a teenager and wishing they'd had the decency to wear modesty-preserving shrouds. And that was back in the days when it was normal for grown women to come bubble-wrapped in cellulite; before yummy mummys and bmi awareness, and the official cancellation of middle-aged spread. Besides, this lot are so critical! They notice the state of your roots, your toenails, the day, to the hour, that your eyebrows need plucking. They yank at any hanging bits of flesh and absentmindedly flick your bingo wings. Once in a while they will say things like, 'Anna is really skinny,' or, 'Jessie's mum has amazing hair,' and you will panic that this is their way of communicating that your sub-standard appearance is affecting their social standing. But, rest assured, they don't really care. They would rather you scrubbed up a bit for their end-of-term prize-giving day – and answering the door to their friends with a coating of creme bleach on your upper lip would not be a good move – but wearing the same old pair of cords day in and day out, is not one of the ways in which you can torture them.

That said, there are of course ways in which you can embarrass your stepchildren that are strictly appearance related. They fall into three categories: wearing things that make you look as if you are desperate to attract attention (hats like ocean liners, zebra-print coats, red lipstick); wearing things that make you look as if you are desperate to attract the attention of men (very low tops, very short skirts, very tight jeans); wearing things that make you look as if you think you are down with the kids (message bracelets, dresses over leggings, beanies, bandanas, Ugg boots, more of which in a minute).

They will say, 'You Are Not My Mother'

It's a statement of fact and yet all stepmothers dread those five words because what they think they mean is: 'You're just some woman our dad has brought into our lives. You are doing a lousy job. Can we please stop pretending you mean anything to us whatsoever.'

There are only two kinds of stepmother as far as a step-child is concerned: the one who took your dad away from your mother and the other sort. If you're in the first category, you are at a big disadvantage, but all stepmothers are outsiders who become insiders simply by virtue of attracting Dad's attention (and the kids already have reason to doubt his judgement). If you are the wife or girlfriend of a man with children, it's worth remembering – when they are being surly and uncooperative – that this could be because they have a stranger in their midst who gets to make a lot of the impor-tant decisions that affect their lives. No wonder at times the situation might strike them as unfair, or what they would call 'random', because it is. If they do say the fatal words at any point (and the chances are they won't – even children know a lousy cliché when they hear it), what they (probably) mean is, 'I can't believe I am a child of divorced parents and I am having to put up with all this CRAP.' Which is slightly different.

It's also worth remembering that there are advantages to this situation for your stepchildren: for a start, you are not their responsibility. Your real mother is your mother for better or worse. A stepmother is like an ex-boyfriend – if they have redeeming qualities, you can advertise your connection to them, if not, you can deny the relationship altogether.

Think about it. Scenario one: you are at a mixed-generations party and your mother is dancing uninhibitedly to 'Sexual Healing' with a sweaty man in a tuxedo. Scenario two: same deal, only this time it's your stepmother dancing to 'Sexual Healing'. The former is social death. It may actually scar you for life. The latter is something you can snigger about without fear of betraying your (real) family loyalties. Or ignore. Or take in your stride. Either way, it bears no reflection on you, whatsoever. For a teenager, being able to say, 'She's not my mother,' is the purest possible form of stress relief. What's more, because your choices do not automatically affect their image, they can almost, sometimes, take pleasure in them. So, for example, if you buy a Spiewak parka, your teenage son will die a million deaths and refuse to go outside with you, but your teenage stepson might well want to borrow it. Mothers are a permanent potential source of embarrassment. Stepmothers are more like eccentric house guests – it could go either way.

Likewise, they don't feel like extensions of you. When a teenage girl talks to her mother, she is mostly thinking: You're making me feel guilty, you're cramping my style, you're treating me like a child, you're totally missing the point (no one writes thank you letters, no one rings the other people's parents), you have no idea how much things cost, I can't hear you because I am thinking about what to wear.

Meanwhile, underlying all this is a low hum of anxiety – a feeling that she cannot really talk to her mother and yet her mother knows everything there is to know about her. Step-mothers, in contrast, know nothing about their stepdaughters, apart from what they see in front of their eyes. They are able to treat a teenage girl like a teenage girl because they are not thinking, But I've only just given birth to you, my baby. How can you be thinking about a tongue piercing?

You can talk, in other words, without it being about something else.

And it works both ways. When your stepdaughter chooses not to go to the university you went to, you can be fairly sure that it isn't a deliberate slight. When she talks about boys, you don't automatically compare her experiences with yours and panic that she's going to make all the mistakes you did. When she alludes to some anxiety, you don't freak out because you suspect it all dates back to the time you left her to cry in that scary holiday house, only to discover there was a bat on the mosquito net. The very best mothers are able to take a step back and remove themselves from the frame when dealing with their children, but even the most inadequate stepmother can manage this quite easily. And it is an advantage to be able to give advice without the object of your advice thinking: You are only saying that because that's what you wanted for your life.

Note: At some point someone will mistake you for your stepchildren's mother and how you handle this moment is crucial. Your first instinct will be to correct the mistake, immediately, in order to save the child the embarrassment of having to do it themselves. Your logic is that if you leave it to them then it will look like they have a problem ('*she's* not my mum'), so, better for you to take the lead. This makes perfect sense until the moment you leap straight in ('stepmother actually') and then, trust me, it sounds like you're the one with the issues. It sounds like you have just said, 'Er, hang on a minute. Not a chance. I don't even like kids. I am married to their father and this was the one non-negotiable.' The only way to avoid this awkwardness is by correcting strictly on a need-to-know basis. If the sales assistant in the shoe shop happens to ask, 'Did your son want the blue or the green Converse?' just answer her. No need for clarification. However, if the teacher at parents day/mother of his new best friend/police make the same error, you might want to correct them. Anyone you are going to see again will need to be put straight, in due course, but there is no particular hurry (and not rushing to put them right will translate as, 'I am blissfully happy being mistaken for their mother, however they might feel about me,' which can only be a good thing).

There will come a point when you all have the routine off pat: hotel receptionist – none of you can be bothered. Noisy woman at party – better clear it up before things get messy. Dentist – probably should put him straight, and so on.

❀ Some Stepmothering Tips (or, How Not To Screw Up Too Badly)

Children/teenagers are quite tolerant of all forms of incompetence. They will, for instance, put up with:

- Wearing clothes that are ludicrously oversized, because they were cheap.

- Swimming in their underwear because you forgot their swimming trunks/suits.

- Having the cut on their head cleaned with vodka because you have no antiseptic.

- Having their hair cut like a marine's because you were engrossed in *Vogue* during the crucial stages.

- Allowing themselves to be clutched by a sobbing au pair for half an hour (because you have had to let another one go).

- Watching cartoons for five hours with children six years their junior, because you are getting drunk in the next room with their parents.

- Subsisting on two T-shirts because you have shrunk all the others.

However, they will not tolerate screw ups to do with their schooling, for example, you washing their daily conduct card for the fifth time in a row. This is a conversation Younger Stepson knows only too well:

YS: 'Why are you trying to stop the washing machine?'

You: 'I just want to check something.'

YS: 'It's in there again, isn't it?'

You: 'I'm not absolutely sure.'

YS: [*Face pressed up against the glass of the washing machine*] 'I can't believe it's in there! That's the second time this week! Is my phone in there too?'

You: 'Oh! *That's* the clunking noise!'

Incompetence in this area never goes down well. You can just about get away with it in other areas so long as you get this one sorted. Here are some other pitfalls to avoid:

Don't make rules that are hard to uphold

You think rules are really simple when you first come to this job. Take off your muddy shoes. That's one. Keep your school-bags there. That's two. Have a shower after football. That's three. These all work as rules should. Great. But then there are the rules you make up on the spot in response to a particular incident. For example, the No More Food Or Drink In The TV Room Because The Coca-Cola Has Been Spilt Yet Again rule. This is a rule that any experienced mother would realize, immediately, was going to rebound on her. It is a bad, unworkable rule, because *you* want to have a glass of wine in front of *Nigella Express*. And does a tangerine count as food? What about a glass of water which, after all, if spilt, will not stain? The rule, as it has been adapted now, if you are interested, is no food or drink in the TV room apart from: takeaways on Sunday nights (served in big bowls, to avoid spilling) and ice cream (also because in bowls). Fruit with a plate is allowed (with the exception of clementines, which may be consumed in the palm of the hand) and tea, at weekends, if the speech has been delivered that begins 'If you spill it . . .' The rule is forever under review and remains a glaring example of the perils of hasty legislation, not to mention the incredible negotiating skills of teenagers when there is something to be gained. They are always saying things like, 'But it's in a tin, which you said was okay, if I keep it by the fireplace,' or, 'This doesn't need a plate because it has peel, remember?'

Sex and nudity

The worst thing about divorce for children (besides blaming yourself, and feeling rejected, and living in two houses, neither of which are anything like as nice as your old house, and no longer seeing the children of the people who were your parents' best friends, and having to sleep in bunk beds, and having to entertain your parents at weekends and demon- strate that you are okay all the time) is that your blob-like parents, who existed only as Mum and Dad, become adults who have sex. One minute they are faceless facilitators of your happiness, who sometimes link arms in the park, whose conversation is all about getting petrol and picking up your sister from ballet. Next thing you know they are buying Diesel jeans and Keane CDs and permanently whispering into their mobiles, and then they bring home someone of the opposite sex and act exactly like teenagers, snuggling up on the sofa and the rest. You never dreamt you would see your father behaving like a sap and now it is a normal daily state of affairs.

The stepmother's duty, in this scenario, is to not make

matters any worse than they already are by wandering around naked or forgetting to lock the bathroom door. (There's something else that separates parents from the rest of the adult population: their children can glimpse them in the buff without feeling sick.) Engaging your older stepson in conversation while you are semi dressed in bra and opaque tights is just about acceptable, but only if you are wearing knickers, or, alternatively, the opaque tights are Wolford and therefore solid, impenetrable black. Otherwise you will wonder why he is staring determinedly at the light fitting above your head throughout the exchange, and, later, when you catch sight of yourself in the mirror, and it appears that you have a spider trapped down the front of your tights, you will feel bad.

In this situation, and at any point when you have mortally embarrassed one of your stepchildren, you must go directly and apologize and explain (for example: 'I thought they were Wolford, but they must have been those ones I got on offer in the supermarket. God! Just goes to show! Never economize on opaques!'). If you don't speak up, straight away, they will imagine far worse indiscretions down the line and before long they will be barricading themselves into their bedrooms. (Note: When it comes to their nudity, you are not in a privileged position. If they need to get naked in your presence, you must do as a gentleman in a nineteenth-century novel, turn your back momentarily and talk about something distracting.)

The only thing more unpalatable to your stepchildren

than seeing you naked is any suggestion of you having a sex life. Apart from taking the obvious precautions, it is totally forbidden to have saucy conversations and dancing cheek to cheek in the kitchen will cause them to make retching noises.

Don't be too much 'Fun'

Just as you want a mother not a 'best friend' (please), you want a stepmother not a whacky older sister. Never be tempted to strike up cool, down-with-the-kids conversations ('Arcade Fire, how great were they?'), especially not involving their friends. Don't sing along to their music. Don't be more into their TV programmes than they are. Don't know more about their friends and their lives than they do – as in, 'I thought Jenny was going to Bar Eight and then on to Fabric, I can't believe she went straight to Fabric! What a loser.' Don't use words like 'loser'. Don't be tempted to tell the story about when you were really out of it and your tent caught fire. Don't try to start food fights. And, as a general rule, it is not a good idea to own something that your stepdaughter owns. Even if you got there first. Even if you really believe a pair of Minnetonkas is just what you need to pull together your wardrobe, don't even think about it.

This generation of teenage girls has never known a time when grown-up women looked gratifyingly horrified as they came downstairs in a sliver of frayed denim skirt (as opposed to cooing, 'I love it. Is it Jack Wills? Do they do one just a teeny bit longer?'). They are remarkably sanguine about the fact that their world has been squatted by old people and your stepdaughter is used to shopping with you in Topshop and you buying the higher heeled shoes with the ankle strap. (That's okay, she doesn't do heels.) But that doesn't mean you don't have to be very careful not to encroach on her turf. Don't push it.

Stick to the truth

Don't lie, or exaggerate. Not even about something small like having been hit by a tiny piece of meteorite; not even if you're only doing it to make them think you're interested ('I love *South Park*.'). These people are piecing together clues about you in order to decide whether or not you are worthy of their respect and maybe affection – for God's sake, don't give them reason to doubt the stuff that's real.

Some general tips for living with a teenager

• Don't bother trying to get them to understand the error of their ways with words. They can't hear you anyway.

• Talk to them about meaningful stuff while out for a walk, or cooking, or in the car, or on the phone. Any situation that allows them to avoid eye contact is good. You can even talk on the phone when you're in the same house – who cares – they find it ten times easier.

- Don't tell them bad news before you need to. For example, if you are going to stay with the family who don't have TV, they don't need to know until you are ringing their doorbell.
- If it works for you, buy a dog. Dogs support children and adults in different subtle ways.
- Now and then, cook with them. It's as close as you can get without hugging.
- Watch TV with them. It is reassuring to find yourselves all howling with laughter at the same things.
- Feed them earlyish. Guaranteed you will reduce the number of outbursts by sixty per cent.
- Leave them in bed at the weekend for as long as it takes.
- Blow up occasionally. There is no harm in them knowing that you can be a terrifying monster.
- Buy them one super-cool article of clothing.
- Remember they soak up your anxiety and throw it right back at you.
- Avoid the manners conversations when you are all tired.
- Screw up, burn the supper, drop the china, lose your keys. Every so often it's good for them to take on the role of calm, cool rescuer.

❀ *The importance of him*

All divorced men feel guilty when it comes to their children, as well they might. They know that shuttling between two parents and maintaining a wardrobe/games section in two separate places is no fun, and they know that they are at least partly responsible. This guilt, combined with the gaps in their hands-on practical experience, makes the average male divorcee quite poorly equipped for solo parenting duties. Generally he will oscillate between intensely spoiling his children, and taking time out to reward himself for all the unrelieved childcare. He will be spending zillions on Thai takeaways, and PS3 games, and trips to the cinema, and all-in holidays and, when he's not, he'll be ratcheting up bar bills and bingeing in Gap and Habitat. This much is inevitable. All you can hope for by the time you meet him – correction, the absolute minimum you should expect – is that he is not so guilty that he isn't open to changing . . . everything.

Super-guilty Dad is as bad news for the novice stepmother as an Asbo teenager (and often the two go together). He will have persuaded himself that he and the kids are a tight, fighting unit, welded together by adversity, and that the normal conventions of family life no longer apply to them. 'You can't expect them to eat with a knife and fork after what they've been through,' is more or less his attitude. (Part of him believes this line, but a bigger part of him is too bored, and too busy dating, to enforce a whole load of little rules.) The upshot is that the children of Super-guilty Dad are officially exempt from civilized behaviour. You can't expect them to get a kick out of being taken to *Billy Elliot,* let alone to say thank you, because they have been to the dark side, and it is his duty (and yours) to respect this and learn to accommodate it.

Some novice girlfriends/stepmothers get bamboozled into accepting this line and imagine they have no right to interfere in something this delicate, but forget it. There is only one rule of getting involved with a divorcee with children and that is you are the priority. He must love you enough to swallow his pride, change his world view and let you rule the house. Anything less and you are in trouble. Whenever you hear about a woman having 'a difficult time' with her partner's children, that usually means she is involved with a Super-guilty Dad – a man who is not prepared to support her one hundred per cent just in case that makes his children blame him more. He doesn't need to announce this, of course; his children will pick up on it automatically, and then he might as well just stick you in some stocks in the garden and leave them to it.

Making a home

All men, unless they are art collectors or architects, will leave their marital homes and automatically embrace male divorcee interior style. They will own, without fail, a pair of leather armchairs; a glass coffee table; a gas log fire; a Smeg fridge; a Dualit toaster; a six-foot-square bed with leather head-board; lots of framed black-and-white photographs of body details that you are supposed to mistake for peaches, or swans, or lilies, and some that genuinely are lilies; a bathroom modelled on an en suite in an Amman resort, only in an area one eighth of the size, with dodgy grouting; a downstairs lavatory featuring humorous framed cartoons and his (premarital) history documented in photographs. If he doesn't have a Bang & Olufsen wall-mounted CD player, he will have a plasma-screen TV with surround sound and speakers the size of traffic bollards. All of this, naturally, has to go. The first rule of second marriages is that you cannot be expected to accommodate divorcee style. Besides, this is just his decompression chamber – a holding pen that allows the divorced man to lick his wounds, flex his bad taste and wait to see what happens next. None of it really matters to him (even the leather chairs, which cost I dare not tell you how much), which is good, because you get to choose everything now.

It's only fair. You are the one giving up your boudoir flat and your cafe-breakfast lifestyle. Shortly you will be required to sell, on eBay, endless boxes of Jimmy Choo boots and an entire railful of satin Voyage dresses and cardigans, Mongolian lamb-trimmed coats, Agnès B leather jackets and APC corduroy trouser suits. Because a) that part of your life is officially over, and admittedly has been for some time, and b) in the house you own together, every inch of storage space will be taken up with cricket stumps, golf bags, sleeping bags, two-man tents, badminton sets, wet suits, surf boards, picnic rugs, punch bags and baskets seething with plugs, remotes and various bits of vital electric cabling. He owes you. It is his first duty to make sure that your living environment is as close to your ideal as possible, and, if your heart is set on the Neisha Crosland wallpaper made with actual gold leaf, then so be it. In the long, drawn-out days to come, when you find yourself yet again bent over a sticky sausage pan, or sadly dabbing at the biro stains on your once-white sofa, it will be better for everyone if you haven't compromised on the kitchen cabinets.

Unconditional back up

In the normal course of events, regular father would say to regular mother, 'Darling, just checking, when you said he had to get off the computer did you realize he was working on an essential bit of course work that has to be handed in tomorrow?' And regular mother would say, 'Oh, darling. What was I thinking? My mistake.' But the husband of novice stepmother must stand by everything she says, no matter how crazy or impractical, and be ready to pick up the pieces when things go wrong. (A few years down the line you will have enough confidence for him to question the wisdom of something you have said. But not for now.) For now it goes something like this:

You: 'Right. You are both going outside to get some fresh air.'

OS: 'What?'

YS: 'But . . .'

You: 'Now. I don't want a fight.'

OS: 'I refuse. Have you looked out of the window?'

OS and YS: [*Together to husband who, having heard commotion, arrives on the scene*] 'She wants us to go outside!'

Husband: [*Familiar expression of bafflement swiftly followed by resignation*] 'You heard. Out you go.'

YS: 'But, *Dad.* There's a hurricane warning. The country is being lashed by eighty-mile-an-hour winds. It's been raining for ten hours solid and the street is sealed off.'

Husband: 'I don't want to hear another word.' [*Opens door on to street with debris flying through the air, trees uprooted, cars overturned.*]

You: 'Well . . . maybe . . .'

Husband: 'Whatever you think, my love.'

Unconditional back up is the only way to build the confidence of the novice stepmother. Similarly the husband of the novice stepmother should be very careful not to make innocent comparisons or suggestions, such as: 'They seemed to love whatever it was Caroline made them for supper. Maybe you should get the recipe?' It's not that you care so much. You just need to feel only one person is judging your performance.

Escape time

From this point onwards your holidays, which were entirely hedonistic affairs, or total rest cures, or life-changing experiences, will be focused on some kind of sporting activity, and probably take place in Cornwall. It turns out that you cannot sunbathe all day on a family holiday. There must be activities, plans, excursions and things that take you away from reading your book. There may be beauty treatments, but only if you can find them in Polzeath. There can be shopping, but only in Asda. For this reason you need a husband who is prepared to whisk you off on minibreaks devoted exclusively to the sinking of cocktails and the purchasing of pointless, hot-weather accessories like decorative flip flops and straw bags with interesting linings.

Note: It is counterproductive to be a martyr to your new role. Don't think you have to be there all the time in order for this step-relationship to gel. It is not just sensible but healthy to get away from all your family responsibilities for one week a year (and it's nice if you take your new husband with you).

Significant moments in step-parenting

- The moment when they first treat you as dismissively as their dad, as opposed to making a slight effort in your presence, so as not to offend their dad. This means you've graduated from visitor to one of the family.
- The first time you lose your temper with them.
- The day your stepdaughter borrows your shoes. Hurrah! Approval!
- When you find yourself feeling jealous of the au

pair. You've been to bloody India. You've read the
works of the Buddha.

- The day they ask to bring home friends.
- The moment you realize their friends think of you
as a parent whose permission must be asked if they
want a glass of water.
- The first time they voluntarily give you a kiss.
- The first time they ask you to come to some
school event for which your attendance is not
required.
- The first home-alone supper, without him. (You
get through it. No one says, 'Hang on. What are we
doing sitting in a kitchen eating with YOU? Clearing
the plates when YOU say?')
- The first time you walk into your house and
think – Mmm, my home – as opposed to
feeling a little like Clarice on a visit to
Hannibal Lecter's cell.

✽ *There Will Be Tears*

Look. I can't tell you that there won't be tears. There will
definitely be tears. And the cause of the tears will almost
certainly be the inability of your new family to live up to your
ideal.

One of the perks of being single is that you get to sit in

judgement over other people's marriages and their child-rearing methods, so, long before acquiring a family of her own, novice stepmum has clear views as to how it should be done. You have spent years watching from the sidelines and you've seen it all: the 'routine, routine, routine' lot; the 'no routine, no bedtime, no rules' lot; the 'wild but housetrained' lot; the 'one hundred per cent feral' lot. You know the sort of children you would never have had and the sort you would automatically have had (mischievous, charming, bright, attractive) and now you find yourself with a ready-made family that's the one thing you didn't bargain for: unhappy. As in not having any fun. It's the only behavioural problem they don't feature on *Supernanny* because there is no naughty step, no privilege removal or pocket-money fine that can deal with bare-faced misery. And that can lead to feelings of frustration, self-pity and blame.

My tears (the big ones) happened in a mountain restaurant, on a family skiing holiday (goggles still on to conceal swollen eyes). We were in a beautiful place, supposed to be having deluxe fun, but the children were silent and resentful and suddenly I cracked. I sat in the loos and wept for the dysfunctional mess I found myself in and genuinely despaired of us ever being a normal, happy family who loved each other. And then my husband suggested a possibility I hadn't considered: that the children were miserable because it was cold and snowing and they needed a hot chocolate. Miserable in the way that any children get, even the ones whose lives are straight out of fifties comic books, whose worst ever experience was losing out on the blue rosette at the gymkhana. Miserable (though he didn't actually say this) in a way that didn't altogether justify losing faith in our future. This was roughly the moment when I realized the following truths the novice stepmother must cling on to:

• There will be misery. However hard you try to avoid it, and it will not always be traceable back to the word 'broken'.

• Building a new family takes time. It takes a year for it to feel like a genuine concern, two to feel like it's really working and even longer to be rock solid (who knows how long it takes for them?).

• You must relax. If you are happy, they are much more likely to be happy. As opposed to being extremely tense and willing them to be happy in order to justify all the effort you have put into making this holiday-stroke-life choice a happy experience.

• Family holidays are weird. It was the same for you. You are either too old for them, too young for them or you are missing something really good at home. And your parents expect way too much enthusiasm, all the time.

• It doesn't matter so much what other people think. Give yourself a break. Or write a message on the palm of your hand: 'We are making changes. Thank you for your patience.'

• You can't blame him. Yes, you do, when it suits you. That's like him blaming you for having old ovaries and not much in the way of a pension. This is just the way it is.

• And finally: don't take anything too personally. You think it's about you; the chances are it really isn't.

Epilogue

It's two years on. My cooking repertoire has broadened to include drop scones. My stepdaughter has gone away to university (I've had the concertinaed family experience – from beginner parenting to the start of empty-nest syndrome). It seems bizarre that just a couple of summers ago I was single and standing looking out of the window of my flat, waiting for the lift to take me to the party where everything would change. But I don't look back and dwell on all that freedom and spare time (which is what my long-term married friends imagine). I don't regret not having talked to The One at that first lunch, three years previously (because it was too early for him, and it was still too early for me). I don't wish it had worked out differently in any way because now I appreciate that some of us are just late developers, and you can't rush this stuff. Besides, the longer you wait, the bigger the happy ending.

If you find The One nail-bitingly late in the day, when the most you were hoping for was Mr Gigantic Compromise, then it is better than any snowy Richard Curtis finale. Bitter divorcees well up at the news, cynical philanderers grin from ear to ear, your parents, God bless them, break out the more expensive of the cavas. Everyone you have ever met will be delighted for you, personally, but beyond that your story will confirm something we all want to be true – that it's never too late to find what you were looking for. Late Love is a small miracle that brings out the very best in everyone and restores your faith in men, life and our ability to risk our hearts, even when we have wrapped them in straw and put them on a very high shelf in the garage. And, although you didn't deliberately remain single for all these years, you will still feel like the heroine of a gripping thriller, with several twists and turns, and a long boring bit in the middle. Because, in a way, that's exactly what you are.

Acknowledgements

I would like to thank my great friends, and agents, Felicity and Sarah, my phenomenal editor, Juliet Annan, and my mentor and sternest critic, Nicola. Thanks to Tiffanie for her indulgence and inspiration. Also, and especially, thanks to Caroline for giving me sanctuary and being the best friend possible. Last but not least, I have to thank my husband without whom this book would not have been possible, on several levels, and my stepchildren, Harriet, Tom and Guy, for putting up with more than usual levels of neglect.

He just wanted a decent book to read ...

Not too much to ask, is it? It was in 1935 when Allen Lane, Managing Director of Bodley Head Publishers, stood on a platform at Exeter railway station looking for something good to read on his journey back to London. His choice was limited to popular magazines and poor-quality paperbacks – the same choice faced every day by the vast majority of readers, few of whom could afford hardbacks. Lane's disappointment and subsequent anger at the range of books generally available led him to found a company – and change the world.

'We believed in the existence in this country of a vast reading public for intelligent books at a low price, and staked everything on it'
Sir Allen Lane, 1902–1970, founder of Penguin Books

The quality paperback had arrived – and not just in bookshops. Lane was adamant that his Penguins should appear in chain stores and tobacconists, and should cost no more than a packet of cigarettes.

Reading habits (and cigarette prices) have changed since 1935, but Penguin still believes in publishing the best books for everybody to enjoy. We still believe that good design costs no more than bad design, and we still believe that quality books published passionately and responsibly make the world a better place.

So wherever you see the little bird – whether it's on a piece of prize-winning literary fiction or a celebrity autobiography, political tour de force or historical masterpiece, a serial-killer thriller, reference book, world classic or a piece of pure escapism – you can bet that it represents the very best that the genre has to offer.

Whatever you like to read – trust Penguin.